## DATE DUE

NOV 2 1 1992

| | | |
|---|---|---|
| DEC 5 1992 | | |
| JAN 11 1993 | DEC 19 1992 | |
| | | |
| APR 29 1993 | MAY 06 1993 | |
| | | |
| | | |
| | | |
| | | |
| | | |
| | | |
| | | |
| | | |
| | | |
| | | |

Demco, Inc. 38-293

| | | |
|---|---|---|
| CT 27 1990 | BIRD SEP 2 9 1990 | |
| | APR 8 1991 | |
| APR 21 1992 | APR 2 6 1992 | |

Demco, Inc. 38-293

*Books by Gladys Denny Shultz*

HOW MANY MORE VICTIMS? *Society and the Sex Criminal*
JENNY LIND, *The Swedish Nightingale*
LETTERS TO JANE
IT'S TIME YOU KNEW

*By Gladys Denny Shultz and Daisy Gordon Lawrence*

LADY FROM SAVANNAH: *The Life of Juliette Low*

# HOW MANY MORE VICTIMS?
## Society and the Sex Criminal

### Gladys Denny Shultz

J. B. Lippincott Company
Philadelphia · New York

# Preface

This is a book that, when it was first proposed to me, I did not want to write. From a personal standpoint, I would much have preferred to put behind me the incident that inspired it. I was reluctant to call attention afresh to the "Jack Smith" of the narrative which opens the book. At last reports he was doing well. I did not want to do anything that might possibly impede his full and permanent recovery.

I found, however, that I could not put behind me the knowledge I had gained, through his attack on me, of the vast misunderstanding that exists regarding the problem of sexually sick males and the dreadful consequences this brings upon women and children. I knew that the mindless, motiveless desecration and slaughter of the innocent will continue as long as the problem is not solved. I had come relatively unscathed through an experience many women do not live to tell about. I had not been raped, I had no need to hide from the world in shame. I had been faced with an apathy appalling to me, after my narrow escape, on the part of both officialdom and my fellow citizens toward protecting the community against the repetition of a sex crime of violence. I had witnessed the inadequacy of the laws of my state to deal with the problem. I am a professional writer, with a lifelong interest in anything that concerns women and children. I decided at length that I had an obligation to do what I could to waken the public to the consequences of apathy toward sex crime.

Once embarked on my task, it became an exciting adventure. It meant delving into the darkest recesses of the mind and emotions, it's true, and into most gruesome and horrible crimes. But this was counterbalanced by my discovery that a vast amount of thought has been devoted to the problem and that, in several places, something effective is being done about it. Veriest tyro in the field of sex crime though I was, I received the most generous cooperation from leading experts who have concerned themselves with the problem for many years. Now I am glad that I put personal considerations aside. As a citizen and voter I needed to know the things I have learned, and I believe my fellow voters and citizens should know them too.

I should like to acknowledge my very great debt to Dr. Manfred S. Guttmacher and Dr. Frederic Wertham, who not only gave me gracious permission to draw heavily on their own writings but rendered personal help and advice on the manuscript; and to staff members of the National Council on Crime and Delinquency, who gave me my first leads toward sources of information and the freedom of their extensive library. My special thanks to Dr. Ralph Brancale, head of the New Jersey Diagnostic Center, and Dr. Bernard C. Glueck, Jr., who headed the second Sing Sing study, for helping me find the right path; to Dr. Seymour L. Halleck, Chief Psychiatrist to the Division of Corrections, Wisconsin's Department of Public Welfare, Dr. David B. Robinson, formerly of the Psychiatric Section of the Mayo Clinic, and the *Journal of the American Medical Association* for permission to quote from important papers published therein; and to the officials of the Youth Board in California, the Youth Agency in Massachusetts, and the New York State Department of Mental Hygiene who patiently answered innumerable questions. I cannot adequately express my gratitude to the officials of the Corrections Division of the Wisconsin Department of Public Welfare, to Dr. G. Lee Sandritter of Atascadero State Hospital, and to their respective staffs, for their fine cooperation and the pains they took to enable me to get a comprehensive picture of the admirable Wisconsin and California systems for handling serious sex offenders. I am grateful also to the attorneys general and other state officials who supplied me with information about the statutes of their states concerning serious sex offenders.

Last but not least, I want to express my appreciation and best wishes to the sex offenders in Waupun Prison, Wisconsin, and Atascadero Hospital, California, who opened their hearts to me so that the public might have a better understanding of the reasons behind sex crimes. It was from them I learned that sex offenders are human beings like the rest of us, only with graver problems than most of us have.

The way in which our society deals with these men will determine how many innocent women and children must suffer outrage, how many suffer death, at their hands. That is why I had to write this book. If it can speed help to the men who must have it to rid them of their incubus of hate and sex violence, the ordeals "Jack Smith" and I went through in our different ways will have served a good purpose.

*Gladys Denny Shultz*

# Contents

# ONE
# The problem

# A shocking story

The first intimation I had that someone was in my house was the clicking of the latch on the door of my first-floor bedroom. I am a professional woman, in my late fifties. My house is in a rural section, and I live alone. There are neighbors not too far away, but none within the sound of my voice, none in a position to see or take alarm at any unusual happenings in my house. In our quiet little community, there are several of us women who live alone in houses out of sight and sound of neighbors. We had not considered that we were living dangerously.

This particular evening, though, I had felt an unaccustomed uneasiness. Some time after I turned out my light at 10:30, I thought I heard movement outside, something brush against the house. I raised myself in bed and looked out of the window nearest me. It was a clear, cold winter night; the moon was very bright. I saw nothing except my car, sitting by the house in the bright moonlight, so I lay down again but remained fully awake. I even heard, later on, the dull, booming sound my ancient, heavy, outside cellar door makes when it is opened, though it was muted. I listened intently, then, but heard no sound afterwards. Deer come up to my very door; dogs and raccoons investigate my garbage can. Trees and old houses can produce strange sounds of their own, especially on a winter night. I finally attributed this sound, too, to some innocent cause or to my imagination.

It was perhaps twenty minutes after that, still with no further sound, not even the creak of a floor board, that the latch rattled on my bedroom door. I think it must have been around midnight then.

That sound could not have been made by the wind or an animal. I came up out of my bed by reflex action and started toward the door, calling out, "Who is it? Who is there?"

The latch clicked more decisively. There was no attempt at secrecy now. I had nearly reached the door when it was thrown open boldly. A man entered with a long, pantherlike stride, half crouching. A man in shirt sleeves, young, lithe and completely strange to me. It was as though he had materialized, in shirt sleeves, out of the winter night. It was nightmare. But it was real, and it was happening to me.

Seeing me standing there, momentarily paralyzed, the man straightened to his full height and catapulted himself upon me, forcing me back across the room to my bed. Through my mind flashed the certainty that this was an insane rapist, that I would be murdered. I remember thinking, as he picked me up to throw me on the bed, "I hope, when they find me, they will realize that I fought as hard and as long as I could."

Much of the detail of that struggle has grown dim in my mind. Partly, perhaps, because there was much I do not want to remember, I thrust resolutely away whenever it threatens to return. But mostly, I believe, because the whole thing had such an aspect of nightmare that it vanished from my mind of itself, in the same way that one forgets much of the detail of even a striking dream, soon after waking.

Next day, when it was fresh in my mind, I figured the struggle had lasted for around half an hour. The first shock passed off quickly. I had never been more alert. I found a strength in my body I had not dreamed I possessed. Believing I was going to die, I concentrated all my forces on giving the best account of myself that I could before I was killed. But how I fought, and what I did in those first confused moments, I could not say now.

The first clear memory I have is of his face bending down to mine. He had thrown me on the bed with my head at the foot, under the window. The moonlight was streaming in. I realized that he intended to kiss me and pushed his head up frantically away from mine. I can see his face now above me in the moonlight, completely expressionless. I got a hand in his mouth, pulled at it hard and knew I was hurting him. I thought, "This will make him angry; he will start now to hurt me." His expression did not change. Or rather, there was no expression. That did not change.

But his hands came down and, joined on my throat, began to press. I thought, "This is it. Now he will kill me." There was no sense of shock or fear, for I had already accepted the idea that I would be killed. I just didn't propose to die tamely. I seized his hands, pulled them from my throat.

That was the only intentionally hurtful gesture he made, and he did not repeat it. He appeared to be in a trancelike state. Above me was the always expressionless face: forehead and cheeks white in the moonlight, the eyes round black holes. No matter what I did to hurt or circumvent him, that face displayed neither anger nor frustration. At the same time his body worked with machinelike persistence, yet cunningly, too, to accomplish its purpose. It seemed to have a mind and will of its own.

After I realized that it was not his intention to kill me, at least not at this point, I began talking to him while we struggled. Throwing out questions, such as where had he come from, who was he, was he not someone in trouble, repeated over and over. I told him I was an old lady, a grandmother, asked him if he had a mother, anything I could think of that might possibly get through to his mind and take his attention from what he was doing. These were the first sounds that had been uttered since he entered my room. He had said nothing, just thrown himself upon me. It had not even occurred to me to scream. It would have done no good, for there was no one to hear me.

I kept telling him over and over that I believed he was someone in trouble. I offered to get him something to eat—while fending off his advances with all my might. I kept asking him where he came from, if he wasn't cold, hungry. On and on. He paid no attention for quite a while. Finally, in reply to the often-repeated question, "Where do you come from?" he paused long enough to say in a little, uncertain, small-boy voice, "What do you want to know for?" I said I wanted to know about him, that I felt he was someone in trouble.

After this he would answer me, and sometimes the struggle would halt while we exchanged several sentences. Then it would start up again as he would renew his efforts, I would renew my counterefforts. His answers sounded as though they were torn from him. Sometimes they were nothing more than a groan. He told me that he had come from a nearby hostel for homeless men; that he was 20; that he had no mother. He wasn't cold, he said. (And he was not, to the touch, when he threw himself upon me.)

The conversational interludes gradually became longer and longer. Several times I thought I had reached his conscious mind. Then he would return to the attack as persistently as before. The struggle became even more strenuous as more effective ways of fighting occurred to me—much to my own surprise, for I am not violent by nature. But faced with deadly peril, my body, too, seemed to develop a cunning of its own.

I managed to squirm off the bed. He seized me and threw me on it again. As he stood stooping over me, I kicked him away, hard, with both feet.

I remember three separate episodes of this kind. Once I slammed him against the dresser, another time against the wall, so hard that the iron foot of the floor lamp was bent out of shape when he crashed against it. I can see him now on the floor, looking up at me with that expressionless face, then springing up, throwing me on the bed again. I lashed out at him quickly with my feet as he stooped over me. That was the first time in my life I ever kicked anybody! But when one is fighting unspeakable degradation, one cannot afford to be ladylike.

Finally, he threw me down on the bed very hard and my head hit the window sill. I was partially dazed. I recognized that the end of my effective resistance was drawing near. I had escaped the rape so far only because my reactions had been quick. If I were slowed down, I would be done for. I was half lying, half sitting against the wall, trying desperately to get my wits back, when he collapsed onto the floor. He stayed there, sitting on the floor, leaning against the bed.

Somehow I knew the battle was over. I must have said something to him about not reporting the affair if he would leave the house now. For he snarled, "Yeah, you would just get me for breaking and entering," and reeled off a long string of charges to which he evidently knew he had laid himself open.

I stood up, then, and he made no motion to stop me. He got to his feet, appearing very young. I repeated my assurance that if he would leave the house now I would tell no one of the encounter. He snarled at me again—in this phase he seemed a young guttersnipe—using a coarse expression. I think I stiffened, showing my distaste. He seemed to recognize that he had offended me, to pull himself together.

Before my eyes, I saw an entirely different person appear. The man who stood in my room now looked mature and poised, tall, straight, with a lithe, athletic build, like a tennis player, I judged him to be around 30. The first thing he said in his new personality was, "Of course you know who I am."

I replied that I did not, that I had never seen him before. He seemed to accept that.

We both knew that, in this guise, he did not wish to harm me in any way. But he didn't want to go to the penitentiary either. He was afraid that as soon as I left I would call the troopers.

I assured him I would not. I told him I would let him out of the house the front way. "You came in through the cellar, didn't you?"

He told me he had, and admitted that he had been lurking under my bedroom window before he entered my house. If I had looked through the other east window, I suppose I would have seen him. I did not ask him what had brought him there. I did not feel in a position, just then, to conduct a cross-examination.

"Why don't you keep your cellar door locked?" he demanded accusingly.

I told him I had never dreamed anyone would molest me. "I'll keep it locked from now on." He nodded approvingly.

I went to the outside door nearest us, took off the spring lock. It was this action that saved me, later on.

Then I walked into the kitchen, just opposite the outside door and adjoining my bedroom. He followed me. We still had to work out how he could be sure of his safety, in return for mine.

As we entered the kitchen, I started to flick the light switch, then took my hand away. It bothered a member of the grand jury, later on, that the man had been in my house for around two hours and no light had been turned on. That had been part of my strategy. In that isolated spot, in the middle of the night, I hadn't a chance in the world to get help from outside. I had to convince him that he would not put himself in danger by leaving me unharmed. I said to him, "I won't turn on the light. That way I won't be able to give a description of you."

We didn't need artificial light, anyway, with the moonlight flooding into the kitchen, too, through the bay window in the south wall. He picked up his suit coat from a chair and slipped it on. Evidently he had stopped in the kitchen as he came through and prepared himself for the attack. He had no overcoat or cap or gloves, though it was January and the night was very cold. I made no comment, nor did he. The door to the cellar was standing wide open. I closed it, shot the bolt home; also without comment.

I realized that my mouth was extremely dry, as happens in times of stress. I went to the sink and drank glass after glass of water. Presently he joined me there. Bending far down over the counter, till his head almost touched it, he exclaimed, in an agony of shame and self-loathing, "Would you believe that I was married once to a good woman?" I said I could believe it.

Then he said, "Why, you're scared half to death!"

I was in fact shivering violently, partly from nervous reaction, partly from cold. I had on only a nightgown and was barefoot; I had turned down the furnace when I went to bed.

I replied, "Well, this is the first time anything of this kind ever happened to me!" Then matter-of-factly, "I'm going to get on a robe and slippers."

I will admit that it took courage to go back into the bedroom. I didn't linger. I got a warm robe out of the closet by touch. Not finding my bedroom slippers where I had left them—I discovered next day that they had been kicked far under the bed—I snatched a pair of sneakers out of the closet and put them on. This was my second lucky break, for my bedroom slippers would have been poorly adapted to that later desperate dash up the road. He sauntered after me but remained in the doorway, keeping me always under observation.

Decently covered now, I walked briskly back to the kitchen; he followed me again. We returned to a discussion of our problem. He told me he had been on the road for four days; told me, in answer to my questions, that he would go over to the railway and hop a freight. He recognized as clearly as I did that he would have to leave my house, after what had happened. I felt truly sorry for this young man. I offered to get him something to eat before he left, to make coffee. He said he didn't want anything to eat, but that he would like some coffee.

I was not afraid of the man in his present guise. Nevertheless I knew nothing about him, and the situation was still very uncertain. I decided the thing to do was to behave with complete naturalness. I went about the kitchen, putting the coffee on the stove, getting out the necessary utensils, with the ease and authority of any older woman entertaining a young person in her home.

He leaned against the counter, watching me. "Why, you're in complete command, aren't you?" he commented wonderingly. "You know, I could have killed you in there. I don't think you cared a whole lot, one way or the other."

It was true that I had been prepared to die rather than accept any type of caress from this stranger who had obtruded himself on me so outrageously. But I thought it best not to dwell on the idea of killing. I answered, "I didn't think you were a bad chap. I thought you were someone in trouble and didn't really know what you were doing."

He said, "That was it. I didn't know what I was doing. I would give anything if I could undo it."

Now he appeared ready to go. We both had forgotten the coffee. I offered him a package of cigarettes, which he accepted. My children had left at the house a variety of coats. I offered him one; he put on a foul-weather jacket that I got out of the kitchen closet. I told him I had around $10 in my purse, that I would like to give it to him. He replied that he wouldn't take my money.

We were standing now at the kitchen door, just across from the outside door which I had unlocked. If I had been cleverer, perhaps I would have contrived to get him out of the house then. But if he had gone then, I would not have recognized how dangerous he was. I believe he would have returned, and I would not have been prepared. Or that if he had not come back to my house, some other lone woman might have been attacked.

Just then, though, the coffee pot boiled over, and I ran back to the stove automatically to turn off the gas. He followed me. There was an awkward pause. Then he said earnestly, "I wish I could talk with you."

Perhaps this was where I made my big mistake. But in so unprecedented a situation, one must be guided to a great extent by instinct. Undoubtedly my training and long experience in dealing with problems played their part, but I had had no experience of situations like this one. It was instinct, rather than conscious thought, that had led me to show interest and concern for this stranger as a person, while resisting the bad thing he proposed to do with all my strength. My instinct appeared to have served me well, so far. It told me now that I ought not to rebuff so innocent a request. Besides, the interest and concern I had used first as a device had become real. The young man's remorse, the respect he showed me after he returned to his proper self, had touched me.

I believed he was in trouble of some kind. He had indicated that he was a homeless wanderer. I thought I could understand that under the combined effects of hardship, emotional turmoil and liquor—I had smelled liquor on his breath during the struggle—a man might be impelled to a type of behavior he would ordinarily abhor. If liquor had played any part in the original attack on me, the effects had worn off completely. Since emerging from the trancelike state, he had shown, in various subtle ways, an innate gentlemanliness. I hesitated only briefly before replying that I would be glad to talk to him.

In this way began the strangest interlude of my life. As the trooper who accompanied me back to my house later on that night expressed it when he phoned the barracks: "Well, this man tried to rape her but didn't succeed. So then they went in the kitchen and drank coffee!" I thought they would consider me a very queer kind of woman indeed, at the barracks.

I poured the coffee, and we sat down at the kitchen table across from each other. First, my visitor slipped off the foul-weather jacket, saying he would not take it after all. I suppose it had occurred to him, though it had not occurred to me when I gave it to him, that to be picked up wearing that jacket would be damning. It is ironic that this gesture of mine, motivated entirely by good will, enabled the blood-hounds to trail him; established one link in the case against the man whom I shall call Jack Smith.

The man sat in the shadow, the moonlight reaching only as far as his ankles. I scrupulously refrained from trying to get a look at his face when he lighted a cigarette. I was sure I would recognize him, after that long session on the bed in the moonlight. But I didn't intend, then, to report him to the police. I didn't try to find out anything that might identify him.

Actually, it did not seem as strange to me as one might think, to be sitting there, holding a friendly conversation with a young man who had so recently attempted to rape me. I have worked a great deal with young people. Many have brought their problems to me. I know of no gratification greater than now and then to be able to touch a troubled young heart in crisis; now and then to be able to divert a young life into more productive channels. I had never before dealt with a young person as deeply disturbed as this one. Under the circumstances, I could not be of any material help to him. But I have learned how much it can mean, in a time of trouble, just to be able to talk to someone who sympathizes, and tried to understand.

What may be hardest of all to comprehend—I don't believe I could do so myself if I had not experienced it—was the feeling of kindliness between us. It was as though he, too, had been saved from something that he would have looked back on always with shame and regret. I was grateful to him, because he could have done me great harm and had not; because he had abandoned the sex attack of his own accord. To feel gratitude under such circumstances is illogical, I know, but I believe it is human.

He apologized again, saying he wished we could be friends but knew we could not be, because of the way things had started out. I told him we would forget that. "We will figure our friendship began when we came into the kitchen." And I meant it.

He replied, "Maybe I could forget. But I know you never could."

He betrayed intense curiosity about me, asking many questions about who I was, what I did. He asked me to tell him why I was "untouchable." I took it that he wanted *me* to tell *him* why he had been moved to abandon the sex attack. I answered, feeling my way, "Maybe I'm wrong about this. But I would say that it is because every man with decent impulses—and I believe you have decent impulses— respects a decent woman and doesn't want to do anything to harm her."

He nodded his head. "I believe you're right. I believe that was it."

He asked me many questions about my work; when I finally told him that it was vocational guidance, he wanted to know what my training had been, why I had gone into it in the first place. He asked me about my children. As we talked, I sized him up as a young man who had not had a great deal of formal education—I later told the troopers he might have finished high school but I did not believe he could have gone beyond that. He seemed to have good native intelligence, with a lively, inquiring mind. I appeared to be quite as much of an odd specimen to him as he was to me. Now and then he would say, "You're just stringing me along." I would reply that I was truly interested in young people, that I would truly like to help him if I could. He said once, "You're sort of the mother type, aren't you?"

I hadn't minded answering his questions, for they had been entirely respectful and, I felt, had been prompted by an intellectual curiosity in encountering someone in a category new to him. But all at once I realized how tired I was. I had risen at 5:30 that morning, had had a busy day before the violent half hour or so of physical combat. (Next day my body was a mass of muscle aches, in addition to the bumps and bruises acquired in the course of the struggle.) I stopped talking, leaned back wearily in my chair.

That was when I saw his feet, in the moonlight, and realized that he was wearing soft-soled moccasins, which explained why he had been able to move so quietly. When Jack was picked up, he had on shoes of the kind I had described to the troopers.

He said, "You sighed just then. Why did you sigh?"

I thought it unwise to display any weakness, so I pulled myself together and told him that this was a new kind of experience for me and I felt rather inadequate. "You said you wanted to talk to me, but I don't want to pry. If there is anything you would like to say to me, I will be glad to listen."

He told me his trouble had been that he never had been able to adjust to society's requirements. "I don't seem to be able to find out what they want of me."

I asked if he had ever had anyone to help him with his problems. He said he had not. I know now that Jack Smith had been loved, that attempts had been made to help him. But perhaps in a deeper sense what he said was true. For love, mistakenly applied, may stand in the way of the kind of help the Jack Smiths need, until it is too late.

Suddenly he said, "Go to the phone and call the troopers!"

I asked, "Do you really want me to?" I could not make a phone call unless he was willing for me to. Besides, at that point I did not want to turn him over to the police unless I was sure that that was what he wanted.

"I may as well go and give myself up to the cops. I've got to face this thing sooner or later. It has happened over and over again." Then bowing his head low again on his hands, he exclaimed in that voice of shame and self-loathing, "Oh, I'm a mess, an awful mess! I'm a sick man!" He did not again tell me to call the troopers, however, and so the moment passed.

If I had called the troopers then, if he had surrendered himself voluntarily, would the outcome for him have been any different? Knowing what I do now, I doubt it. For the troopers would have had to turn him over to the local authorities just the same. And I imagine the treatment accorded him would have been the same.

I asked if there was any chance that he might go somewhere new and make a fresh start. He said, "I tried that once, out in———" — naming a distant state—"but they were after me like a pack of rats."

Thus far his conversation had been completely rational, his questions sensible and well phrased. I was unprepared for the fantasy element when it suddenly appeared. The first sign that something malign was taking place was his question: "What I would like to know now is why have you been haunting me all my life?"

I laughed at that, told him I had not known he existed until that night. "You must be thinking of someone else. Your grandmother probably." For I had been laying great stress on the age difference between us.

He said, a querulous note in his voice, "No, not my grandmother. At least, I don't think so." He kept repeating that he would like to know, before he died, why I had been haunting him all his life. His talk became disconnected, his questions ceased to convey what he was trying to express. Presently he said, "I am surprised that you work at the kind of things you do. I would have thought you would be interested in murder—murdering me." The last sentence seemed very hard for him to get out. He stumbled over the words, his tongue awkward, his voice thick.

I took this, too, as though he were joking. "Why, I wouldn't hurt you or anyone else!"

He said, moving his head in a tortured way, "You were cruel to me. You hurt me in there"—nodding toward the bedroom. Previously, he had respected me for my resistance. More ominous still, he began to talk in a flirtatious manner, completely at variance with the deference he had shown me up to that time.

I knew now that I was in very deep waters indeed but felt that I must not let him see I knew it. I said firmly, as I would have to any male who had overstepped the bounds of propriety in my home, "I think the time has come for you to go." I stood up; he, too, got to his feet, reluctantly.

As we stood there facing each other, he took both my hands in his. He apologized again for his actions, told me it had helped him a great deal to talk to me, asked if he might come to see me.

Gently disengaging my hands, I answered, "You may, if you will come in the daytime and will telephone me first."

Then he asked me to kiss him good-bye. I said "No," emphatically.

He asked wheedlingly, "Why not?"

"Because it wouldn't be right!" He made a move toward me and I stepped back, saying sharply, "Don't start that again! We have made a friendship. Don't spoil it!"

He stood there, swaying a little, a foolish, uncertain grin on his face.

Now I was afraid—utterly, terribly afraid. By his repeated expressions of remorse, his respectful attitude after he had returned to his proper self, the man had erased to a degree the sordidness and indignity of his initial attack. Now the full horror of it swept over me. I could not go through that again, I could not. I doubted that I would be able to talk my way out a second time. My instinct told me that the expressionless automaton of the struggle, taking possession in front of me, would be prepared for that. I saw only one chance—to get him out of the house, if I could, before the automaton took over entirely.

I grasped him by the arms, turned him around and marched him toward the outside door. He let me. His body under my hands felt rigid, poker-stiff. He walked with the jerky step of a robot. But he let me propel him to the door. I reached around him, turned the doorknob, opened the door wide. Just then he turned and faced me. His arms clamped around me with the mechanical motion of a trap when the spring is released. For an instant that expressionless face, with the round black holes for eyes, looked down into mine.

But we were by the door, and it was open. I reached my hand way down, seized the door jamb near the floor, used its leverage to pull myself downward out of his arms—I could not have broken that rigid embrace—and through the door. I ran to the nearby road and up the hill crying, "Help, help!" I knew no one would hear me, but I thought he might think someone would. Part way up the hill, I glanced back. He had followed me out of the house and was standing beside my car, looking after me.

I turned then and ran on, as fast as I could. I did not look back again until I was well over the brow of the hill. I could not see him at all, then, but continued to run until I reached the nearest neighbor's house. They telephoned the state police.

After the troopers had left, I walked back and forth through my house for many minutes, saying, "Thank You, God, thank You, God, thank You, God!"

Our state police are a wonderful organization. The nearest barracks is fifteen miles away, but two patrol cars were at the neighbor's door within twenty minutes, and the troopers were very much on the job in the week following, trying to find a lead to the stranger.

Two days after the attack, someone thought of the dogs occasionally used by our county sheriff's office. Two deputies came in a station wagon with a couple of huge, mournful-looking English bloodhounds. One was placed on a long leash and given the scent from the foul-weather jacket, which Jack had worn so briefly. The dog picked up the trail outside my door, and, following him, we could reconstruct every move of my assailant from the time I had last seen him, standing beside my car.

The hound showed us that the man had gone to the highway but had soon left it, taking a dim wood trail up a hill overlooking my place. Here he had evidently lain and watched while the troopers came and went. Then the trail led back to the highway and south for nearly a mile. We could see where the man had swerved into the ditch from time to time, probably to hide while a car went by, then had turned into an entrance which led to an old deserted barn. Inside were recently made tracks of an automobile. There the trail stopped, for the time being. With a car, a man could get very far away, in two days' time.

The sixth night after the attack, two troopers called and, without saying anything, handed me a thick pile of photographs of men who, I assumed, had records of sex crimes. I went through the pile quickly, discarding each one at a glance. For these were older men, heavier men, men who appeared either dull or brutish. I was about halfway through when I came to the picture of a good-looking young chap with a rather cocky, self-conscious smile but confused, troubled eyes, a striking contrast to the dreary rogues'-gallery faces that had preceded it. I said at once, "This is the man."

The troopers said, "That is Jack Smith."

Jack, who had grown up in my county, had been in three mental institutions and was an escapee from the third. His story, as I came to know it, confirmed and intensified the tragedy I had sensed during my talk with my then unknown attacker. Jack had been a promising lad, it appeared; had graduated with honors, at the age of 16, from a well-rated private academy and soon afterwards had enlisted, with his parents' consent, to fight in World War II. His illness had first shown itself after he was discharged, when our armies were disbanded following the end of the war. He was then only 18.

The diagnosis was schizophrenia, the mental disease of "split personality." He had gone through several periods of seeming improvement, only to regress. Between commitments to institutions, he had married a fine girl of the community, as he had told me. There were children.

It is not a pleasant duty to have to deprive a young man, the father of young children, of his liberty. It is harder still after you have had a glimpse into his tortured heart, after he has cried out to you for help. When a trooper took me to our local Justice of the Peace to swear out the warrant for Jack's arrest, the three of us discussed the sad features of this case. Jack was obviously a sick man, we agreed. My charges would serve to keep him confined safely in a place of treatment until he was pronounced truly cured.

I was told that, when Jack was picked up, he would be sent away for thirty days' observation. If found mentally unbalanced, he would be placed at once in a treatment institution. If found sane and accountable for his actions, he would be brought back to stand trial on my charges. But we all considered the second alternative a very remote contingency indeed.

As the trooper drove me home again, I felt that a great weight had been lifted from me. In the six days that had elapsed between the attack on me and my identification of Jack's picture, there had been four rape murders in the big city not far from me. In every case the police were looking for, or had already apprehended, a man who had served one or more terms in penal or mental institutions. Society had had its chance at a sick man; had bungled it. An innocent girl or woman had paid the penalty. It seemed to me that we had been given an opportunity possibly to avert a sickening tragedy of this kind. The seriousness of Jack's illness had been made apparent before he had become brutalized, before he had done any irreparable harm. He had been observed in his fantasy state and out of it. During his talk with me, he had admitted his condition and recognized that he must face up to it. There was pathos in the fact that, in his disturbed state, he had been led back to a house associated with his childhood—to his undoing, as it had proved. But all these things would furnish important clues to the doctor or doctors in whose hands he would now be placed.

I thought I would tell Jack, when he was brought to me for identification after his arrest, that I had been sincere in what I had said to him that night, that I would not have reported him if that other, malign personality had not assumed control again. I wanted him to know that I was his friend, that I would help toward his cure in any way that I could.

I hadn't learned, then, how little help or hope there is for the Jack Smiths of this world, once their behavior has laid them open to the "due process" of the law.

Jack Smith was not brought to me for identification, nor was he sent away for observation. He was placed at once in our county jail. The kindly Justice of the Peace before whom I swore out the warrant told me that Jack had been brought before him after the arrest and had waived examination. That permitted our local authorities to hold him in the jail for thirty days without confrontation—positive identification, that is to say, by the complaining witness, myself. (I learned later that Jack had not known what waiving examination meant, nor would I have known, in his place.)

In the end, Jack Smith sat in the county jail for almost three months without having been identified, without a psychiatric examination, without treatment. He was held on purely hearsay evidence, for during that time no one with authority over Jack ever saw me or heard my story. The various attempts I made to be allowed to identify the man they were holding on my charges, to gain information about the case or to pass on the information I possessed, were either brushed off or ignored entirely. I was advised by lawyer friends that I should not, on my own motion, go to the jail to identify the prisoner or ask to see the county attorney. I should wait until I was sent for. Nor could I do anything toward having Jack's mental state established. Only the defense counsel or the county attorneys have the power to ask for a psychiatric examination of an accused man, under our law.

I was haunted by a conversation I had had with Jack's mother, just after his arrest. A well-dressed, pleasant-appearing woman, somewhat younger than myself, she had displayed all the shock and horror any mother would feel when she learned what her son had done. She had exclaimed, when I told her what Jack had said about being a sick man, "It's the first time he has ever admitted it! That has been one of our troubles, that we couldn't get him to admit he was sick. Oh, I hope the officers will realize he is sick!"

"They do realize it, Mrs. Smith," I had assured her. "They told me they did."

As the weeks dragged by, I worried more and more about the identification. If Jack were to be tried before a jury, as appeared to be the intention, would not the long delay in confrontation be a weakness in the prosecution's case, something the defense counsel could seize on, make much of? I would have liked to make the identification, also, for my own peace of mind. I had little real doubt that Jack Smith was my assailant. Nevertheless, when a man has been arrested on your charges, charges that can blast a man's life and make him an outcast from society, you want to be very sure the police have arrested the right person. When I called the county attorney to express my anxiety about this, he replied that there was no need to worry, the case was "in the bag." A letter I wrote him later on was not even acknowledged. I could only hope this indicated that Jack had confessed or in some other way had been proved, beyond a shadow of a doubt, to be the man who had attacked me.

In the end, the confrontation was left until ten minutes before I had to go into the grand jury room to testify. It could hardly have been carried out in a way better calculated to defeat its purpose. I had seen my assailant only once, nearly three months before, and by moonlight. On this occasion I was taken to the jail and directed to stand on one side of a double set of bars. The sheriff led Jack out on the other side of the bars, to stand directly beneath a brilliant neon light. I had talked with Jack for a long time; his inflections and manner of speech would have been revealing if we could have had the conversation I had hoped we might have. But nothing was said except when Jack, evidently not informed as to what was taking place, exclaimed to the sheriff in an explosive gabble, "Who is she? What's she doing here?"

I was too appalled and heartsick to say anything myself. I had impressed upon the troopers, in describing my assailant, that we were not dealing with a brute but with a thinking man, a man of some sensitivity. I had recognized Jack's picture instantly as the man I had seen in the moonlight.

But in the man before me now, I could detect little resemblance either to the good-looking, smiling young man of the photograph or to the moonlit, masklike face graven on my memory. This man glared down at me out of cruel, cold eyes. His face was deeply grooved, furrowed with bitterness and hatred. I had described my assailant as lithe, athletic. This man was bulkier, starting to run to fat. He seemed a good ten years older than the man who had been in my house. He was indistinguishable, in fact, from those lost men whose pictures I had thumbed through so quickly before I came to the smiling, handsome young fellow Jack Smith had been such a short time before. Had some of those men, too, been lithe and good-looking once? Had they, too, possessed a potentiality for good that had been turned needlessly into brutality and hatred?

I cannot describe the shock and horror of that moment. Not so much at the realization that, if this was the man, my danger had been even greater than I had thought. But at the realization that if this was the man, a possibly salvageable human being had been destroyed. Worse yet, I could not say that this was the man who had attacked me, or that he wasn't.

(When I asked one of the troopers who made the arrest if there had been a change in Jack's appearance since then, he replied, "Well, let's look at it this way. Suppose *you* had been sitting in that jail for three months. Don't you suppose you would be feeling mean and bitter? It isn't surprising if he has put on weight, just sitting in a cell month after month. Men often do.")

"Has he confessed?" I asked the county prosecutor who was handling the case, after Jack had been led back to his cell.

No he had not, I was told. Neither had any evidence been found to connect Jack Smith directly with the crime.

"But I can't identify him," I said. "What am I to do?"

"You will just have to tell the grand jury you can't identify him," the prosecutor replied.

I learned later that Jack Smith was the man, and I am convinced I could have identified him unhesitatingly if I had seen him soon after his arrest. But I had to go directly before the grand jury, confused, heartsick and unsure in my own mind that the man I would be talking about was Jack Smith. Nor had I any idea what portions of that two-hour-long session in my house would be germane to the grand jury session, because no one from the county attorney's office had ever gone over my story with me. The prosecutor couldn't help me, because he had no idea what I had to say until he heard me say it to the grand jury.

The members of the grand jury listened attentively; the questions they asked me were searching and to the point. I failed to recall certain details which came to me later and which previous questioning might have brought to the surface in time to be of some good. To the vital question, "Did you identify Jack Smith as the man who attacked you?" I had to answer that I had not been able to do so.

When the prosecutor and I left the grand-jury room, I felt the jury must have been left with grave doubts. I myself was in the dreadful dilemma of not knowing whether an innocent man had been terribly wronged, or whether, as a result of the ineptitude with which matters had been handled, a dangerous man might be released into the community. I asked what would happen if the grand jury failed to return an indictment. Could not the authorities then order a psychiatric examination of the prisoner on the grounds that he was an escapee from a mental institution?

The prosecutor replied regretfully, "Unfortunately, we find that the institution has marked Jack down on its records as having been released. That was to make them appear better, I guess."

I looked at this pleasant man in consternation. Knowing these things, our county officers had left the identification to the last possible moment; had left the part I must play in his indictment entirely to chance. That lives could be disposed of so casually, that responsibility toward the safety of the women of the community could be held so lightly—to me this seemed the most incredible phase of the whole incredible affair. In the process a sick and troubled man had been made sicker yet, and loopholes had been left through which he might escape back into the community, possibly filled with a hatred and desire for revenge that he had not possessed before.

As it happened, the grand jury did return an indictment and Jack was arraigned. But he sat in the jail for another month before he was examined by state psychiatrists and pronounced a paranoid schizophrenic, unfit to stand trial. (A paranoid is an insane person who has delusions of persecution.) A month and a half after that, he was sent to a state hospital for the criminally insane.

Might Jack get some special therapy there? "Not a chance," I was told. "The hospital is too badly overcrowded and understaffed. He'll be there the rest of his life. It's too bad, really. He was a nice chap to begin with."

Would Jack Smith escape again or be released prematurely? Would some other woman be victimized, perhaps someone not as vigorous and lucky as I had been?

Possibly Jack's case was already hopeless when he entered my house. But could he have been saved if he had been treated as a sick man from the moment of his arrest, with thorough psychiatric study and treatment begun at once? Might those other Jack Smiths have been saved if their disturbance had been treated when it first showed itself?

I have asked myself these questions many times. The answers leave me deeply concerned.

# Aftermath to
# "A shocking story"

"A Shocking Story" appeared anonymously, somewhat edited, in the April, 1960, issue of the *Ladies' Home Journal* and was soon after that excerpted in *The Reader's Digest,* also anonymously. I was the writer. I had not signed the story because I had a natural shrinking from publicizing such an experience in my own person, and because I had no wish to pillory any individuals by name before the entire country. I did not believe that anything had been done or left undone, in the Jack Smith case, through malice or evil intent.

In order to preserve my anonymity, we had changed a few unimportant details. For one thing I am a professional writer, instead of a vocational counselor. But the greater part of my writing has been in the field of child rearing and guidance of young people. Thousands of mothers, teen-agers and young men and women of college age have brought their problems to me. The events of that night, however, and Jack's subsequent handling by our county authorities were as I had described them, with one exception. I have been told since that Jack did have several treatment sessions with a psychiatrist while in our jail. They did not seem to have done him much good, though, in such a setting. (One of the problems of the schizophrenic is withdrawal into himself. To leave Jack so long in what amounted to solitary confinement was about the worst thing for him that could have been done.)

I had been urged to publish my story by lawyer friends, who had been certain that the county attorney's office must have the case well in hand, that the prosecutor would surely counsel with me before presenting the case to the grand jury. When events befell as they finally did, my advisers were as shocked as I was.

As one of them put it, "The ordeal you have gone through will serve a purpose if it wakens the public to the consequences of society's indifference and callousness toward sexually sick men. Perhaps it is too late now to save Jack Smith. But there are many others who can be saved, and saving them is the only way to save the women and children who would otherwise be their victims." Mr. and Mrs. Bruce Gould, then editors of the *Ladies' Home Journal,* of which I was a staff member, agreed that the story should be published.

Even though it ran long for a magazine article, much had to be omitted. I dwelt only briefly on the mental and emotional turmoil I went through as I waited for word from our county seat that never came. My background and experience, while by no means qualifying me as an expert in psychiatric matters, nevertheless had given me a deeper understanding of the psychiatric issues involved than is possessed by the average citizen and hence, I felt, a more than ordinary responsibility. On the other hand, I knew only enough about the law to be aware of the damage laymen can do when they barge into a legal situation without expert guidance. I dared not take any action on my own lest inadvertently I should bring about the very thing I wanted to prevent—the release of a dangerous man on some legal technicality.

Actually, I suffered far more from my experience with the law than I had from the attack itself, for I recognized that Jack was not responsible for what he had done. My friends began to worry about me when it became evident that Jack's case had been handled with the same blindness to future consequences that had characterized those of the rapists and sex murderers I had been reading about. There were even times, after the grand jury meeting, when I was a little worried about myself.

In my distress, I consulted one of the country's leading psychiatrists, to learn if there was still something I might do to help Jack Smith. He agreed that the handling accorded Jack had been inexcusable. "That sort of thing has been a subject of controversy between psychiatry and the law for many years." But he considered it doubtful that a case of schizophrenia, so long-standing and severe, could be permanently cured under the most favorable circumstances, though schizophrenics frequently have remissions from time to time when they appear to be cured.

In any event, he advised that there was nothing I could do. "They would just say to you, 'Well, lady, what do you want? You want the man put where he can't do any harm, don't you? We've put him where he can't do any harm. So what do you want?' " I could hear "them" saying it. It was my understanding that the inmates of the hospital for the criminally insane, where Jack had been sent, were treated humanely. If Jack would have to be confined for the rest of his life, that seemed as good a place for him as any. So I put the incident behind me and turned my attention to my own affairs.

The shock was all the greater, therefore, when, twenty-two months after his commitment to the hospital, Jack was returned to our county jail to stand trial for the attack on me. It was a little while before I found this out. I had been in New York City, covering the annual meeting of the American Medical Association for the *Ladies' Home Journal,* and had been home only a few minutes when a visitor knocked at my door. We had a new prosecuting attorney now. Unable to reach me by phone, he had had the kindness to come to my house in the evening to tell me that Jack had been released from the hospital as recovered and ready to stand trial. There was to be a meeting on the case at the courthouse the next morning. He had thought I might like to be there.

What filled me with utter consternation was his going on to say that, while a trial would have to be held, Jack would be turned loose however it came out. The jury of laymen would be called upon to decide whether or not he had been sane and accountable for his actions on the night, now more than two years back, when he had attacked me. If the jury decided he was insane, it would have to find him not guilty by reason of insanity, and he would go free. If he was found sane and guilty, under the charges lodged against him he could at most be sentenced to two and a half years in the penitentiary, which he would already have served in our jail and the hospital for the criminally insane. He would go free.

The proceedings the next morning proved to be a hearing on a plea that Jack be freed now on bail, pending the trial. The defense attorney and the prosecuting attorney stood before the judge, presenting arguments for and against. It was plain that not one of the three men believed Jack was cured.

The prosecutor opposed the motion on the grounds that Jack's crime had been one of violence and might have had very serious consequences if the victim had not managed to escape entirely through her own efforts. Jack, he said, had had little if any psychiatric treatment in the hospital for the criminally insane. To turn him loose would constitute a peril to the community.

The defense attorney countered that Jack's family wanted him released so that he might be given psychiatric treatment. There was a chance, he said—a very faint one, to be sure, but still a chance—that with proper psychiatric treatment Jack might be cured. When he had finished speaking, the judge leaned forward, said to him earnestly, "Mr. D——, I wish you would leave the man in jail."

After some further argument by the attorneys, the judge said, "We may as well be realistic about this, gentlemen. We all know that if I deny the plea, Mr. D—— can appeal to the State Supreme Court and have his client out in a few days on a writ of habeas corpus. We may as well turn to considering the amount of the bail." That settled, a tentative date was set for the trial which would make Jack's freedom absolute.

It appeared that my very worst apprehensions had been realized. A man I still believed to be dangerous was being released into the community. If something dreadful were to happen in consequence, I would feel responsible. But what could I do?

"Maybe the man really *is* cured," a friend pointed out. "They are doing wonderful things now in the mental institutions. Why don't you find out before you get worked up all over again?" I had not heard of anything as wonderful as the cure in less than two years' time of a case like Jack's, but through the kindness of state officials I did obtain a report on Jack from the hospital. It did not reassure me. There was no mention at all of psychiatric treatment, sexual disturbance, or the desperate struggle in my home. That incident figured only as Jack's having admitted that he was drunk the night he went to a house—mine, I assumed—and entered it without knocking. A note was added to the report, in answer to a query from me. There was of course no guaranty, it said, that Jack would not break down mentally again. My request for information as to the extent and depth of his psychiatric treatment got nowhere. These matters are private and privileged, I was told. The law forbids their disclosure.

At this point, an official experienced in dealing with offenders advised that I move far away, leaving no traces behind me, and communicate with my friends only through my publishers. I wasn't so much concerned for my own safety, however. I knew the danger, I could take steps to protect myself. But there are literally millions of women within easy driving range of my locality who would not know the danger. No one could foretell which one of them might have to pay the penalty if Jack's release had been premature. I had had no connection with Jack, I hadn't known he existed, until he threw open my bedroom door in the middle of the night.

Attention had been drawn to Jack Smith originally because of rumored attempts on other women in the community, though mine were the first charges ever filed against him. As far as I could learn, the attack on me had been the most serious thing he had done to date, and it had followed a long period of remission which had led his family to believe that he was over his trouble. Only God can know what would have happened if we had not been by the open door when he seized me a second time—I have never let myself think about that—but his previous comments about murder and cruelty indicated that anger and resentment had entered his mind, along with the fantasy element. Certainly no other woman could count on having the luck I had had.

On the other hand, there was the possibility that we were doing Jack and the hospital doctors a grave injustice. How were we to tell?

In the end, a solution was furnished by the defense attorney. When the time came for the trial, I was called into consultation with Mr. D—— and the prosecutor. Mr. D—— said he had heard via the grapevine that I was unhappy about the case. I replied with an emphatic "Yes!"

He told the prosecutor and me that he had been involved in many cases of this kind and spoke of one in which he had gone before a judge—not the one in our case—and expressed the opinion that his client should not be released. "The judge called me into his chambers and said he didn't think I had represented my client's interests very well." The reprimand had stung. But not long afterward, the client climbed out onto the roof of his house and through a window of the bedroom where his 10-year-old daughter and a friend were sleeping, tied both girls to the bed and raped them, then took a gun, went out onto the street and shot several people. We gathered that Mr. D—— wished no such denouement as this in Jack's case.

He had thought of a plan which would give the court power to insure that Jack should receive continued supervision and psychiatric care. He was prepared to propose to the judge, Jack and his family consenting, that the not-guilty plea already entered be changed to guilty, on a charge that would permit a longer sentence than those brought against him originally; that the part remaining after the two and a half years Jack had already served be spent on probation, with competent psychiatric treatment. Mr. D—— stressed the word "competent."

The prosecutor reminded me that Mr. D—— could bring his client off scot free, with no strings attached at all, by retaining the not-guilty plea and going ahead with the trial. He thought Mr. D——'s proposal was very generous, and I agreed.

And that was the way it was done, after the judge had satisfied himself, by questioning Jack closely, that the young man understood the implications of pleading guilty to a felony and did so willingly. For some years to come, Jack must report once a month to a probation officer, wherever he may be, and remain under psychiatric treatment. Should he fail in this, or commit another offense, he will finish out his sentence in the state penitentiary.

Meanwhile I had had a long talk with the probation officer. For the first time since the incident in my house, I was able to tell the full story of what had happened that night, with psychological overtones of the incident itself and background I had since gathered, to an official charged with some responsibility for Jack's handling.

None of us wants to see Jack land, ever, in the penitentiary. "There should be a special institution where such men could be sent and receive the kind of therapy they need," the prosecuting attorney said, after the judge had handed down his verdict. But it was the best solution our state laws and facilities allowed.

"You haven't heard anything yet!" That was the comment of a dear friend of many years, whom I shall call Mrs. Brown, after she had listened politely to my experience with the operation of the law in its handling of dangerous, sexually disturbed men. She went on to tell me what her daughter, Sue, had gone through.

I have known Sue since she was a tiny girl and have seen her grow up into an attractive, brilliant woman, well balanced and sound of judgment, the last to imagine threats that do not exist. Widowed suddenly and tragically, she at length had reached the point of considering her future and had enrolled in a graduate school in California, taking her two small children with her. She accepted several invitations from a fellow student, also working toward a Ph.D., but sensed something peculiar about him and refused his subsequent invitations. He then began bombarding her with flowers, candy and obscene messages, many written on postcards. "Sue couldn't tell her father and me what some of the messages were," her mother said, "they were so vile."

Sue went to the head of the psychiatry department of the university to ask his advice about the situation. "How long have you had these delusions that someone is persecuting you?" the psychiatrist wanted to know.

Presently a long, rambling letter arrived from the man, proposing marriage and stating quite calmly, "I killed my three children." Investigating, Sue learned that her suitor had indeed killed his three children, had been placed in a hospital for the criminally insane and then released as cured, before entering the graduate school. With this information in hand, a male relative of Sue's went to the university authorities and demanded that something be done. They were ready to help now and did interview the man. The next development was a letter addressed to Sue's children and saying, "I don't want to hurt you, but your mother has brought this upon herself."

Sue rushed to the police station, taking her children with her. When the police captain heard her story and read the letter, he told her to get herself and her children on the next plane for her parents' home. She was not allowed even to return to her apartment for the clothes they would need; a policewoman was sent to pack for them. The man had disappeared, and the captain said the police could not guarantee to protect her and her children as long as he was at large.

"I never in my life saw anything as woeful as Sue and the children when they got off the plane," Mrs. Brown said. "Sue had had to drop her college work in mid-term, of course, but the worst was that she still didn't feel safe. Her persecutor had money, and no one can guess what such a man will do. We didn't dare let either Sue or the children out of our sight until word came that the man had been arrested. Sue was asked to return and testify at the trial, and she went back at once, for she felt it was her duty to do so."

But the trial was never held; no witnesses were ever heard. While Sue waited for her summons, a private hearing was arranged before a judge. A psychiatrist testified that he had examined the man and found him sane. The judge dismissed the charges, and the man was turned loose.

"I was so wrought up that I wrote the county attorney myself," Mrs. Brown said, "asking if there wasn't something that could still be done to protect women and children. He replied regretfully that, inasmuch as a judge had dismissed Sue's charges, the law could do nothing until the man had committed another offense! Sue didn't dare resume her college work in California. She has moved to another place, naturally, and we hope she is safe. But what about the next woman who happens to attract this man's fancy?"

A prominent doctor told me his daughter's experience. A young mother, she was attending night classes at a college some blocks from her New York City apartment, while her husband minded the baby. For some time she had had an impression that someone was following her as she walked home from the college. One night the man came into the open, followed right behind her, and pushed ahead of her into the unattended lobby of her apartment building. Afraid to get into the elevator but equally afraid to remain in the lobby, she at last summoned her courage and dashed into the elevator. Fortunately the door closed quickly, and she arrived safely at her own apartment.

The next night they hired a sitter, and the young woman's husband hid himself near the college entrance. When the wife appeared, a man stepped out of the shadows and followed her to the apartment, the husband following both. When the man again entered the apartment house after her, the husband seized him and held him while the wife called the police.

The wife's tracker, six feet four inches tall and weighing 250 pounds, proved to be a patient under psychiatric care. He admitted to the police that he had been attracted to the young woman and had been following her with the idea of grabbing her when an auspicious moment presented itself. But the police had to let him go. They said the law forbade them to take any action until the man actually did grab her!

"My daughter is no glamor gal, you understand," the father said. "She's a serious-minded young woman who wears flat heels and a minimum of make-up. She does have yellow hair, and the psychopath told the police he likes blondes. The only helpful suggestion they made was that my daughter should wear a scarf over her head when she goes out at night!"

But a head scarf does not promise very much protection from a giant who has already marked her down for his prey. Even to give up her college work and to stay at home nights would avail little, since the disturbed man might be lying in wait for her anywhere in the daytime, when her husband necessarily is away at work. Must this young couple find another home, the husband find another job, while a sexually sick man remains free to do whatever he likes?

In both of these cases, the families are prominent, the threatened young mothers are of the finest character, neither is of the type deliberately to attract the wrong kind of attentions from males, neither has been guilty of any offense.

Yet they are the ones who are called upon to flee, to go into hiding, *until* the sick man in California perhaps is moved to threaten another victim, *until* the sick man in New York State actually grabs some unsuspecting young woman.

I saw now that the release into the community, over and over again, of the sexually disturbed man with a propensity for violence is a much bigger matter than the degree of assiduousness with which individual officials carry out their duties.

When Jack Smith's case came up the second time, our local officials had been as anxious to protect the community, and Jack's own best interests, as anyone could have wished. They would have been barred from doing it by the very law itself if the defense attorney had not had an unusually keen sense of his own obligation to the community.

In the other two cases, a known child killer and a known sexually sick man remain at large with the blessing of a law which offers no protection to the innocent ones they have chosen as their victims.

However, I had not dug very far into the subject before I learned that merely revising old laws, or passing new ones, is not enough. In fact, my own state, New York, though not the best, is among the better ones in this respect. And California, where Sue's unhappy experience took place, was the first state to provide a special, separate institution for the care and treatment of sexually disturbed offenders. In both these great states, a sincere and intelligent effort has been made to bring the statutes regarding sexually sick men into accord with scientific progress. If it can happen this way in New York and California, what must the situation be in states where no such effort has been made?

# 3
# How big
# is the problem?

But had I let my imagination run away with me, as a result of my own experience? Were my doctor friend and Sue's parents worrying about something that is never going to happen? There are writers who contend that there is no reason to get excited about these men. The violent, dangerous sex offenders are relatively few when compared with the general crime population; the rapist seldom repeats his offense, they claim. J. Edgar Hoover has been severely excoriated for an article by him which appeared in the *American Magazine* for July, 1947, "How Safe Is Your Daughter?" Such articles only arouse needless fears, his critics maintain.

To prove how minor the problem is, one writer stated that he had gone through *The New York Times* for the years 1930, 1935 and 1940 and had found only seventeen murders of women and children by "unknown sex fiends" reported in the entire three years. Sex attacks short of murder were not counted. I myself, in making inquiries at diagnostic and treatment clinics, have been told repeatedly that they get few men or boys who have committed sex crimes of violence. Is the problem truly such a tiny one that there is no point in making a fuss about it?

I decided to make a little newspaper survey of my own, to see how prevalent sex violence is in more recent years. But I did not employ *The New York Times*. One might even find some significance in the use of *The New York Times* for this purpose, if the investigator is acquainted with newspapers, for that admirable paper habitually plays down, or ignores entirely, the more lurid aspects of the local crime scene. I often hear, over the morning radio, of sex murders in New York and adjoining states which are not reported at all in the edition of *The New York Times* that comes to me every day. For my survey, I started with the *New York Post* which pays more attention than does the *Times* to the more gruesome facts of life, but without concentrating on them to a disproportionate and sensational extent. Following is the record of attacks on women and children by sexually disturbed men—most of these men unknown to their victims—as found in the *Post* for January and February of 1960. Unless otherwise indicated, these crimes all took place in one of the five New York City boroughs.

January 4: A 50-year-old grandmother is raped by an unknown man who forced his way into her apartment at knife point when she stepped outside her door to put garbage in the incinerator. He first demanded money and took it, then threw her on her bed, raped her, and left her tied to the bed.

January 5: A 16-year-old girl, who had been beaten and raped, is found unconscious in a hallway of a housing project where she lived. Her condition is serious. The *Post* reports several days later that she is still unconscious.

January 11: A cab driver signs a confession to having attempted to rape the daughter of a prominent writer, after she got into his cab at La Guardia Airport in New York City. He confesses also to sex attacks on five other women.

January 24: Murder is suspected in the case of a 12-year-old Boy Scout found hanging in a wood in Connecticut, with a woman's nylon stocking on his right leg in place of his own shoe and stocking. The feminine garment here hints at a particular kind of sex aberration. Nothing further reported in this case.

This same issue contains the first report of an attack made on January 9, on an 18-year-old Hempstead, Long Island, mother. A man about 28 years old, and weighing around 200 pounds, had seized her at a shopping center parking lot, thrown her into the trunk of a car, driven to a lonely spot, raped her, then set her free. The incident is reported at this time because the victim had received a letter from the man, expressing his regret and remorse and saying that he had visited a doctor, but that it was hard for the physician to understand "the type of mental problem or block upon which the devil played and turned me into some kind of animal."

January 28: A 22-year-old man is charged with the rape murder of Margaret O'Meara, a 77-year-old Brooklyn spinster. The man allegedly told police that he had also raped a 29-year-old housewife. He had served reformatory terms for auto theft, burglary, and grand larceny and had been placed on probation after being charged with unlawful entry and malicious mischief.

In the same issue: Police are seeking a man, 35 to 40 years old, who had forced a 12-year-old girl at knife point onto the roof of the apartment building where she lived, made her undress—this was January, mind you—and then raped her. He is believed to be the man who raped two other girls in the same neighborhood.

February 2: A grade-school principal in Hartford, Indiana, walks into two different classrooms and, in the presence of the pupils, shoots and kills the woman teacher in each room, then shoots himself. He had been complaining of headaches and sleeplessness and imagined there was gossip connecting him with one of the teachers he had killed. There was no sex molestation, but, as we shall see later, sexual disturbance may cause murder without sexual molestation. A community leader is quoted as saying, "Here was a potentially dangerous man. He should have been given medical aid. Now it's too late. We let him slaughter two fine citizens in front of children who will always carry this horrible memory."

February 5: A 20-year-old college student in Mississippi is arrested for the murder of a socially prominent neighbor, 31 years old and the mother of four children. The husband and children found her body when they got home from church. She had been strangled with a wire coat hanger. Though again there was no sign of sexual molestation, the circumstances indicated that her attacker was sexually disturbed.

February 7: A 19-year-old Brooklyn youth is arrested for the fatal stabbing of Mrs. Estrella Matos when she resisted his attempt to rape her in November, 1959. Recognized on the street by a woman he had raped and robbed on January 18 (not reported in the *Post* at the time), police said he had confessed to both crimes. He is reported to have told detectives, with regard to the murder of Mrs. Matos, "I was drinking that night, but I remember what happened. Every time I drink, I get the urge to rape and rob people."

Police reported he said he had seen Mrs. Matos as he walked down the street, seized her, and dragged her across the street toward a park. What a plucky woman Mrs. Matos must have been! She bit the hand he put over her mouth to stifle her screams, pulled out of his grasp, ran back across the street, but fell when she reached the sidewalk. He caught her again and stabbed her twice. Momentarily the knife thrusts deprived her of power to resist, and he pulled her back to the park, but there she broke away again and ran up the street, only to fall once more. He stabbed her twice more, there in the street, this time fatally, but a crowd was beginning to gather, so he ran. Police were planning to question the youth about two hitherto unsolved rapes and a murder, also unsolved, that had occurred in the vicinity; nothing further on this case in the papers reviewed.

February 21: The case of Caryl Chessman, sentenced to die by a California court for a number of rape murders, is very much in the news, with so much agitation from citizens for and against commutation of the death sentence to life imprisonment that it has become a political issue. (Chessman was eventually executed.)

The police admit no headway has been made toward finding the killer of the invalid wife of a prominent New Jersey surgeon, her maid, her companion and housekeeper and a New Jersey taxi driver who happened to be at the house, the lack of any apparent motive for the mass slaying having been a serious handicap to the authorities. (Cash in the house amounting to $1000 was not taken.) I list it here because it is typical of the apparently motiveless crimes of men who are incited to murder by their aberrant sexual impulses but do not molest their victims sexually.

February 22: A 13-year-old Delta, Ohio, boy stabs to death a neighbor girl as she gets out of the school bus in which both were riding. The boy could not say why he had killed the girl; he declared that he liked her. Several months before this, he had fired several shots at the girl's home. The sheriff found then that the boy owned eight other guns besides the one he had used in this incident. A juvenile court judge had ordered psychiatric treatment for the boy, but it had not been given him.

February 25: A search is reported for a youth who raped and robbed the 46-year-old wife of a Presbyterian minister on a deserted subway platform in New York. The youth is described as around 19 to 21 years old (nothing further on this case in the papers reviewed).

February 26: A Brooklyn father and his three sons trap an intruder who had attempted to rape the 13-year-old daughter of the family in her bedroom. The man is identified as the one who had raped a 28-year-old woman in her home on January 31. (The January 31 rape was not reported in the issue I read of that date.)

February 28: Police are hunting a youth accused of attacking a 40-year-old Brooklyn woman in a vacant lot only three blocks from her home, at 8:50 P.M.

So much for the first two months of 1960, as reported in the *New York Post*. For a similar sampling of 1961, I decided to use the *New York Journal-American,* another middle-of-the-road paper in its treatment of crime. I found only two apparently sex-inspired crimes of violence noted in the *Journal-American's* January issues. On the fifteenth, two sisters, 27 and 20 years old, were both stabbed in the back as they were walking along a New York City street after bowling. The 16-year-old boy who was arrested for the stabbing had a previous record of three arrests and had been confined in Creedmore Hospital.

A 20-year-old San Francisco girl had sustained a fractured skull and other injuries when she leaped, nude, from a second-story window in order to avoid being raped by her stepfather, on parole from San Quentin prison.

February, 1961, was a different story, however.

February 14: A 32-year-old New York City man admits to having killed three mistresses in one evening. The body of the most recent addition to his harem, a 16-year-old high school girl, was found on the roof of the building where he lived. The man's mother, going to get her son because the police wished to question him, found the bodies of the two other women in his room.

February 15: In California, a pretty, blond 8-year-old girl is being searched for. She got off the school bus and then vanished (nothing further on this case in the papers reviewed).

February 22: A 33-year-old Long Island woman reports that she woke at 12:45 A.M. to find a man standing over her, holding a knife and a flashlight. She says she screamed, the man slashed her face, then fled. The victim's husband was away, but her two children and a maid were in the house.

February 23: Fifty-five detectives and uniformed police have conducted an all-night search, combing roofs, cellars and hallways in a section of Flatbush, Long Island, for 4-year-old Edith Kiecarius, who had vanished from the sidewalk in front of a relative's apartment during ten minutes that she had not been under direct observation by the relative. With the story, which appears on page 3, is a photograph of Edith, plump, pretty, sparkling-eyed. Readers are urged to be on the lookout for a little girl forty inches tall, weighing forty pounds, with honey-blond hair and hazel eyes.

In the same issue, it is reported that Marvin Rees, 32 years old and a former University of Maryland student, has been found guilty of wiping out an entire Apple Grove, Virginia, family—father, mother and two small children. The prosecution charged that Rees had killed the father and 18-months-old baby first, in Virginia, then had taken the mother and 5-year-old girl with him to Maryland for sexual gratification. There he had beaten and strangled mother and child and left their bodies on a rubbish heap. Tried first in a federal court in Baltimore for the two murders committed in Maryland, Rees had been convicted and sentenced to life imprisonment. He had then been tried in a Virginia court for the two other murders and sentenced to die.

February 24: The story about the still-missing Edith Kiecarius has moved to the front page as the search for her intensifies. Three hundred policemen and 125 detectives are now in the area. Police helicopters are flying low over the rooftops. A policeman speaks to a *Journal-American* reporter about the deep concern of the officers. "She is such a little girl," he says.

February 25 and 26: The search for Edith Kiecarius continues, with 3000 officers and detectives now engaged. Reports from many places that she has been seen prove false. Fears grow.

February 27: The body of Edith Kiecarius, beaten, raped and strangled, has been found in a squalid room filled with empty beer cans, only three blocks from the New York City Hall. People in the neighborhood are horrified to learn that a man who could rape, torture and kill a 4-year-old child has been living in their midst. Will he strike again?

February 28: The man who was later convicted of killing Edith Kiecarius has been caught already, identified by fingerprints in the room where Edith was found. Fifty-nine years old, married, with three daughters, Fred Thompson is a man without skills who has eked out a living as dishwasher, porter, handyman. In 1945 he had been confined in Pilgrim Hospital in Brentwood, New York, after beating one of his daughters in a drunken rage. (At this time, according to the newspaper, he had been diagnosed as having an alcoholic psychosis but was found to be free of any incipient sex deviation.) Thompson was said to have told the police, "with an air bordering on unconcern," that he had been drinking when he went out on the street, saw Edith, and wanted to have intimacies with her. She had gone with him readily "to see his little sick girl." She was frightened and screamed when he attempted to touch her body, he said, and he told how he had beaten her head against the wall and floor until she was quiet, then had thrown her on the bed and raped her. She had been dead for at least one of the four days during which he had stayed with her in the room.

Thompson told police that Edith was not the first child he had molested, that he had "been this way" for over a year. "In subways I kept trying to get women and little girls to come with me. I'd say filthy things to them and expose myself. I guess most of them were too scared or embarrassed to tell the police."

Thompson was indicted by a grand jury within a few hours after his capture and charged with first-degree murder and kidnaping a child subsequently found dead, the latter charge in New York State carrying a mandatory death penalty upon conviction. He was sent to Bellevue Hospital for psychiatric examination and pronounced sane after a few weeks of observation, tried, and convicted on November 17, 1961. In January, 1962, he was returned to Bellevue upon representations of his lawyers that he had become insane after his conviction. The Bellevue psychiatrists concurred and recommended that the man be sent to the Matteawan State Hospital for the Criminally Insane, which was done after the judge had ordered an independent psychiatric examination. Thompson was still in Matteawan in early 1965. Under the New York law, if he should recover his sanity he will be returned to the court for sentencing, but there will be an automatic stay of execution until his case is reviewed by the New York State Court of Appeals and the governor.

These are the gleanings from two different New York City newspapers in just two months of each of two different years. I have ignored so-called "crimes of passion" caused by marital troubles; the murder of a wife by a husband so that he might marry someone else; slayings in connection with robberies; and cases where a girl or woman accused some acquaintance of rape.

The files I have maintained in somewhat desultory fashion since the attack on me in early 1959 are bursting with further newspaper stories of rape and murder, some of them supplied by friends in other parts of the country and not all dated.

It is stated by reputable sources, one of them being J. Edgar Hoover's Uniform Crime Reports, that murder has the lowest repeater rate among crimes and rape the next lowest. This does not mean, however, that the rapist can be counted on not to repeat, if left free to do so. As was pointed out by the late Dr. Benjamin Karpman, formerly chief psychotherapist at St. Elizabeth's Hospital, Washington, D.C., the forcible rapist, among the various types of sex offender, is most likely to be apprehended and put out of circulation at least for a while. My clipping file indicates that, if not apprehended, or if turned loose after a term in the usual jail or prison, the forcible rapist is very likely to repeat. In the great majority of the cases noted there, the man arrested or convicted had had a previous record of conviction or had perpetrated a number of rapes before being caught. Also worth noting is that a number of murderers had carried on a considerable career of rape or other sex offenses, short of murder—though so many of the rape murders remain unsolved that it is hard to be sure about that—before being caught.

Some had actually been convicted of murder and then released, before the sex killing. A notable instance from my file was the rape murder in April, 1959, in the Bronx, of a 65-year-old grandmother, the mother of five grown children, one of them a nun, as she was walking home after a visit to a relative not far away. Her body—she had been beaten, her ribs kicked in, raped and finally choked to death—was found in a vacant lot only three blocks from an alley where an 18-year-old girl had been brutally attacked, less than three months before, and a half mile from the spot where another woman had been attacked in the month preceding assault. The man arrested was a giant Negro, six feet five inches tall and weighing 300 pounds, who had been sentenced to twenty years in West Virginia for killing his wife, paroled after a few years, picked up again three years later, and again paroled in 1954. A warrant had been issued for his arrest on a charge of attempting to poison a second wife in 1955, but he had vanished, and it was not served until he was arrested in Boston for the rape murder in New York City.

In the case of one of four women killed by rapists in New York City during the week my own assailant was at large—that was when I first became vividly aware of these crimes—a police artist had drawn a picture of the man suspected of the slaying, made up from descriptions of an "unknown sex fiend" which were furnished by twelve victims of rape in the same area, preceding the murder. I did not observe in the papers that the man was ever found.

Cases in my files for 1960, aside from the ones already noted, included the rape murder of Nina Thoeren, the 19-year-old daughter of a Hollywood screen writer, on the campus of Los Angeles City College where she was a student. The murderer, a Bible salesman, was arrested on the scene. He had been paroled by California authorities in 1958, following a previous conviction for rape (*New York Herald-Tribune*, July 13).

On August 18, the dismembered body of 11-year-old Avril Terry, the daughter of a prominent Boonville, Indiana, doctor, was found in the Ohio River, downstream from the spot where 53-year-old Emmett Hashfield, an ex-convict, allegedly had admitted to police that he had thrown the pieces into the water. Hashfield's record of crimes against children stretched back many years, according to Indiana authorities. Hashfield had been paroled in 1958 from a fourteen-year-sentence for sodomy. According to the *New York Herald-Tribune* for August 19 and 20, Avril's father asked, "What manner of man, what type of motivation, directs a parole commission knowingly to turn loose a beast in the streets?" (This case is extensively discussed in Chapter 6.)

In October, the life of a 5-year-old Philadelphia girl was being fought for by doctors after she had been gagged, bound with wire mesh, and stabbed twenty-one times by a 14-year-old neighbor boy. He had lured her into the basement of the housing project where they both lived with a promise of candy and attempted to rape her. Her screams and struggles made him angry, so he had tied her up and stabbed her again and again with his pocketknife. The boy had served more than a year at the Philadelphia Protectory for Boys, a corrective institution, on charges of assault and battery with a stick and robbery. He was said to have been a troublemaker and very serious problem in his neighborhood by the time he was 10, had been examined psychiatrically at that time, and had been sent to the Protectory because there was no other place to send him. The judge before whom the boy appeared on that occasion was reported to have said, "We don't have a place in Pennsylvania where a defective juvenile can be sent" (Philadelphia papers for October 10 to 12).

I find a clipping from the *New York Herald-Tribune* for January 25, 1961, of a crime not noted in the edition of the *Journal-American* that I went through. According to New York State Police, a 37-year-old escapee from the Polk State School, a mental institution in Pennsylvania, had admitted killing a 5-year-old boy at the New York State fairgrounds the preceding August. The victim belonged to a family of acrobats appearing at the fair; the slayer was a roustabout employed there. Police said he confessed that he had molested the little boy sexually and then had strangled him for fear he might tell.

As I proceed through my clipping file, it occurs to me that J. Edgar

Hoover might justifiably have titled his article, "How Safe Is Your Daughter, Your Little Son, Your Sister, Your Wife, Your Mother, Your Grandmother?" Where females are concerned, there is no safety either in old age or in extreme youth. There are men, in fact, who specialize in older women for their victims, such as the Boston Strangler, who has raped and strangled ten women, most of them elderly, in Boston and its environs as this is written, if indeed the Boston Strangler is one man. The oldest rape victim to come to my attention was 81, while at the other end of the scale we have 3½-year-old Becky Holt of Philadelphia, strangled by a 15-year-old neighbor, a "model" boy and honor student. This case, however, would have attracted little attention outside of Philadelphia—there are, alas, so many similar ones—had not Becky's father, a professor at the University of Pennsylvania, appealed to the public over the radio to recognize that his little daughter's slayer was a sick person, and that the true tragedy lay in the fact "that it was possible for this boy to go through his whole fifteen years without *anyone* who was responsible for his upbringing— such as his school or church—having taken note (out of uncaring or lack of understanding) of the danger signals before the tragedy."

Countless women are attacked in their houses or apartments by men who gain entrance on plausible pretexts. An undated clipping from *The New York Times* describes an attack on a 71-year-old woman and her 28-year-old daughter in their home at 9:30 in the evening, by a man who had delivered a motion-picture projector to them a few weeks previously. The mother let him in when he said he wanted to examine it, and she stated that he at once began beating her about the face and head with a revolver. In this case, the women's screams brought neighbors, and the man fled after having knocked the mother unconscious, looting her handbag, tying the hands of both women and attempting to rape the daughter, according to the clipping. Police were seeking a man who had served a year in the penitentiary for burglary.

The rape is reported of a 21-year-old housewife in Levittown, New Jersey, in her home, by a man who held a knife at her throat, thrust a handkerchief into her mouth to stifle her screams, pushed her into her bedroom and tied her with her husband's neckties. The family had moved into the house only the day before. The young woman was expecting a maintenance man and had let her assailant in because he was dressed in work clothes. The arrested man, a former cab driver, had been at large on probation under a one-year sentence for a morals offense committed about five months previously (Philadelphia *Evening Bulletin,* January 16, 1963).

Women and children have been attacked with no provocation, or murdered, when going about on the most ordinary occasions of life. Another undated clipping from *The New York Times* describes the vicious, unprovoked beating of a 51-year-old female office worker in the elevator of an office building at Fifth Avenue and 25th Street, New York City, during office hours. The thug was in the elevator when she entered it, on the first floor, and began at once to beat and kick her. A man got on at the tenth floor and went to her assistance, whereupon the thug knocked both the woman and her defender unconscious, then left the elevator and escaped down the stairs. It appeared that robbery was not the motive for the attack. For good measure, this same item tells of an attack on a New York State female employee, as she was coming up out of the subway at the corner of Broadway and 40th Street, just off New York's famous Times Square, at 4:15 in the afternoon. The man knocked out several of the young woman's teeth and pushed her down the stairs, then tried to grab her handbag, but her screams were heard by a patrolman who stopped the man from doing further damage. This would appear on the surface to be a case of mugging and theft, of which there is a great deal in New York City, but the recklessness and unnecessary savagery of this attack, made in broad daylight in one of New York City's most congested areas, seems abnormal, even for a mugger.

Still another undated item, paper not identified, tells of a charge brought by an 18-year-old girl against a clerk in the personnel department of a large New Jersey company where she had applied for a job. She said that he told her a girl was needed at the company's plant at Bristol and offered to drive her there in his station wagon. Near Williamstown, New Jersey, she charged, he pulled off to the side of the road, took a knife from his pocket, tied her hands behind her and, holding the knife at her throat, raped her. Police said the man had been put on probation in January of 1959, after he was found guilty of aggravated battery and assault on a woman.

Phyllis Ann Jones, a pretty 24-year-old girl from Norristown, Pennsylvania, died as a result of striking up a conversation with a 41-year-old Trenton, New Jersey, printer who was surf fishing at a New Jersey beach where she had gone swimming. It is believed that he represented himself as an airplane pilot, owning his own light plane, and had tricked the young woman into entering his car on the pretext that he would show her an aerial view of storm damage over the area. The confessed slayer had been given a long penitentiary sentence in 1949 for tying a 21-year-old Hopewell, New Jersey, girl to a tree stump and criminally attacking her, had been transferred to a mental hospital and re-sentenced to the penitentiary after that, then released (Philadelphia *Bulletin,* June 11, 1962).

A 31-year-old female commuter was slashed with a knife by a 24-year-old man in New York City's Pennsylvania Station. The man had had no previous connection with his victim; he could not say why he had attacked her (*New York Times,* July 7, 1962).

The raped and strangled body of a 4-year-old girl was found in the areaway of the apartment house of which her father was the superintendent, only a few feet from her parents' door. The police were rounding up all the known sex perverts in the neighborhood, as is always done *after* a crime of this kind has been committed (*New York Times,* June 7, 1963). Nothing further was seen on this case.

One elderly rape-murder victim was killed as she was walking home after Wednesday night prayer meeting. A Washington State Girl Scout was brutally slain while going around her own neighborhood, selling Girl Scout cookies. Women have been attacked in brightly lighted laundromats, and several attacks have taken place in the parking lots of supermarkets.

The attacks and murders take place in luxurious suburban homes as well as in city apartments and on city streets. A 31-year-old Negro, six feet tall and weighing 195 pounds, was convicted of the murder of a woman in her home in an exclusive section of Westport, Connecticut, and the kidnaping and raping of her 14-year-old daughter. A handyman who had raked leaves for the family, he entered the house in the morning after the husband and father had departed for his work, strangled the mother in the upstairs hall, then seized the daughter and drove around with her in his car, raping her several times in the course of the day and night that he kept her captive.

There is not even safety in numbers. Three Illinois women, wives of prominent businessmen, could not have dreamed that they were running any risk when they set out for a walk together in an Illinois state park. All three were clubbed to death and sexually molested when they refused sexual favors to a man who came upon them in a secluded spot. Two New York City society women lost their lives when their Cadillac stalled on a city street at night, and two youths who came along helped start it, then jumped into the car. An added macabre touch in this double rape murder was that the Cadillac was the death instrument used on its owner, the murderer driving it over her several times. There are many instances of rape where a male escort of the victim has been rendered helpless by the attacker.

The New York housing projects, designed to wipe out the crime-breeding conditions of the slums, have become happy hunting grounds for men and boys who prey on women and girls. In one housing project, a 24-year-old laborer was identified by twelve women as their attacker. Of these, six charged they had been raped.

In another, a number of women were beaten by a "well-dressed stranger," one so badly that her husband and daughter did not recognize her. In a third, a similar reign of terror culminated in the rape slaying, by stabbing, of a 12-year-old girl in her parents' apartment. The police said that no rapes had been reported previously from this project (Manhattanville), though several charges had been made of felonious assault. But tenants of the project said that between January 1 and September 14, when the murder occurred, there had been at least thirty instances of violence, including mugging and rape. These had not been reported to the police because of the embarrassment of the victims or fear of reprisal.

In still another New York City housing project, a 16-year old boy was arrested on January 23, 1963, as the rapist of eight girls, 10 to 14 years old, within the confines of the project in which all of them lived, in a single month. At the time, the youngster had been released from custody by a court, pending hearings on two charges which had been brought against him, one for rape. His technique was said to have been to loiter in the grounds of the project and, when he spotted a likely victim, follow her into her own building. There he would draw a knife and force her onto the roof or into the basement or under a stairway.

One of the most dramatic cases of 1962, so spectacular that it made the front page, under a two-column head, of *The New York Times,* was the shooting of the rape slayer of two women, when he came back to kill a third woman whom he had previously raped but had left alive. The rapist, Charles Gomby of Brooklyn, had entered the apartment of his third victim, a nurse, through a bathroom window. The nurse woke as Gomby began throttling her, then was choked into unconsciousness. She soon regained consciousness, however, and, recognizing that her attacker was mentally disturbed, talked to him quietly through the two rape attacks which followed, saying she would pray for him and promising to keep her eyes averted so that she would not be able to identify him. He left her apartment without harming her further, but his fingerprints matched those found in the apartments of two Brooklyn women who had been raped and murdered sometime before, 57-year-old Mrs. Lea Auster and 60-year-old Mrs. Wilhelmina Tinsdale. The police believed Gomby would regret that he had left a witness against him alive and would return to kill her.

No report of the rape was printed at the time. The police hid the nurse in a place of safety and surrounded her apartment with one of the biggest "stake-outs" in the history of the New York City Police Department. The night Gomby did return, policemen and detectives were hiding behind cars parked along the street, detectives waited in the nurse's apartment, and a woman detective lay on the nurse's bed, with the bedroom door partly open. Gomby entered through the bathroom window, as he had done before. He drew a gun when challenged by the detectives and was shot to death.

Since Gomby's three victims were elderly women and all had had some connection with hospitals, the police thought at first that Gomby was the Boston Strangler, a number of whose victims have also been elderly and have had some connection with the medical world. But the Boston Strangler has claimed more victims since Gomby's death. Gomby might have claimed more victims, too, before he was caught, had it not been for the presence of mind of his third victim and the vigorous and astute action of the police.

The 1963 crime which attracted nation-wide attention was the slaying, on August 28, in their apartment in a fashionable section of New York City, of two career girls, one the niece of a famous writer, the other the daughter of a Minneapolis surgeon. One girl had been molested sexually, both had been brutally beaten and repeatedly stabbed.

In September of 1962, Mayor James H. J. Tate of Philadelphia, aroused by the mounting number of rape cases in that city, blasted as "a public outrage" the dumping of sex criminals back upon the public by prison officials, correctional institutions, and parole boards, adding that he did not exclude the courts from blame. Three Philadelphia women and girls had been killed by rapists in a little more than a year; 225 rape cases had been reported in Philadelphia during the first eight months of 1962. Of the 175 men who had been arrested for these crimes, 140 had records of previous crimes and of commitments to correctional or mental institutions. Mayor Tate had ordered extra police protection but declared this was of little avail so long as courts and institutions "keep releasing men who have been convicted of rape, bodily assault, or other violent crimes" (*Philadelphia Inquirer,* September 19, 1962).

I daresay the reader has long since grown weary of this gruesome catalogue, but I could cite many more.

Let us not forget that these are things that have happened to real women and children, not fictional ones, who had done nothing to provoke the assaults upon them, who had no reason to suspect the grave danger that lay in wait for them. These are not alarmist theories; they are sex crimes as they occur and will keep on occurring so long as we remain indifferent to the problem of the sexually sick man or boy.

Let us remember also that the ones noted here for the most part took place in a limited area, and the record barely scratches the surface of the serious sex crimes committed in that area, let alone the country over.

Taking the country as a whole, J. Edgar Hoover said in his *American Magazine* article that a criminal assault occurs every forty-three minutes, day and night, in the United States. That was in 1947. The latest report issued by the F.B.I., for 1961, indicated that an assault of this kind was occurring every twenty-eight minutes, day and night.

Many authorities state that only a small proportion of rape attacks and child molestations are made known to the police. Some say only one fourth are reported, while Dr. Karl M. Bowman, of the Langley Porter Clinic in San Francisco, reporting on the California Sexual Deviation Research Project, put the proportion as low as one fifth. The very first finding of the staff which carried out the first New York State study of sexual offenders in Sing Sing was:

> The problem is much more complex than had been thought. The spectacular cases which arouse so much public concern are numerically only a small part of the problem of sex crime. It involves not only thousands who are convicted but other thousands never discovered except by social acquaintances who never complain, and millions more who are borderline cases of maladjustment.

The California and New York State reports were issued by highly trained, competent and respected authorities, after searching investigation. The as yet unsolved rapes and rape murders and molestations of children indicate in themselves that a considerable number of sexually disturbed and dangerous men and boys are running loose, with or without the sanction of some court or institution. Many more contain the emotional components of violence, awaiting the event which will explode them into action.

"The big problem with regard to the serious sex offenders is that people don't realize how terribly sick many of these men are," Dr.

Bernard C. Glueck, Jr., told me. Dr. Glueck headed the second study of serious sex offenders in Sing Sing. (The two Sing Sing studies will be discussed in Chapter 11.)

Meanwhile, no list of sex offenses can be kept up to date. You will have read in the newspapers of several shocking new sex crimes committed while this chapter was being printed.

# 4
## The law, medicine
## and the sex offender

The sickness has been recognized in a few places, and measures have been taken to handle it intelligently. At time of writing, Baltimore, Chicago, Cleveland, Cincinnati, Detroit, Philadelphia, Pittsburgh, Toronto and Washington, D.C., have psychiatric clinics in connection with the criminal and juvenile courts, and New York City has one in connection with its General Sessions Court. Massachusetts has a statewide system for furnishing psychiatric facilities to all its courts, the only state at present of which this is true. Dr. Manfred S. Guttmacher, head of the famous Baltimore court-connected psychiatric clinic, tells me that Los Angeles officials have recently consulted him about organizing a similar one there.

As I write this there are two special institutions for the study and treatment of sexual psychopaths, or sex deviates, or mentally disordered sex offenders, as the men we are concerned with in this book are variously called—one in California and one in Massachusetts. Wisconsin has had a special facility for sex deviates in its Waupun Prison since 1951 and is planning to build a special institution for these men in the middle 1960's. Several states have special facilities for the treatment of sexually sick men in their mental hospitals, as will be seen in the description of laws and procedures of the fifty states regarding sex offenders in the Appendix of this book.

Maryland has a special institution where "defective delinquents," offenders of all ages and types who have shown a propensity for dangerous behavior, can be sent and receive effective psychiatric treatment. California has psychiatric wards in its institutions for youthful offenders where sexually disturbed youngsters can be kept separate and given therapy. The New Jersey State Diagnostic Center, headed by Dr. Ralph Brancale, provides residential facilities for children from 8 to 18 and, in addition to its work with offenders for the New Jersey courts, offers preventive treatment to patients on private referrals.

The foregoing is not very much, to be sure, in the richest and one of the scientifically most advanced countries of the world, but it is something. Yet when I wrote my article for the *Ladies' Home Journal,* in 1960, we were unable to learn of any place where the problem was being attacked along the lines advocated by the experts in the field, except for the New Jersey State Diagnostic Center. No one to whom we applied seemed to have heard of the Sing Sing studies, made in our own state of New York, the second of which was reported on as recently as 1956, or of Dr. Guttmacher's Baltimore clinic, or of the excellent work carried on for years in California and Wisconsin, not to mention the other court clinics and numerous studies. The reason was that we applied to the wrong people—persons responsible for the actual handling of these offenders after they are caught. It was not until I started my research for this book and was referred to the National Council on Crime and Delinquency that I gained any idea as to what is being done and the vast amount of information that is available.

So far as the general public, the law enforcers, and even much of the medical world is concerned, Dr. Glueck's statement—that the great problem is a failure to understand how terribly sick many of these men are—still holds true. This failure to understand affects the handling of dangerous men and boys throughout our whole judicial, corrective and medical fabric, except for the places just noted.

Attempts have been made in other places but have proven largely ineffective because of a failure to understand the problem. In the late 1940's or early 1950's, around half of our states added to their statutes an indeterminate sentence for sexual psychopaths, as sexually sick men were then generally called, which ranges from one day to life and permits indefinite custody of men deemed by the committing court to have a potential for danger. But with only a few exceptions, the legislators failed to provide for effective treatment for the men given this sentence, and the indeterminate sentence is little used in the states which have not done this. Judges are reluctant to invoke what could be life imprisonment, on the mere presumption that a defendant might do something terrible at some future time, without assurance that he will receive proper therapy.

As for prosecutors, the late Professor Paul Tappan of New York University, a recognized authority on the legal side of the sex crime problem, says they appear to be inclined to utilize the law only where the state's case is too weak for a criminal conviction. "Moreover, prosecutors are clearly affected by their interpretation of and reaction to the statutes—where they disapprove the policy involved, they employ the law little or not at all."

There is as grave a lack of therapy for sexually disturbed youngsters as for adults. Even Massachusetts, which shares honors with California for the excellence of its handling of youngsters who have got into trouble, still has no place where juveniles who are both offenders and disturbed may receive the kind of medical treatment they need. The mental hospitals are not equipped to handle offenders; the training schools are not equipped to handle disturbed boys. This is the situation the country over, where youngsters in need of special help are concerned, except for a few states. In the others, clinics and private psychiatrists are hard put to it to find places where the youngsters can get help who need it most. And yet Dr. Glueck told me that by early adolescence a boy with a serious sexual disturbance is already too sick to be cured except by the most intensive psychiatric approaches.

I visited a private school in New York State, run by a religious group, which has established an enviable reputation for its program of treating and educating boys and girls who are both disturbed and delinquent. But in fairness to the rest of the school population, it had to refuse a 15-year-old boy who had fantasies of killing people and cutting them up and who replied, when asked what one does with girls,

"You grab them and hurt them." My own state, big and rich as it is, has no public institution equipped to deal in a beneficial way with a boy as dangerously sick as this one.

The tragic results of the lack in Pennsylvania were called to public attention in October of 1960 when the 5-year-old Philadelphia girl was bound with wire mesh and stabbed twenty-one times by a 14-year-old boy who had first appeared before the court in 1956, when he was 10 years old (described in Chapter 3). You may recall that the judge was reported to have spoken then of the fact that Pennsylvania had no place where a defective juvenile under 15 years of age could be sent.

In April of 1963, Ephraim R. Gomberg, then executive vice-president of the Crime Commission of Philadelphia, was deploring the lack of treatment for adult Pennsylvania offenders, before they are allowed to return to society. *The Philadelphia Inquirer* quoted him as saying, "Not only do we not cure sex offenders, we don't even make the attempt."

Statistics on sex crime are misleading. Lack of understanding of the problem renders those regarding forcible rape, for instance, practically meaningless. In many instances no differentiation is made between forcible rape, where a man overpowers a completely unwilling subject, and statutory rape, which is intercourse with a girl past the age of puberty and under the age of consent—an age which varies widely in the different states and in some is higher than the age permitted for marriage. A girl in the "jail-bait" age range may have actively invited the man's attentions, may have lied about her age, may be a professional prostitute, but it is still called rape if the man yields to her seductions.

But what throws off statistics even more, for all types of sex crimes, are the rather prevalent customs of not convicting men or boys charged with sex offenses and of permitting men charged with serious sex offenses to plead guilty to a lesser, non-sex offense, so that many of the convictions obtained are on charges not ostensibly connected with sex.

The report of the first Sing Sing study called attention to the fact that, of 1285 men charged with sex offenses in New York City in 1948, only 115 were ever sentenced. Many were turned loose; many others pleaded guilty to lesser charges, such as disorderly conduct, and were sentenced to a jail or penitentiary for short periods. Among these last were many repeaters. "Few persons charged with sex offenses are found guilty as charged."

The second Sing Sing study called attention again to the important error in the practice of offering a man under indictment for a sex offense the opportunity to plead guilty to a lesser offense, such as assault, which then becomes the crime of record, and disguises the nature of the crime both in the statistical report and the man's record. (Two of the supposedly non-sexual offenders used as a control group in the second Sing Sing study were found to have committed serious sex crimes as well.)

Around the time when the first Sing Sing report was made public, Dr. Karl M. Bowman of the Langley Porter Clinic in San Francisco was citing another New York City sex crime docket, in reporting on California's Sexual Deviation Research Project. He had reviewed the cases of 1219 New York City men accused of rape. Six hundred and thirty were either acquitted or their cases were dismissed without trial. Of the 589 who were convicted, only 123 were convicted of rape, though 15 men who had been charged with other crimes were convicted of rape as well, bringing the total convictions to 138. Presumably the other 451, or many of them, had pleaded guilty to lesser offenses. Of the 138 convicted, 28 were placed on probation, 11 were given suspended sentences, and 4 were merely fined. In the end, only 95 of the 1219 charged originally with rape were removed from the community. Similar studies in other states bear out the foregoing figures.

Accepting a plea of guilty to a lesser charge may occasionally be justified, as was pointed out to me by a state attorney general. Upon investigation, the district attorney may not find a basis for the more serious charge. But often the device is used to avoid the expense and bother of a trial, and it is employed most frequently in the big cities, where the dockets are most crowded and the sex crime rate also is heaviest. This could very well account for the fact that so many sex offenders have previous non-sex crimes listed on their record, but no sex crimes.

In January of 1959, mothers of 13- and 14-year-old girls stormed a

Brooklyn court when they learned that, without any notice to the complainants, it had accepted pleas of guilty to third-degree assault from youths who had been carrying on a reign of terror among early teen-age girls in a Brooklyn neighborhood and had been charged with first-degree, or forcible, rape, which is a felony. One youth had been indicted for eight different offenses. Third-degree assault is a misdemeanor in New York State, carrying a maximum sentence of one year, which frequently is suspended. In this case, the Brooklyn Children's Society, usually found on the side of the young offender, joined the mothers in urging that at least one felony charge should stand against each youth.

According to former New York City Magistrate Morris Ploscowe, there are few fields in which it is more difficult to enforce the law than in cases of sexual tampering with children, and many other authorities agree. Large numbers of these cases never come to the attention of the police. Children often do not tell their parents of these occurrences, and when parents become aware of them they are reluctant to subject the child to questioning by police or to testifying in a courtroom. As a result, comparatively few persons are arrested for sexual offenses against children. When they are arrested, they are frequently charged with less serious offenses than the ones they committed. It is easier to obtain convictions in minor cases than in major ones, which require a jury trial, and the problem of convicting a man and imprisoning him on the unsupported testimony of a child is a serious one.

Hence in New York State, according to Judge Ploscowe, the charge of impairing the morals of a minor, which is a misdemeanor in New York State, is frequently used in cases of attempted rape, carnal abuse of children, and incest, which are felonies. Once the charge has been altered to a misdemeanor, the offender cannot be sentenced to more than one year, whatever the nature of his offense. In actual practice, persons convicted of misdemeanors are frequently placed on probation.

Surely the public officials who permit these kinds of law evasion would not intentionally release dangerous men to prey again upon the women and children of the community. They simply do not understand the nature of the problem of the sexually sick man.

So far as the question of sexual sickness is concerned, in most states psychiatric examination of a man charged with a serious sex offense is left to the discretion of either the defense counsel or the court. (In at least one state, it rests entirely with the defense counsel.) As was shown by the second Sing Sing study, the deviates have a great fear of being sent to a hospital for the criminally insane, where they will have to stay, presumably, until the staff has reason to believe they are cured. There is also the stigma that is associated in the minds of many with mental illness.

Should the question of mental status be brought up by either side, in a large proportion of our states the examining psychiatrists are required by law to be governed by the M'Naghten Rule in determining whether or not the man is sane and accountable for his actions. The M'Naghten Rule grew out of questions asked prominent judges, in the British Parliament in 1843, before mental illness had been studied in the modern sense. It holds that to establish a defense on grounds of insanity, "it must be clearly proved that, at the time of committing the act, the party accused was laboring under such a defect of reason, from disease of the mind, as not to know the nature and quality of the act he was doing, or if he did know it, he did not know that he was doing wrong." This is usually interpreted as the ability of the accused man to distinguish right from wrong.

The M'Naghten Rule was generally adopted as the standard for determining insanity in American jurisprudence, in spite of a standard set up in New Hampshire in 1870, more in accord with modern thinking, which requires the judge or jury or medical examiners merely to determine whether the accused individual, at the time the crime charged against him was committed, was suffering from a mental disease and whether the crime had been committed as a result of this disease. You may see which of our states still go by the M'Naghten Rule by consulting the section on state statutes regarding serious sexual offenders in the Appendix of this book. The inadequacy of the rule of "right or wrong" was brilliantly exemplified by Jack Smith.

That he realized he was doing something both wrong and illegal was evidenced by the string of charges he reeled off, when he was returning to his proper self, and his remorse during his lucid interval.

Yet he had been diagnosed as a psychotic and had already been in three mental institutions.

I am told that men who are sexually disturbed, but not psychotic, are not welcome in mental hospitals, anyway. We shall see a little farther on that the great bulk of sex offenders are not insane in the ordinary sense, just as they are not criminals in the ordinary sense. Directors of mental hospitals feel they have enough to do in caring for the insane and mentally deficient without taking on men who are not insane or mentally deficient within the meaning of the statute. The treatment of sexually sick men in such institutions tends to be purely custodial, according to Dr. Karpman, with no real effort made to cure and rehabilitate them.

The great majority of convicted men, however, are sent to civil prisons, on fixed sentences. The Massachusetts Governor's Report found, as did the Sing Sing studies, that any fixed sentence protects the public only during the time of confinement. "Imprisonment with non-sexual offenders does more harm than good to the sex offender, other inmates and society." We shall see later that this is not necessarily true where an intelligent, devoted effort is made to supply special treatment to sex offenders in a prison, but one can count the states where this is done on the fingers of one hand.

Another difficulty, when sex cases are handled by "due process," is the wide variation in the sentences imposed in different states, and by different courts within a state, for the same kind of sex crime. In 1950, in New York State, a homosexual offense between two adults was downgraded from a felony to a misdemeanor, while in the same year California increased the penalty to from ten years to twenty. Two years later, California lawmakers revised this again to an indeterminate sentence, with a minimum of one year.

A research group from Yale University, studying the population at the Connecticut State Prison, reported that 25 per cent were sentenced for sex offenses, while only 10 per cent of those in New York prisons were so charged. This was probably due to the fact that a number of offenses considered misdemeanors in New York State, not involving consignment to penitentiaries, are placed under the head of felonies in Connecticut.

There is a wide difference also in the reactions of prosecuting officials to the sex criminal. In some states, the district attorney or county attorney or prosecutor, as these men are variously designated, may ask for a death penalty for rape. In all it is up to the local official whether he presses any charges. A doctor friend told me that, in five rape cases where he had been called in to examine the victims and give them medical treatment, the district attorney in his county had refused to prosecute.

By contrast, the police, in general, emerge creditably in their attempts to track down an offender, after he has committed a serious offense. I could not have asked for greater devotion to duty than was displayed by the various police officers in the Jack Smith case, and no reports have come to me of lack of assiduousness in the functioning of this branch of the law. The men who have to view the mangled bodies, or talk with a distraught victim directly after she has suffered an attack, are inclined to have a special loathing for this type of crime and a greater determination to put the perpetrator behind bars.

The police, however, are limited by the law in making arrests of those who have not yet done anything terrible. And the men who attack women and children unknown to them are the hardest of all criminals to track down, because of the very motivelessness of the crime and lack of any previous connection with the victim.

Many women do not report attacks to the police or testify against their attackers, out of shame or fear of reprisal in case the man should be released. Such fear is not entirely groundless. One of my newspaper clippings, from the *New York Post,* tells about the woman in a western state whose husband, meeting a man who appeared to be down on his luck and feeling sorry for the new acquaintance, brought him home to dinner. Not long after this, the guest broke into the house and raped the wife. She brought charges, but a jury found the man not guilty. He lay in wait for her and beat her up. When she appealed for help the police, probably discouraged by the finding of the jury in the rape case, said they could do nothing. The wife bought a revolver, so that she might protect herself. When her husband was away on a business trip, she had her mother come to stay with her. Her persecutor broke into the house again, but he had a revolver too.

Before the wife could get her own gun, he shot and killed both her and her mother.

The problem finds little better understanding among members of the medical profession, taken as a whole. Dr. Benjamin Karpman once said that the average psychiatrist would rather treat ten cases of anxiety neurosis than one sex disturbance, and that to the average general practitioner the sex offender, as to the public at large, is a degenerate, not deserving of pity or help. We have already heard the testimony of the man who raped the Long Island housewife and, in his remorse, took his problem to a doctor, and reported that the doctor "found it hard to understand."

My researches have given me a strong impression that the sexually sick man with a bent for violence has the least chance of any to get preventive help outside an institution. I visited a psychiatric clinic which is doing a marvelous work in rehabilitating offenders, 70 per cent of whom are sex offenders. But the head of the clinic could tell me nothing about the chances of rehabilitating those who commit acts of violence. "We don't see those men. They are sent to prison."

The number of men and boys who commit horrid, motiveless assaults soon after release from a mental institution would indicate that even here the true seriousness of their condition is not always properly appreciated. One wonders if the underlying sexual cause of the disturbance has been elicited at all.

The lack of understanding on the part of both the law and medicine is shown most starkly when a sexually sick man has finally reached the stage of brutal, outrageous murder, after a series of incarcerations in prisons and mental institutions from which he has been released, unrepentant and uncured, to prey again and eventually to kill.

# 5

# The law, medicine and Albert Fish

A great many men have carried on quiet—and, to them, eminently satisfactory—careers of sex crime with very little interference. They may have had to suffer brief interruptions—here or there a year or two in a prison or maybe a mental institution—but nobody really bothered them. Nobody really cared when the doors of the prison or mental institution opened to let them out, to pick up their aberrant practices again where they had been temporarily forced to lay them down. Nobody asked, "Is this man getting worse, instead of better? Is it possible that he is dangerous?"

Then a particularly horrible murder occurs, the man is arrested, and how the picture changes! His mental condition becomes a matter of absorbing interest. To save his client from the electric chair or gas chamber or hangman's noose, the defense attorney enters a plea of insanity. He hires psychiatrists to examine his client, and, by some odd coincidence, to a man they find him to be insane. The prosecutor calls in other psychiatrists who, by another odd coincidence, to a man find the defendant to be just as sane as anybody.

The courtroom frequently becomes the scene of a Donnybrook. The two psychiatrist teams are pitted against each other, and opposing counsel treats the psychiatrists on either side as though the experts were the persons on trial.

The long hypothetical question is a favorite device of counsel. If a psychiatrist victim feels it is unanswerable in the present stage of scientific knowledge, or fumbles any part, he is made to appear an ignoramus. Such goings on tend to bring psychiatry into disrepute, and it is little wonder that many psychiatrists are reluctant to subject themselves to an ordeal of this kind.

When the murder has been gruesome and shocking enough to attract nationwide attention, the courtroom scene then ensuing can be one to make Justice weep bitter tears behind her bandage. There are of course many defense attorneys who genuinely believe, as the law itself decrees, that a man who has committed his crimes because of mental illness should not be executed. There are prosecutors who feel, along with much of the general public, that a man who commits such a crime should be done away with, regardless of his mental state. But one wonders in some instances whether counsel is actuated so much by a desire to serve the ends of justice as to gain kudos from winning a case that is being tried before the whole country.

Edmund Pearson, in his sardonic rules for murderers and murderesses, advised that, if one aspires to murder, to be safe from punishment one should either go in for mass murder or make the single murder a particularly cruel and unusual one. "The person who kills some one obscure individual, who does it quietly and with moderate civility, is in a rather perilous position, perilous, that is, for a murderer. There are about three chances in a hundred that he may be executed."

But the person who indulges in wholesale poisoning or commits the shockingly cruel and unusual murder "attracts the sob sisters and sob brothers of the yellow press; causes quack alienists to rally to his defense like buzzards around a carcass, invites the wildest oratory and the most unmitigated flapdoodle from his attorneys; and finally, if he be convicted at all, makes thousands of persons move heaven and earth, slander the living and vilify the dead, in order to save his precious body alive."

It might be legitimately argued that persons who plot murders for cash benefits are simply carrying business methods too far. But how can there be any question about the abnormality of a murderer who has already been institutionalized because of mental illness, or one who tortures, desecrates, murders and mutilates total strangers for the sole purpose of gaining sex satisfaction from his horrid act? Yet when such a man reaches the point of murder, in many of our states "due process" requires that a lay jury shall decide whether or not the man is insane, and it may perforce base its decision, since few of us laymen are qualified to give an expert medical opinion, on the kind of court-room act staged by the opposing counsels.

Robert Irwin, whose murder of three innocent people was one of the spectacular cases of our era, before this had several times committed himself to mental hospitals on the advice of Dr. Frederic Wertham.

When Irwin gave himself up and was taken back to New York City, where the murders had occurred, he refused to say anything to the police. Because of Dr. Wertham's previous connection with the young man, the police commissioner called the physician, who went to police headquarters. The psychiatrist talked to the young man in private and advised him, as a physician, in the way he should conduct himself. As a result Irwin answered freely the questions put to him by the police.

In spite of Irwin's record of hospitalization and Dr. Wertham's opinion, based on long observation, that the man was insane in every sense of the word, the trial was a grotesque legal battle, with the sanity or insanity of the defendant the question at issue.

A lunacy commission sat for seven months and came up with the conclusion that Irwin was sane, that his trouble was due to "poorly digested reading in philosophy and psychology."

Three psychiatrists engaged by the district attorney's office stated that Bob had no mental disease, two psychiatrists engaged by the defense—Dr. Wertham being a third—stated that he had. Dr. Wertham's diagnosis was that Bob suffered from a mental disease which Dr. Wertham was the first to describe, catathymic crisis, a classification now used generally in modern diagnosis. It indicates an obsessive fixation, continuing after the stimulus has been removed. However, the district attorney in this case wanted to understand, and the charge finally brought against Irwin was murder in the second degree, which did not carry the death penalty. Convicted by the jury as guilty and sane, Irwin was sentenced to 139 years in prison and sent to Sing Sing. But he only remained there ten days. The prison psychiatrists, who were not bound by legal technicalities or other obstacles to un-prejudiced diagnosis, very quickly determined that the young man was psychotic and sent him to a hospital for the criminally insane, where he has remained until time of writing. We shall have more to say about this fascinating case in Chapter 10.

The "due process" system came to full flowering in another New York State case, that of Albert Fish, the most notorious torturer and murderer of children in our country's history, described, along with the Robert Irwin case, by Dr. Frederic Wertham in his absorbing book, *The Show of Violence*. Albert Fish was in his sixty-fifth year when he was brought to trial in New York's Westchester County in March of 1935 for the murder some six years previously of 10-year-old Grace Budd. He was the father of six children and felt a particular attachment to his oldest grandchild, a girl of 12. Despite what would appear to have been an ample outlet for his sex needs in marriage, throughout his adult life he had gained sex satisfaction through torturing children and through practicing every variety of known sexual aberration and some that seemed to be original with him.

A small man, gray-haired, he had a gentle, benevolent facial expression. Dr. Wertham tells us little about Albert's childhood background, beyond saying that in his branch of a distinguished family there had been a high incidence of mental illness. Several members had died in mental institutions, and Albert's mother was said to have been "very queer."

Between official laxness and the man's kindly outward appearance, Albert Fish probably would never have been stopped in his sadistic, murderous career short of his natural death, had he not been impelled to let Grace Budd's parents know what had happened to their child.

Grace had come to Fish's notice as a result of an ad her 18-year-old brother had put in the paper, in 1928, asking for work in the country. Fish went to the Budd home in New York City, giving the name of Frank Howard. He said he had a truck farm and wanted to see if the young man would work for him. But during the visit, he remarked that his sister was giving a birthday party for her children and asked if he might take Grace to it. He added that he loved children. Mrs. Budd demurred, but the father, deceived by the mild appearance of the stranger, gave his consent.

Grace was never seen again, and the police search that followed her disappearance failed to turn up any trace of her or of "Frank Howard." In November, 1934, a letter came to Mrs. Budd recalling the incident of the pretended birthday party and continuing, "Under the pretense of taking your daughter Grace to a party at my sister's, I took her up to Westchester County, Worthington, to an empty house up there, and I choked her to death. I cut her up and ate a part of her flesh."

Though the letter was unsigned, there was a partially obliterated address on the envelope and the symbol of a benevolent organization. Through the clues presented by the envelope, Fish was easily tracked down, and, when taken to New York City police headquarters, he readily gave the details of the murder to the police. Then he went to Worthington with the police and led them to the stone wall where he had deposited what was left of Grace's body, in three sections, six years before. The police found bones which the People contended were those of Grace Budd, and the defense never denied it.

Fish told the police that he had left a bundle containing a knife, saw and butcher's cleaver at a newsstand before going to the Budd house, and that when he came out with Grace he picked up the bundle again. Since the murder had occurred in Westchester County, the trial was held there. The district attorney, in his opening statement, cited the concealment of the murder tools as evidence that, while Fish was sexually abnormal, legally he was sane.

> His acts were abnormal, but when he took this girl from her home on the third day of June, 1928, in doing that act and in procuring the tools with which he killed her, bringing her up here to Westchester County, and taking her up to this empty house surrounded by woods in the back of it, he knew he was wrong to do that, and he is legally sane and responsible for his acts.

In short, the good old M'Naghten Rule, still being cited in the same way in many of our states.

Dr. Wertham was called in by the defense counsel, before the trial, and had many interviews with Fish, in which he elicited from the man the macabre story of his outer and inner life. His sexual pattern, Dr. Wertham says, was one of unparalleled perversity. For the court Dr. Wertham listed eighteen different kinds of perverse sex practices. "I did research in the psychiatric and criminological literature and found no published case that would even nearly compare with his." Fish confided that he had always "had a desire to inflict pain on others and to have others inflict pain on me." He showed considerable ingenuity in inflicting pain. Two of his practices mentioned by Dr. Wertham were to take bits of cotton, saturate them with alcohol, insert them in his rectum, and set fire to them; and to insert needles into the tender portions of his body adjacent to the genitals. He did these same things to the children who were his victims.

Dr. Wertham had X rays made of Fish, and they revealed in his body many needles, some nearly rusted away, indicating that the man had practiced this particular aberration for many years. Another of Fish's habits, significant of regression to an infantile level, was all manner of play with his bodily excreta.

He preferred boy victims and told Dr. Wertham that when he went to the Budd house, leaving his bundle of butcher's tools at the news-stand, it had been his intention to take Grace's brother to the deserted house, called Wisteria Cottage, castrate him, then leave him tied up in the cottage, go back to his room, pack up and leave town. It was what he had done with little boys before. When the brother turned out to be no little boy but a youth of 18, Fish took Grace, instead, and explained that it was with a desire to protect her from harm. "I knew that this child would eventually be outraged and tortured and so forth," he said, "and that I should sacrifice her in order to prevent her future outrage."

Fish gave Dr. Wertham full details of the ways in which he had preyed on at least 100 children, either by seducing, bribing or forcing them. His trade of house painter, which he contrived to carry on in public buildings as much as possible, gave him an excuse to dodge away to cellars or garrets. He wore nothing underneath his painter's overalls, so that he could undress and dress again quickly. After particularly brutal abuse of a child, he would move to another address and never returned to the same neighborhood. He told Dr. Wertham that he had lived in twenty-three states in the course of his nomadic life, "and I have had children in every state."

> He felt driven to torment and kill children [Dr. Wertham wrote in *The Show of Violence*]. Sometimes he would gag them, tie them up, and beat them, although he preferred not to gag them, circumstances permitting, for he liked to hear their cries. He felt that he was ordered by God to castrate little boys. "I had sort of an idea through Abraham offering his son Isaac as a sacrifice. It always seemed to me that I had to offer a child for sacrifice, to purge myself of iniquities, sins, and abominations in the sight of God."

Dr. Wertham estimated that Fish had murdered at least five children. A detective who worked on the case stated that Fish had killed three other New York City children, in addition to Grace Budd, and a New York Supreme Court justice put the number as high as fifteen. Fish had actually been arrested for one of the other New York City child murders but had been released because he looked so innocent. When asked how he had managed to escape detection so long, though he had been picked up by the police a number of times because of complaints that he had abused children, Fish replied that "it never came out. Children don't seem to tell. I always manage to cover it up."

Fish in fact had been in the hands of the authorities at least eight times, for offenses ranging from grand larceny to sending obscene letters through the mail; he had twice been sent to psychiatric hospitals for observation, yet no one had spotted him as being dangerous. The first hospital experience occurred two and one half years after he had killed and eaten parts of Grace Budd, because a court had been appealed to by Fish's daughter on the grounds that he showed signs of mental aberration. He was returned to the court from the hospital as being not insane but merely a psychopathic personality, sexual type, whereupon the judge put Fish on probation for six months.

A year later, he was arrested for sending obscene letters. The officers who made the arrest found in his room a cat-o'-nine-tails, and he told them he used it to whip himself. (He also whipped his child victims with it.) He had such a "weird" look on his face, in the words of one of the detectives, that an ambulance from a psychiatric hospital was called. The intern who came with the ambulance said Fish was clearly a mental case, a sadist, and took him off to the hospital, but Fish was only kept there two weeks and then released as sane, though the nurses reported several times that he was restless and confused. "During his stay in the hospital," Dr. Wertham says, "no one asked him a word about the cat-o'-nine-tails, no investigation was made, and the one psychiatric examination that was carried out consisted of a thirteen-line superficial quotation of Fish's remarks and three words: 'Quiet, co-operative, oriented.'"

In addition to the arrests, Fish had been picked up many times by the police, usually for impairment of the morals of minors.

> Yet [says Dr. Wertham] the attention of the authorities to this man, whom his family, many neighbors, and many past employers knew to be constantly after children, was neither penetrating nor persistent. Nobody ever made any attempt to pick up the pieces or put them together. At no time was he ever referred by anybody even to a mental hygiene clinic for examination or proper disposition. This was true although he made no secret of his interests or of his predilections.

This is the briefest outline of a psychiatric—and legal—history bizarre almost beyond belief. It included a kind of perverse religiosity, hallucinations and other evidences of an unsound mind, in addition to the sexual perversions and the sadistic practices with children. You may read the whole story in *The Show of Violence*.

Fish displayed a dreadful kind of relish in describing to Dr. Wertham Grace Budd's murder and the subsequent cannibalism. After the arrival at Wisteria Cottage, Fish had gone into another room and removed his clothes. When he appeared before the child naked, she cried out that he was bad, she would tell her mother on him. Then he strangled her, and he told the precise way in which he had cut up her body and cooked her flesh during the nine days following the murder, "with carrots and onions and strips of bacon." During the entire time that he ate the human flesh, Fish was in a state of intense sexual excitement.

Dr. Wertham says:

> He spoke in a matter-of-fact way, like a housewife describing her favorite methods of cooking. You had to remind yourself that this was a little girl that he was talking about. But at times his tone of voice and facial expression indicated a kind of satisfaction and ecstatic thrill. I said to myself: However you define the medical and legal borders of sanity, this certainly is beyond that border.

At Fish's trial, in which Dr. Wertham testified in support of the defense contention that Fish was insane, the psychiatrist detailed the material he had obtained from Fish and presented the results of a Rorschach test and the X-ray pictures of the needles Fish had inserted into his own body. Two prominent psychiatrists who had made independent examinations of Fish confirmed Dr. Wertham's diagnosis.

But the district attorney produced four psychiatrists who testified that Fish was sane. Dr. Wertham describes them thus:

> One of them was professionally associated with a district attorney's office. Another was a regular psychiatric adviser to the district attorney of the county. One was the chief of both the public psychiatric hospitals where Fish had been "observed" some two years after the Budd (and other) murders—while he was still being sought "high and low" on that account by the police—and there declared both harmless and sane. . . . Two of these psychiatrists based their testimony on one joint interview they had with Fish one evening.

The trial, as described by Dr. Wertham in his book, might have been taken for one of Dean Swift's savage satires on human idiocy if it had not actually happened in a New York State courtroom in the year 1935.

There was no contest as to Fish's guilt. He had signed six different confessions, and the defense attorney did not question that the bones which were brought into the courtroom in a cardboard box were those of Grace Budd. The battle was to prove either that Fish was sane—this by the state—or insane—this by the defense—when he had killed Grace Budd.

Nevertheless the courtroom show included frequent rattlings of the dead child's bones by the district attorney, introduction of a *World Almanac* to determine whether or not the moon had been full at the time of the crime, a 15,000-word hypothetical question, and the war records of both the contending attorneys. Spice was added by the diametrically opposite diagnoses presented by the psychiatrists called in by the state and the defense, respectively, and the questions fired at the psychiatrists on both sides in cross-examination, many of which bordered on the ludicrous.

If psychiatry has some reason to be suspicious of the law as sole arbiter of a sexually sick man's destiny, the Fish case gave grounds for legal reluctance to turn the entire matter over to psychiatry. Dr. Wertham in his book quotes some of the statements made on the stand by the state psychiatrists, to prove that Fish's eccentricities were not signs of mental illness, that he was merely a psychopathic personality.

"I should say," said one expert, "that the proportion of those who walk the streets who are psychopathic personalities is at least 25 per cent, if not more."

Other quotes were:

"Danger has nothing to do with the commitment of mental cases."

"A man might eat for nine days that [human] flesh and still not have a psychosis. There is no accounting for taste."

"I know of individuals prominent in society—one individual in particular that we all know. He ate human feces as a side dish with a salad [referring to one of Fish's many eccentricities with regard to excreta]. . . . I had a patient who was a very prominent public official who did that."

"If a man takes alcohol and puts it on cotton and puts that into his person and sets fire to it, that is not masochistic; he is only punishing himself and getting sex gratification that way."

The jury found that Fish was sane, one of them remarking later that most of them felt the man was insane but that he should be electrocuted anyway. The judge sentenced him to death in the electric chair; the Court of Appeals upheld both the verdict and the sentence. Dr. Wertham appealed to the governor of New York State to commute the death sentence and confine Fish to an institution for the criminally insane. The court was bound by the M'Naghten Rule; the governor was not.

Dr. Wertham's appeal to the governor cleared up something that had puzzled me after I began my serious investigation into the handling of sexual offenders—the great indignation expressed by a number of leading psychiatrists when men of Fish's type were pronounced sane so that they might be given the death penalty. It had seemed to me that much worthier subjects might be found on which to base a protest against capital punishment. But when I read Dr. Wertham's argument, I saw I had missed their point. It goes to the heart of the weakness in our whole system of handling sexually sick men. If there is such a thing as insanity, Albert Fish was insane. Dr. Wertham felt the blame for Grace Budd's murder should rest on the officials, including medical men, whose function it was to protect the public, and who had had a sadistic, homicidal maniac in their hands time and time again but had let him go.

He began his argument by sketching briefly his reasons for believing that Fish had a definite mental illness, illustrated by the X-ray pictures of the needles Fish had inserted into his own body. He then made it clear that his plea was not dictated by any soft-heartedness toward Fish, whom he considered to be unpunishable, as well as incurable and unreformable, that Fish might indeed even welcome this ultimate form of punishment because of his marked impulses for atonement.

"I was appealing on behalf of his many child victims," Dr. Wertham says in *The Show of Violence.* "I was also appealing on account of the many victims, past and future, of such men as Fish."

He pointed out how easy it would have been for the case to be dropped, through some technicality, when the district attorney chose to fight it through on legal grounds. If, for instance, doubt had been thrown on the identity of the victim, of whom nothing remained but the bones. In that case the community would have had to wait until

Fish had tortured and killed still another child—and been caught—before the community could safeguard itself.

> If you uphold the judgment of sanity implicit in the death sentence of this obviously ill man, you uphold, officially, the policy of psychiatrists who on two different occasions have had under observation a man who had butchered and eaten more than one little child . . . and who have the temerity to declare now that such a man was not a suitable case for commitment to an institution for the insane. . . .
>
> If he is electrocuted as sane, then you—to whose personal conscience the law entrusts this case at this moment—will give your stamp of approval to all the callousness and unconcern of those whose duty it was to protect the children of the community.

Dr. Wertham asked the governor not just to deny his stamp of approval to such practices, by committing Fish to an institution for the criminally insane, but also to "make this case an example and a starting point for a real scrutiny not of individuals nor individual institutions, but of the whole haphazard and bureaucratic chaos of the psychiatric prevention of violent crimes."

Dr. Wertham comments that as he made his plea the governor's face betrayed nothing, "no shade of feeling, no interest." When the psychiatrist had finished, the governor nodded, rose and left the room. "His impassive face remained with me—the symbol of cries unheard."

Albert Fish was executed in due course. This was in the mid-thirties. Nearly fifteen years were to go by before New York State, at a later governor's urging, was to take its first steps toward a more enlightened handling of sexually sick men. There is still no protection for citizens, that I know of, against inept procedures in releasing dangerous men from mental hospitals.

I too have experienced the lack of interest or concern that Dr. Wertham speaks of, the ears closed to the cries of future victims. When they ring in one's own ears, the indifference of the sane and normal and educated and fortunate can be hard indeed to bear.

# 6

# The law and
# Emmett O. Hashfield

But the Albert Fish trial was held in 1935. Surely it couldn't happen in the same way today! Let us see about that.

It was on the morning of August 16, 1960, that 11-year-old Avril Terry, the daughter of Dr. Robert H. Terry of Boonville, Indiana, disappeared from Boonville's Courthouse Square on her way to a dreadful death (noted briefly in Chapter 3). As in the case of Grace Budd's disappearance, a birthday party was involved, but this was a real one. Avril's younger sister, Candace, was 8 years old that day; the Terrys were having a party for her that afternoon. Avril had gone to the square at ten o'clock to buy a present for Candace and candles and decorations for the birthday cake, telling her mother that she would be back by eleven.

Avril was so scrupulous about keeping her promises that when she had not returned by eleven, a search for her was begun at once, and the *Indianapolis Star* of that same day carried a story about the hunt that was being conducted by 300 men, aided by two Civil Air Patrol planes, in the area of strip mines and rugged country north of Boonville.

Avril's father, the story said, doubted that she would have accepted a ride from a stranger or have permitted herself to be led away by someone she did not know. She was a very dependable child and had been thoroughly instructed in the dangers presented by child molesters. Avril was described as being five feet tall and weighing ninety-five pounds, with dark brown hair and an olive complexion. She was wearing red plaid "slim Jim" pants. When she left home she had two pet chameleons on her blouse, which was white, with a red strawberry design.

On August 18 the story erupted in papers all over the country, for, the afternoon before, Avril's body had been found in the Ohio River, cut into seven pieces. Already in custody, charged with her murder, was 53-year-old Emmett O. Hashfield, who had spent most of his adult life in jails or prisons for offenses against children and who was out on parole at the time of the slaying, after having served a little over ten years of a fourteen-year sentence for sodomy.

It was Hashfield's record which had first directed the police officers' attention to him. At a fish fry held the evening of August 16, the day Avril disappeared, someone mentioned that an ex-convict named Hashfield, who had served time for offenses against children, had not showed up that day at his job in a toy factory. (An expert wood carver, Hashfield made a specialty of hand-carved miniatures of pieces of furniture. Avril's little sister, Candace, collected furniture miniatures. It has been conjectured that he might have induced Avril to enter his car by suggesting that one of his miniatures would make a nice present for Candace.)

The word was relayed to Paul Houston, at that time Boonville's chief of police. (At time of writing, he is the sheriff of Warrick County, of which Boonville is the county seat.) Chief Houston called Hashfield's employer and got confirmation both of Hashfield's prison record and of the man's absence from work that day. The police chief, together with Warrick County Sheriff Robert Shelton (at time of writing employed by the Indiana State Department of Education) and Sergeant Wendell Opel of the Indiana State Police, went to Hashfield's house to "check him out," in the police phrase, as they had been checking out known child molesters ever since Avril's parents had reported her disappearance.

Hashfield had moved to Boonville from nearby Yankeetown only about a week before and was living in a shack that had been slated to be torn down, but which he had been able to rent for a small monthly sum. It was ten o'clock at night by the time the officers arrived at the shack, and Hashfield was rubbing his eyes when he opened the door, after a considerable delay, as though he had been asleep. The bed, however, was made up, and the officers later believed that they had interrupted the man in the task of washing blood out of his and Avril's garments. An officer who had stationed himself at a corner of the house while the other two men went to the door—a routine police precaution when they do not know what their reception may be— thought he had even heard the splash made when the wash water had been hastily thrown out of a window.

Hashfield's unbuttoned shirt appeared stained, and there were scratches on his chest and hands. The officers later testified in court that, seeing these things, they asked the man if they might search his house and that he gave them permission to do so, a point which was to have great significance in the legal proceedings that followed.

The officers found stains on the floor, with evidence of an attempt to wipe them up, but Hashfield said they were grease, from a grease gun he had dropped. The only light in the shack came from a kerosene lantern and was so dim that the officers could not say the stains were not grease. But in Hashfield's car they found a brassiere, bloodstained and cut into two pieces.

Now came the second action of the police which was to have great significance in the legal proceedings. The officers had Hashfield get into their car and put him off at the jail in Boonville along with Sheriff Shelton, who began questioning him, while Chief Houston and Sergeant Opel took the brassiere to the Terry house. Robin, the eldest of the Terrys' three daughters, identified it as Avril's. She went to Avril's room and came back with one just like it, which had been bought at the same time.

A more thorough search of Hashfield's shack was indicated. The officers testified that this time they procured a search warrant and that they also obtained Hashfield's oral permission to search the shack again. "Go ahead and search all you like," they claimed he said. "You won't find anything."

Around one o'clock on the morning of August 17, Chief Houston and Sergeant Opel, accompanied this time by an F.B.I. man from the Indianapolis office, returned to the shack, bringing lights with them. Now they were able to determine that the stains they had noticed on the first visit were blood. In a drawer they found two chameleons, one dead, with a string around its neck, the other still alive.

They took the covers off the bed, turned the mattress over. It was still wet with blood—Chief Houston later testified that he had estimated it contained at least a quart of blood—and the officers could see the imprint of a slight body. Outside the window from which the sound of the splash had come was a man's shirt, which apparently had been used to mop blood from the floor, and a girl's shoe was found outside the back door.

The officers noticed an attic space in the shack and an aperture in the ceiling through which it could be entered. The other two officers boosted up the F.B.I. man. He discovered, pushed back from the aperture as far as a man could reach, a bundle of clothing tied up in a man's T shirt. It contained a girl's panties, red plaid "slim Jim" pants, a white blouse with a red strawberry design, and several articles of men's clothing. All showed signs of having recently been in water, but they still contained a considerable quantity of blood. The articles of girl's clothing completed the list of garments Avril had been wearing when she left home, except for one shoe, which was never found. Neither did the officers ever find the decorations for the birthday cake which Avril was known to have bought.

They felt they had enough, however, to connect Hashfield with her disappearance and probable murder, and the questioning continued throughout the night of August 16 and the next morning. Hashfield at length admitted that he had helped a young girl pick up some pennies she had dropped in the Courthouse Square, had persuaded her to enter his car, and had thrown her body into the Ohio River—he said nothing about mutilations or dismemberment—but insisted that he had "blacked out" after getting the girl into his car and had no recollection of what had happened until he found himself with the body at the riverbank.

A considerable crowd was milling around outside the jail where Hashfield was being held, and reporters, photographers and television people were swarming inside, causing so much confusion that it interfered with the questioning (a striking similarity to the Lee Harvey Oswald case). On this account, Hashfield was removed for a time during the night to the State Police post at Evansville, seventeen miles away. All of these seemingly natural actions by the officials were subjected to severe scrutiny in the later legal proceedings.

The next morning, that of August 17, Hashfield, back in the jail at Boonville, was still maintaining that he could remember nothing of what had happened between the time when he picked up the child on the square and the throwing of her body into the river. However, he did consent, on August 17, to show the officers the spot where he had thrown the body in. The crowd outside the jail, which had consisted mainly of searchers when Hashfield was brought in, had been considerably augmented by the merely curious, who wanted to get a look at the suspect. The officers slipped him out of a side door to avoid the crowd and, following his directions, drove him to Rockport, Indiana. There he appeared to undergo a change of mind and directed the officers to Grandview, in the opposite direction from the place where the dismembered body was later found. But his car had been seen the day before on a road on the other side of Rockport. The officers followed this road to the Ohio River and there came upon the first of the grisly discoveries awaiting them—some viscera at the water's edge.

Thinking they might be able to scan the bank better from the river itself, the officers got a boat and rowed out into the stream. From this vantage point, they saw something bobbing up and down within a network of willow branches which drooped into the water. It proved to be the chest portion of a young girl's body. Caught by the willow branches, it had remained afloat because of its air sacs.

River experts were called in, and at four o'clock that afternoon, August 17, search boats and skin divers found the other six pieces into which the body had been cut some miles downstream, near Owensboro, Kentucky, but on the Indiana side of the river. Within half an hour after that, Hashfield, barefoot and with tattooed arms, was taken before a justice of the peace, charged with Avril's murder, and ordered held without bail at the Warrick County jail.

At news of the ghastly development, the crowd outside the jail grew threatening. "If they had had a leader, they would probably have taken Hashfield out and strung him up," an officer who was on the scene believes. But no leader appeared, and, after a couple of particularly vociferous members of the mob had been arrested and put in the jail too, the crowd dispersed.

In the eyes of the press and public, Hashfield already stood convicted of the murder of Avril Terry—he was frequently designated as her murderer in newspaper accounts—but the police continued to tighten the case against him. Through appeals issued in the newspapers and over radio and television, witnesses came forward who, in the opinion of the officials, pretty well established what Hashfield's movements had been after he picked up Avril on the square. It was believed he had driven first to the wooded, mine-pitted section north of Boonville and that Avril's missing shoe and the cake decorations had been lost there. Failing in an attempt to rape the child, as the state was later to claim, Hashfield had then driven her to his shack on the edge of Boonville.

A man had an appointment with Hashfield there on August 16. Hashfield had come to the door but had put him off. The officers thought Avril was in the shack at the time and that the slaying and dismemberment had been carried out in broad daylight. There were houses both in front of the shack and behind it. The officers considered it likely that the dismemberment had been done so the body could be removed without exciting the neighbors' suspicion. The blood found throughout the shack was proved to be of the same type as Avril's. (The body had been so completely exsanguinated as a result of many cuts inflicted before death, dismemberment and immersion in water that it was necessary to squeeze the heart in order to get blood for typing.)

Finally, not only had Hashfield's car been seen on the road to the river the day of the murder, a flat tire Hashfield had left at a filling station to be fixed matched the marks of a flat tire found on the river road.

Exactly what happened in the shack was still not known to authorities at the time of my visit to Boonville in 1963. Hashfield had never confessed, at least not to them, the actual killing, and he was not put on the stand in the trial proper. But they thought a hair-line fracture on the severed head had probably been caused by a broken catsup bottle found in the shack—blobs of catsup were mixed with blood.

The officers believed the dismemberment had been carried out on Hashfield's mattress.

Dr. W. A. Ratcliff, an Evansville pathologist who examined the remains soon after they were taken from the river, pronounced the killing a lust murder. (This type of sex crime is described in Chapter 9 of this book.) He based his opinion on the many severe injuries, including multiple cuts (aside from the ones he considered a cause of death), sexual violation and disfigurement. (Among other mutilations, the uterus had been cut out; it was never found.) There were six nonfatal cuts on the head alone.

The coroners of Warrick County, where the crime allegedly occurred, and of Spencer County, where the body was recovered from the river, examined the remains, and their finding was that the child had been raped. The pathologist, however, stated that rape could not be proved, in view of the hacking about that the body had suffered, but said there was a strong presumption that it had occurred. He found the cause of death to have been strangulation and lacerations on the neck and blood vessels.

Confirmation of Hashfield's guilt was afforded to the public mind by his identification, on August 17, as the man who had abducted an 8-year-old girl from the fairground in adjacent Spencer County on July 24, less than a month before Avril's murder. The man had offered to take the child for a ride in his car. When she refused, saying her mother had forbidden her to go off with strangers, he persuaded her to get into the car by suggesting that they would go find her mother and see if it wouldn't be all right. He drove her to a deserted place where ordinarily no one came, had her get out of the car, then said to her, smiling, "Now I am going to kill you."

Just then the miracle happened that was withheld in Avril's case. A couple who had lost their way drove into the place, the child ran to their car, the stranger jumped into his car and drove away. The season had been dry, dust thrown up by the wheels had obscured his license number, and though a report had been made to the police they had had no clue to the identity of the stranger. But when Avril's body was discovered, the little girl unhesitatingly picked Hashfield out of a five-man line-up as the man who had abducted and threatened to kill her.

Hashfield's record, too, counted heavily in the public mind, not only against him but against the officials who had turned him loose.

It was testified at his trial that Hashfield had served successive sentences of thirty days, five years and six years for rape or attempted rape before he was given a fourteen-year sentence for sodomy in 1947, and the Indiana Parole Board came in for strong condemnation for paroling him in 1958.

A signed article in the August 21 issue of the *Indianapolis Star* attempted to explain how it could happen that, although Indiana has a law allowing indefinite custody for sexual psychopaths, "the chances are good that a sexual psychopath can go to prison in Indiana for a crime such as attempted rape and come out in a few years unchanged in his twisted make-up—a constant menace to all around him." The writer, Paul M. Doherty, attributed this partly to the fact that Indiana still followed the formula of treating the crime, rather than the criminal, and partly to the fact that it treats crime "under a system which carries a burden of politics from top to bottom." He quoted several officials with regard to the inadequacy of the training required for parole and probation officers and also with regard to the inadequacy of the psychiatric treatment provided in Indiana prisons. This in spite of the fact, he pointed out, that nearby Wisconsin and Michigan presented examples of sane and enlightened ways for handling criminals. (The Wisconsin system for handling serious sex offenders is described in Chapter 15 of this book.)

A member of the Parole Board defended the board's action in paroling Hashfield in 1958 by pointing out that the suspect would have had to be released unconditionally when he had served his full sentence. The board had had to choose between releasing him provisionally, ahead of time, while some control could be exercised over him, and seeing him go out from prison with no controls, after he had completed his term.

It is not the province of this book to try to determine the motives and political purity of officials in our various states, but it must be admitted that there is justice in the contention of the Parole Board member. Hashfield could not have been given an indeterminate sentence when he was convicted of sodomy in 1947, for the indeterminate sentence was not placed on the Indiana statute books until after he had been sentenced. If Hashfield was the murderer of Avril Terry —and no one ever seriously contested that—holding him for his full sentence presumably would only have delayed a dreadful tragedy, not have prevented it.

Nor could Hashfield's parole officer properly be charged with failing in his supervision. The accused man had not been connected with the abduction of the 8-year-old girl in Spencer County until after Avril's murder, and I was told on excellent authority that other suspicious behavior of Hashfield's was not reported to the parole officer, nor was the man's removal to Boonville reported to him. As soon as Hashfield's parole officer, Everett Beasley, learned that Hashfield had moved to Boonville, he called the jail there to ask where Hashfield was, only to be told, "Hashfield is right here, in the jail." It was the morning of August 17, after Hashfield had been returned to the Warrick County jail from his brief detention at Evansville. The officers had still failed to elicit any clue as to what he had done with Avril. Beasley came at once, and it was he who finally persuaded Hashfield to show them the place where he had thrown the body into the river.

It is human nature to look about for a whipping boy when a shocking and preventable tragedy occurs, and in this case the Parole Board provided a handy one for Indianians. An Indiana county official, however, with whom I talked, did not share this view. "Our citizens simply will not pay the cost of the social workers and psychiatrists we need to prevent crimes of this kind," he said. "I keep telling them they are the ones to blame, but they don't listen."

We have already seen that the indeterminate sentence for serious sex offenders proves small deterrent when it is not backed up by an adequate system of treatment. The Hashfield case exemplifies the price a community may be called upon to pay long after a particularly bestial sex murder has taken place, when the citizens of a state have failed to recognize the special nature of crimes against women and children and have been content with a system which permits a chronic sex offender to be freed, time after time, untreated and uncured, until at last he lands in newspaper headlines over the entire country.

Actually, Hashfield's appearance in the national press was brief. After August 19, 1960, I saw no more about the case in the New York City papers. A man was in custody, the evidence against him appeared conclusive, the law would take care of him. If there were lessons to be learned from his record of repeated imprisonment and release, how many of us took them to heart? How many of us, after a shudder of horror at the crime itself and perhaps amazement that such a thing could happen to the carefully reared and protected child of a professional man, put it out of our minds and turned back to our own affairs?

But shock, and fears for the safety of their children, did not end for the Terry family and the citizens of Warrick County with the arrest and detention of the man who was later convicted of torturing Avril Terry to death. They had barely begun and, as I write this, more than four years after Avril's murder, they are still not over with.

This situation was made possible because the Indiana statutes in the early 1960's, like those of the New York State statutes in the 1930's when Albert Fish was tried—and still in 1964—offered the death penalty. Psychiatric examination of an accused man, whatever the nature of his crime, was left to the discretion of the court or of the defense attorneys. The decision as to the accused man's legal sanity, in Indiana in the sixties as in New York in the thirties, was left to a lay jury.

We have seen how this system operated in the Albert Fish case. There, however, the defense placed its hopes, too optimistically as it turned out, on being able to prove to the satisfaction of the jury that the accused man was insane. Fish's attorney appears not to have taken advantage of the many possibilities due process affords, which conceivably could permit a sexually perverted murderer to be released scot free—as for instance by contesting that the bones brought into the courtroom in the Fish case were those of Grace Budd.

To see what use a vigorous and ingenious defense can make of these possibilities, let us trace the Hashfield case as it has wound its weary way through the Indiana courts.

The local officials acted speedily. The sheriff immediately polled lawyers in the vicinity, trying to find one who would represent Hashfield. (Since the request did not come from a court, they were under no legal obligation to take the case.) A grand jury was convened on August 23 and, on August 24, indicted Hashfield for first-degree murder, which in Indiana is punishable by death. The day after that, Jack Broadfield, a recent law school graduate practicing in Indianapolis, agreed to act as the accused man's counsel. He asked to have Hashfield's arraignment delayed to September 20 to give him time to enter a plea, and Warrick Circuit Judge Addison Beavers consented. On September 20 Mr. Broadfield asked for a further delay, and the arraignment was put off until October 4, 1960.

On this date Mr. Broadfield registered a plea of innocent for his client and entered a motion to quash the indictment on two counts. One count was that the indictment failed to state that an offense was committed within the jurisdiction of the Warrick County Court; the other count was that the indictment was ambiguous in its wording and incorrectly punctuated. (The motion claimed that one sentence of the indictment had begun with a lower case instead of a capital letter.)

Judge Beavers overruled the motion to quash the indictment and designated January 9, 1961, as the date for Hashfield's trial. (Three more dates were to be set for the trial before it finally began in September of 1962.)

At the same time that Judge Beavers set the January 9, 1961, date, he appointed a veteran Indianapolis criminal lawyer, Ferdinand Samper, as co-counsel with young Broadfield. Mr. Samper, who took the lead in the defense from that time forward, immediately asked to have the trial put off so that he might familiarize himself with the case. His request was granted, and he attempted to have Hashfield freed on a writ of habeas corpus.

A hearing on the writ began on January 10, 1961. Mr. Samper claimed that Hashfield's constitutional rights had been violated when officers searched his shack without first getting a search warrant, and subpoenaed seven persons, including Warrick County Prosecutor Fred L. Mock, to testify. After vigorous arguments on both sides, the defense dropped this tactic when Judge Beavers set a bail bond of $25,000 for Hashfield—a shock to Boonville residents, who had understood that, under the Indiana law, persons accused of first-degree murder could not be released on bail. There was speculation that Prosecutor Mock had consented to the bail bond in order to avoid having to reveal his whole case in advance of the trial.

The very next day after the bail bond was granted, Defense Attorney Samper moved to have the amount reduced on the grounds, among others, that proof of Hashfield's guilt was not "evident and strong"; that he had committed no crime for which he should be imprisoned or detained; and that he had no money or means for posting a bond of $25,000.

Papers filed by the defense also asked that all the evidence against Hashfield the state had amassed should be barred, on the ground that it had been obtained illegally because, the defense lawyers claimed, the officers had not had a search warrant, when they searched his shack, and had taken Hashfield to the jail before getting a warrant for his arrest.

Every item removed from Hashfield's shack was listed, down to a washcloth and a lady's handkerchief. The defense asked to have barred every conversation Hashfield had taken part in and every admission adverse to his own interests, from the time the officers first went to the shack; all photographs and fingerprints taken from the time of Hashfield's arrest until his arraignment; Avril's body or parts of it; articles removed from Hashfield's car or his person; and all testimony pertaining to Hashfield's condition or appearance that had been gained from his "illegal arrest," as the defense described it, on the night of August 16, 1960.

Judge Beavers having denied the motion to reduce the bail bond, and no one having come forward to post the $25,000—in the proceedings Hashfield was designated as a pauper, Warrick County was paying his lawyers—the defense a few days later returned to its attempt to suppress evidence the state had gathered against Hashfield. Attorneys Samper and Broadfield filed a motion to quash a search warrant the officers allegedly had procured before they searched Hashfield's shack the second time—when the bloody mattress and garments and the chameleons were found—and again asked the court to bar all the evidence gathered in the search. Judge Beavers over-ruled the motion after due consideration, and on January 21, 1961, Attorney Samper entered a plea—not guilty by reason of insanity. At the same time he filed a petition for a court order to transfer the defendant to a hospital for a mental examination.

A hearing was held on the petition, during which Hashfield took the stand. He disclaimed any knowledge of the slaying, complained he was kicked on the shins, jerked and shoved during his questioning at the state police post at Evansville the night of August 16, but said he had not been mistreated by Warrick County officials. He testified that he had spent 28 of his 53 years in jail or prison, for sex crimes.

(In a hearing held within the trial, nearly two years later, Hashfield denied that he had suffered any mistreatment from the officers but said he had been afraid they would beat him up, because of previous experiences he had had with the police. As was mentioned previously, Hashfield did not take the stand in the trial proper.)

Judge Beavers denied the petition to remove Hashfield to a hospital but ordered examinations by two physicians and a psychologist of his own choosing, in their Evansville offices and within carefully deline-ated time limits which required all three examinations to be completed in a single day. This matter settled, as he thought, Judge Beavers set March 13, 1961, for the date of the trial and ordered a venire of 400 citizens to be drawn for prospective jury duty. The venire was drawn. But by the time the trial date had arrived, Judge Beavers had retired from the case at the request of the defense. Judge Francis E. Knowles had been drafted from the circuit court of another county, to take his place, and was unable to qualify by March 13. The trial therefore was postponed a second time.

The defense had objected to an order of Judge Beavers denying both prosecution and defense access to the reports filed by two of the court-appointed experts. The prosecution had asked for, and been granted, permission to have Hashfield examined by three other ex-perts, chosen by Prosecutor Mock. These examinations, too, were conducted within brief and carefully designated time limits, set by the court. On March 6, the defense lawyers had filed a petition for funds to pay for still another examination by experts *they* would select, and Judge Beavers had granted it. Nevertheless, the defense persisted in its efforts to have access to the reports of the court-appointed experts and asked Judge Beavers to reconsider his order empowering the prosecution to have Hashfield examined by *its* group of experts. It was when Judge Beavers denied both these motions that the defense asked for a change of judges.

The matter of access to the reports of the experts appointed by Judge Beavers was wrangled over through the rest of 1961. Writs were filed, hearings were held, three times the matter was taken to the Indiana Supreme Court. Meanwhile, term after term of the Warrick Circuit Court came and went. Emmett Hashfield, still sitting in the Warrick County jail, was apprised of his constitutional right to have a speedy trial but indicated he would not press this particular right.

On November 15, 1961, Special Judge Knowles granted a defense petition to have Hashfield transferred to a hospital for examination by defense-appointed experts—the examination for which funds had been granted back in March—and on December 7 issued an order allowing Hashfield to be taken to the Marion County Hospital at Indianapolis for the examination, with no time limits imposed. (The accused man was not returned to the Warrick County jail until February 8, 1962.) For certain examinations the court permitted Hashfield to be taken, under heavy guard, from the hospital to the Indiana Medical Center at Bloomington. Thus Hashfield was examined by experts not once but three times—very briefly by the teams chosen by Judge Beavers and Prosecutor Mock; at considerable length, by the experts chosen by the defense, and in a hospital setting, as Mr. Samper had originally requested. Just the same, the defense pursued its efforts to have access to the reports filed by Judge Beavers' expert team until December 29, 1961, when the Indiana Supreme Court refused to hear the matter argued a fourth time.

But already another cause for contention and delay had arisen— the place for holding the trial. It was an Indiana custom, when a change of venue was indicated, to transfer the trial to an adjoining county. Defense Attorneys Samper and Broadfield filed affidavits purporting to show that Hashfield could not hope to have an unprejudiced trial in any county in southwest Indiana. Among other things, they cited speeches Dr. Terry, Avril's father, had made in nearby counties, after the murder, and the difficulty Hashfield's lawyers had had to find doctors in the locality who would consent even to examine Hashfield for the defense. Special Judge Knowles, after listening to arguments by both sides, ordered the trial moved to the Circuit Court of Monroe County, of which Bloomington is the county seat, some 125 miles north and east of Boonville. Now it was the turn of Prosecutor Mock to enter petitions and appeals and vigorous protests throughout the first half of 1962. On June 22, he was joined by the Monroe County prosecutor, Fred H. Gregory, in a last appeal to have the change of venue set aside, but without success. In fact, on the previous March 8, Hashfield and all the papers relating to the case had been moved to Bloomington, Special Judge Knowles had stepped down, and Monroe Circuit Judge Nat U. Hill had taken over as presiding judge, the third one to sit on the case. For the third time a date was set for the trial to begin, July 19, 1962, but on June 29 and again on July 6 the defense filed motions for a continuance; both times it was granted by Judge Hill. At a conference held on July 16, however, it was agreed on all sides to start the trial on September 24, 1962, and it actually started then.

The morning of September 24, a venire of more than 600 prospective jurors crowded the Monroe County courthouse, for Judge Hill had ordered a special venire of 500 drawn in addition to the 110 who had been selected earlier in the month. By order of Judge Hill, the Monroe County prosecutor was on hand to assist Warrick County Prosecutor Fred Mock; Attorneys Samper and Broadfield were representing Hashfield as "pauper counsel." Judge Hill also stated that newspaper and television camera men were to be allowed in the courtroom. Observers estimated that the trial would be over in two weeks. It lasted six.

Seven days were spent in selecting a jury of twelve, with two alternates—forty-five minutes of this time being taken by the prosecution, the rest by the defense—so that it was October 8 before they got down to business. Hashfield was brought into the courtroom, handcuffed, between two deputies. Shaved and shod now and wearing a decent black suit and white shirt, he smoked cigarettes and chatted with his lawyers during intermissions.

The defense at once contested Judge Hill's ruling that the jury should be locked up while the trial lasted, on the ground that it would be both inhumane and costly to keep the members shut up in a hotel, and moved that they be allowed to go to their homes each night.

The judge denied the motion but granted a second defense motion that the witnesses be "separated"—excluded from the courtroom when they were not testifying—with the exception of Warrick County Sheriff Robert Shelton and Sergeant Keith Shelton of the Indiana State Police, who were allowed to remain with the prosecuting attorneys. Excluding the witnesses was an act of mercy as well as a legal precaution, for it spared Avril's father, mother and older sister, who were called as prosecution witnesses, the ordeal of hearing and seeing the harrowing disclosures of the weeks to come.

These began with Prosecutor Mock's opening speech, in which he gave a detailed description of the severed portions of the dead child's body. Prosecutor Mock was a close friend of the Terrys; his daughter had been Avril's chum. He had seen the remains when they were taken from the river, and I was told it had fallen to him to break the news to the Terrys of what had happened to their daughter. The judge ordered the jury to disregard this part of Prosecutor Mock's statement.

From then on, the defense never let pass an opening to object and to attack. It challenged the testimony of one of the two coroners who had examined Avril's body on the ground that he was not a medical man. It called for a mistrial when Mrs. Terry broke down on the stand while describing the reason for Avril's errand to the Courthouse Square and, looking straight at the accused man, cried out, "I suppose Candace will never have another birthday party!"

(Later the defense called for a mistrial when Police Chief Houston, asked while testifying what had first directed the officers' attention to Hashfield, answered truthfully that it had been the man's record of crimes against children. Under due process, no reference to a defendant's previous crimes is permissible.)

The trial came to an abrupt halt when Warrick County Sheriff Shelton took the stand as the next prosecution witness after Mrs. Terry. The jury was sent out of the courtroom, and Mr. Samper asked permission to present to the court a motion "to suppress all the evidence, oral or visual, gained from an illegal arrest, from an illegal search of the defendant's premises, from an illegal search of the defendant's automobile, and from the illegal search warrant issued in this case." (The warrant which the officers had presented at the hearing held in early 1961 was challenged then by the defense as having been fabricated after the event.) The judge consented to a hearing on the motion; it began the next day, October 9, and continued through October 16, while the jury remained locked up in its hotel.

The hearing constituted in effect a trial within a trial, with the officers who had tracked Hashfield down and taken him into custody replacing the accused man as defendants. Each in turn was interrogated about every event of the search and the questioning of Hashfield, in an attempt to find that, in some detail, some officer had failed to follow the full routines prescribed by the law. At no time was there any intimation that the garments of the dead child and the bloody traces of murder had not been found in Hashfield's shack, as the officers claimed. The defense effort was to establish that Hashfield's constitutional rights had been violated in the way they had been found.

Sheriff Shelton admitted that the officers had had no search warrant when they went to Hashfield's shack in their search for "a lost child," but said the accused man had invited them in, and Police Chief Paul Houston testified to the same effect. State Police Chief Detective Opel testified that he had signed a warrant for Hashfield's arrest before Justice of the Peace William Bradley, and a warrant signed by Bradley was also produced for the search which had turned up incriminating evidence in the shack. The authenticity of these documents was attacked by the defense. State Police Sergeant William W. Cornette testified that he had had no warrant nor authority from any court when he transferred Hashfield briefly from the Boonville jail to the state police post at Evansville the night of August 16, 1960, to get away from the crowd inside and outside the jail. And so it went, day after day.

When one considers that officers of two towns (Rockport, Indiana, as well as Boonville), two counties, a state and the federal government were involved in the search for Avril and the effort to learn what had been done to her, and that the slightest procedural slip on the part of any one of these officials conceivably could result in the freeing into the community, yet again, of a man whose sexual pattern would seem to have progressed through rape and sodomy to torture and murder, one is made painfully aware that the safety of children hangs on a slender thread indeed. The fact that it was nearing midnight when the officers first went to the shack, that Avril's parents were waiting in agony for word of their missing child, apparently would have been no excuse.

At the end of the hearing the judge overruled the motion to suppress evidence, the jury was called back, and the prosecution was able to place before it the facts the defense had tried to have barred. State Police Sergeant Wendell Opel was on the stand all of October 17, 1962, describing the events of the night of August 16, 1960. He told how the three officers had gone to Hashfield's shack in the search for Avril, said he had advised Hashfield that he need not say anything until his lawyer was present, that Hashfield had replied he would just as soon talk to the officers. He told of retracing Hashfield's journey to the Ohio River with the severed portions of Avril's body in his car, the stop Hashfield had made at a filling station to get a flat tire fixed, and his admission that at the river he had seen a small black boat and had got into it.

Police Chief Houston testified he had heard Hashfield tell State Police Sergeant Opel that he had disposed of the girl's body by pushing it off the back of a boat into the channel of the Ohio River.

This time, the officers' narratives were illustrated, over most strenuous objections by the defense, with color slides and the introduction into evidence of the articles the officers had found in Hashfield's car and house. Twenty-year-old Robin Terry—she was 18 when her sister was slain—wept as she testified that the girl's garments found in the shack were her sister's. Dr. Terry identified, for the third time in a legal proceeding, the chameleons also found in the shack.

The first color slides exhibited were of Hashfield's car and the shack, with stains on the front porch, and there was a picture of

Hashfield taken at the time of his arrest, showing scratches on his chest. Later, tire tracks and bloody clothing found at the riverbank were displayed. When State Police Sergeant Keith Shelton described the recovery of a girl's torso, two arms and a leg from the river, color slides of the pieces of the body, as they floated on the water, were thrown on the screen.

The exhibits went on, in a rising crescendo of horror. When testimony was given by the skin divers and others who had taken part in the recovery of the body, more color pictures were shown of the fragments. Attorney Samper did succeed in having one color picture of the hacked, dismembered corpse excluded from evidence, declaring that it was the most sadistic one he had ever seen and that to exhibit it would be grounds for mistrial, but enough were permitted to have satisfied the most avid sensation-seeker.

A witness who had been present both at the recovery of the body and at the showing of the pictures in the courtroom told me that the color replicas were even more shattering than the reality had been. The *Indianapolis Star* reported that Hashfield viewed them with no sign of emotion.

One of the pictures the judge admitted over defense objections was of the bloody mattress the officers had found in Hashfield's shack. The mattress itself was not placed in evidence, though it had been brought to the courthouse and was outside, in the trunk of a state police car. Hashfield asked to see it, and his request was granted. He looked at it without comment, then was led back into the courtroom.

As the final one of its forty-odd witnesses, the state called to the stand a psychiatrist who had not examined Hashfield but who, when asked a question about a hypothetical slaying closely resembling Avril's, replied that, on the basis of the evidence, the killer in the hypothetical case appeared to be a man who could distinguish right from wrong (the M'Naghten Rule).

When the defense took over, Hashfield's lawyers did not immediately attack the matter of their client's mental status, the determining of which had been wrangled over through most of 1961. Instead, they tried to establish that Avril had died, not from strangulation and cutting of blood vessels in the neck, as the pathologist, Dr. W. A. Ratcliff, had testified on several occasions, but as a result of rape, which had ruptured the uterine artery.

Both Dr. Ratcliff and Boonville's Police Chief Houston, the youngest and least experienced of the officers who had taken part in the search, were questioned rigorously in an attempt to get them to admit that rape had occurred. Chief Houston testified that he had overheard Hashfield say he had not raped the child. Dr. Ratcliff held to his original statement that, while rape could be assumed, the cutting to which the body had been subjected had made it impossible to prove.

This led to various motions on the part of the defense lawyers— that the court furnish it with money to hire a pathologist to rebut Dr. Ratcliff's testimony; that Avril's body be exhumed so their own pathologist could examine it and ascertain, among other things, whether the exterior jugular vein had been severed (as claimed by Dr. Ratcliff); that the trial be recessed and the jury members sent to their homes while the defense pathologist made his examination.

It was not until the judge had refused the motion to exhume the body and recess the trial—though he said he would authorize payment of a reasonable fee for a defense pathologist as long as the trial was not delayed—that the question of Hashfield's sanity, or lack of it, was seriously attacked. Four intimates of Hashfield's had already testified, during an interval in the exhumation attempt, that in their opinion Hashfield was not normal. Now began the parade of expert witnesses. Dr. William E. Demeyer, an associate professor of neurology at the Indiana State Medical Center, testifying for the defense, pronounced the accused man to be mentally sick. He said that X rays had shown Hashfield to be suffering from atrophy of part of the brain and to have an abnormal knot on the left side of his skull, both conditions probably having been caused by a blow in earlier life. Failure of this part of the brain to function, Dr. Demeyer said, had been shown by scientific investigation to lead to sexual aberration. Two psychiatrists who had studied Hashfield during his two-month stay in the Indianapolis hospital also testified to the effect that the man was unable to control his antisocial impulses.

The prosecution then put on the stand the two medical men whom Judge Beavers had appointed to examine Hashfield and whose reports the defense had made such vigorous efforts to obtain. Dr. Jerome Reitman, an Evansville psychiatrist, testified that his examination of Hashfield in February of 1961 had left him certain that the accused man had known right from wrong. He said Hashfield had told him of picking up a small girl on August 16, 1960, taking her to his house in Boonville, and failing in a sexual assault on her. (The failure of the sexual assault was important to the State's contention that Avril had died as the result of strangulation and cuts, as claimed by Dr. Ratcliff, and not of rape, as the defense had tried to establish.) Hashfield had told him that another man came to the house, took Avril to the bank of the Ohio River, and killed her while he, Hashfield, sat in the car, the psychiatrist testified. (Lies or other attempts to conceal guilt are frequently cited by prosecuting attorneys as proof that the accused knew right from wrong.)

When the other psychiatrist appointed by Judge Beavers also testified that Hashfield knew right from wrong, Attorney Samper again asked to have the trial halted and the jury sent home during the time it would take to have a transcript made of the testimony of the two court-appointed psychiatrists, claiming it had come as a complete surprise. The transcript was needed for rebuttal, Mr. Samper maintained. (He had succeeded in having the testimony of the third expert appointed by Judge Beavers excluded on the ground that this expert was a psychologist and not a medical doctor, as required by the law, and that Hashfield was not allowed to confer with his attorneys before he was examined by the court-appointed experts.)

These motions having been overruled by the court, the defense moved for a directed verdict of not guilty by reason of insanity, which was also overruled. Judge Hill expressed his willingness to grant the defense an opportunity to present evidence in rebuttal to the testimony of the two medical men appointed by Judge Beavers, but the defense, saying it had no evidence to present in rebuttal because of the court's refusal to allow a transcript to be made, rested its case. The defense could, and did, cite adverse rulings by the judge as errors, which might permit review by a higher court and possibly bring about another trial.

Closing arguments were given by each of the four lawyers involved,

Prosecutors Mock of Warrick County and Gregory of Marion County for the state and Attorneys Samper and Broadfield for the defense. The attorneys for the state went over in detail the evidence which had been presented against Hashfield. Prosecutor Mock pictured the scene in Hashfield's shack, with the 11-year-old, ninety-five pound girl fighting the heavy 53-year-old man until her fingernails were torn off. He asked for the death penalty, exhorting the jury, when they entered the jury room to arrive at their verdict, to "go with the father of Avril Terry and with her family. Go to the first grave in the Ohio River and go to the second grave in Boonville and write indelibly on the little tombstone that her killer suffered death." Prosecutor Gregory spoke in similar vein.

Messers Broadfield and Samper paid full attention to the testimony in their turn, and Attorney Samper, who during the trial had made three attempts to have the jury members allowed to go to their homes, now begged them to "dedicate two or three days to us, instead of turning in a quick verdict and hurrying home to your children."

At one point, however, Mr. Samper appeared to put aside legal stratagems, of which he had proved himself such a master, and to approach the case from the standpoint of the thoughtful citizen. He expressed regret that members of the Terry family had been submitted to an ordeal in testifying but pointed out that the prosecution had put them on the stand and said that inflammatory material it had introduced had forced the defense to counter as best it could.

Mr. Samper went over in detail the testimony of the medical experts retained by the defense, and especially that of the neurologist, Dr. Demeyer, with regard to the knot found on Hashfield's skull and damage done to his brain, stressing that Hashfield's first sex offense had occurred two years after he had suffered a severe blow on the head.

Then Mr. Samper attacked the true core of the problem before them, which had largely been lost sight of in the two years of legal maneuverings—what *is* the proper disposal of a man who has been allowed to proceed to shocking, sadistic murder, after his progress in disturbance has been clearly revealed by his pattern of sex crimes?

"He [Hashfield] has been in our institutions for twenty-some years," Mr. Samper exclaimed, "and no one has seen fit to do what we did—have him examined! No one, no prosecutor, no judge, no one!"

Hashfield had a physical lesion of the brain, he continued, and a history indicating sexual perversion. "He was a socio-path who had spent many years up there [meaning the Indiana State Prison] and we haven't seen fit to recognize that problem and to begin to give him help. . . .

"The first time a man came up there on a rape case I might forgive their laxity. But how about a second time? How about a third time? He wanted help—who gave it to him? He had never been examined or treated in all those years in prison!"

The defense stood on its medical experts' opinion that Hashfield was insane and hence could not be convicted. So what was to be done with him? "Are you going to turn him loose in the streets? I'm going to be honest with you. . . . He would go out on the street and he would be home free until he reached the outskirts of Boonville, and there they'd kill him."

Mr. Samper next addressed himself to the fear in the minds of many that, if consigned to prison or a mental hospital, Hashfield might be turned loose at some future time, though he did not see how any reasonable person could do that. He suggested that this fear be quieted by giving the now 55-year-old defendant a sentence of twenty years. At age 75, he would not present much menace.

The attorney laid the blame for Avril's murder at the door of the public itself—"it's our fault"—and pleaded that the best memorial for Avril would be for the public to take the lesson to heart and henceforth to elect people to office who would see that the case could not be duplicated.

It was an eloquent plea, but one wonders whether the very vigor and wiliness of the defense, revealing as it did the many loopholes the law affords for the escape of a deadly dangerous man, had perhaps made the jury members feel that the only way to protect children from Hashfield would be to have him dead. After deliberating only an hour and five minutes, they found the accused man guilty as charged and recommended that he should suffer death. Judge Hill accepted the recommendation and ordered that Hashfield should die in the electric chair, Indiana's method of execution, at sunrise of March 4, 1963, at the Indiana State Prison at Michigan City, overruling an objection by the defense that the man was temporarily insane.

But Warrick County residents had scarcely had time to sigh with relief that the long suspense had ended when it started all over again. Judge Hill refused an appeal for a new trial, entered at once by Hashfield's lawyers, but granted a petition to appeal his decision to the Indiana Supreme Court. The defense claimed that 101 errors had been made during the trial.

On February 8, 1963, the Indiana Supreme Court accorded Hashfield an indefinite stay of execution so that a transcript of the trial might be made—it ran to 2,356 pages of legal-sized paper—and the State Supreme Court given an opportunity to study it. September 9, 1963, was set as the date when these things should be accomplished, but later an extension was granted to February 5, 1964. Hashfield's attorneys filed the transcript with the Indiana Supreme Court on April 8, 1964, and it was expected that it would be at least six months more before they filed their brief. An Indiana official wrote me on April 10, 1964, in answer to my inquiry, "At the present time it appears that this case will not be heard before the Indiana Supreme Court for at least a year or more."

If the Indiana Supreme Court decided Hashfield had not had a fair trial, it could order a new one and the dreary business would have to be gone through all over again. If it were to decide that his constitutional rights had been violated in the way his arrest and the search of his house had been conducted, it could dismiss the charges against him. If it were to uphold the lower court, Hashfield's attorneys could appeal the case to the United States Supreme Court, and no Indianian would bet that Attorneys Samper and Broadfield would not do just that.

"Surely it is inconceivable that any court would release such a man!" I exclaimed to a lawyer I talked with in Indiana.

"It certainly is conceivable!" he replied. "Provided the court were to find that his constitutional rights had been violated. I personally would rejoice in that case, for it would prove that in the eyes of the law the rights of the poorest and most despised citizen are as important as those of the wealthiest and most influential one."

"But what about the constitutional rights of children?" I asked. "Not to be tortured to death, for instance?"

"Of course, if he were to kill another child, he would be tried again."

There is one thing, however, of which Boonville and other Warrick County citizens can be certain. They will have to underwrite Hashfield's defense as long as his lawyers can contrive to keep the case before the courts. Owing to the accident that their county, and a child of theirs, had paid the terrible price for the failure "of all of us" to detect Hashfield's potential for danger, the law ordains that they must pay for the attempts to save him from the penalty that has been ordained by the law.

The end of what must now be regarded as the first phase of the Hashfield case came on August 5, 1963, when Judge Hill approved a final bill for costs of the trial held in faraway Monroe County, against the strong protests of the Warrick and Monroe County prosecutors.

The judge listed extra precautions that had been required in order that Hashfield might have a fair and impartial trial and, stating that they were the legitimate burden of Warrick County, ordered that they should be paid by Warrick County, together with "any prior expenses heretofore." This final bill came to $10,597.78. It covered only the cost of housing and feeding the locked-up jury for six weeks, $4322.08; $1850.00 for the nine experts appointed respectively by Judge Beavers, the prosecution and the defense, who testified or were on hand to testify; $2000 to Monroe County Prosecutor Fred Gregory, appointed by Judge Hill to assist the Warrick County prosecutor; $2177.80 in partial payment for the transcript, with another $137.90 for office supplies; and $110.00 to a man whose function was not given.

It did not cover the pay for the extra venire of 500 prospective jurymen summoned by the judge or pay for the jury itself or for the extra bailiffs needed to guard Hashfield and keep order; it did not cover the cost to Warrick County of board and room for its own officials during the trial or the great burden of extra work and expense incurred by its officials before the trial; it did not cover the fees of the defense attorneys which were also Warrick County's responsibility.

When the case was transferred to the Indiana Supreme Court, the Warrick prosecutor stepped out, the Indiana attorney general taking over for the state. But the Monroe County judge had ordered that Mr. Samper and Mr. Broadfield continue to serve as Hashfield's "pauper counsel," and Warrick County would have to continue to pay them.

I was told in June of 1963 that up to that time the Hashfield case had cost Warrick County's taxpayers $60,000. This may well be, considering the heavy expenses incurred inside Warrick County alone, and certainly they should reach that figure, or pass it, before the case is finally over with, if it ever is over with short of Hashfield's natural death.

What has been established by this long, expensive exhibition of legal dexterity? The impartiality and fairness of due process? Or confirmation of Edmund Pearson's cynical comment that in order to commit murder and escape punishment, one should either go in for mass murder or commit the single cruel, unusual and ghastly one? What solace has it provided for those who loved the murdered child, what reassurance for other parents of the community where the crime occurred? To find out about that, I went to Boonville.

Boonville, Indiana, is a typical midwestern county seat, with the courthouse in the center, the stores and shops facing it on all four sides, and tree-lined residence streets extending out from the Courthouse Square to the east, west, north and south.

It is not a town where one would dream there would be any danger for an 11-year-old girl in the Courthouse Square, of a summer day. Everyone knows everyone else. Even at night there is much honking of car horns in the square, as the drivers recognize the cars they pass. There are no places of concealment on the square from which an "unknown sex fiend" might pop out.

It is a friendly, welcoming town. Though the Terrys had moved to Boonville only five years before Avril's murder, they had become leading and affectionately regarded members of the community. At the time of my visit, Dr. Terry was secretary of the Warrick County Medical Association and president of the Warrick County Association for Mental Health, in great demand as a speaker. The residents with whom I talked regarded the tragedy that had befallen the Terry family as a personal one.

Those closely connected with the case were hesitant to voice their feelings about it, more than three years after Avril's murder. It was still before the courts; no one was prepared even to guess when, if ever, it would be settled. What a determined defense could do with any unguarded action or statement by a person anywhere within the periphery of the legal proceedings had been vividly demonstrated. But the "man in the street" in Boonville—the woman, too—were under no such restraint. As soon as Avril's murder and the subsequent legal actions were mentioned, faces would change, men and women would speak in hushed voices and wondering or despairing tones. It was as though this pleasant town had been dealt a blow from which it would never recover, and the citizens could not understand what they or the Terrys had done to merit it.

"I think it's terrible, and I don't believe you will find anyone who thinks differently," one after another said to me. "It doesn't seem like justice."

Tears filled the eyes of one woman as she told me, "Oh, it was dreadful! Mrs. Terry came into the store where I was working that morning, when she was looking for Avril. I will never forget her face. Of course, she didn't know, then.

"I wish you could have seen her before this happened. She is lovely now, but before that she was simply beautiful. A wonderful mother, so quiet and refined. She's a sweetheart, we all love her. She has to go on the stand and tell all about this, and she's not supposed to get hysterical. How could she help getting hysterical?"

"It has done terrible things to this whole community," said a Boonville man. "For weeks after the murder, if you walked down the street at night, someone was likely to call the police. If you went up on a porch and rang the doorbell, you would hear people start screaming inside."

The terror remains, though in lessened form. A pleasant, middle-aged woman told me she had a 16-year-old daughter. "If I do say it myself—and there's plenty of others who will tell you the same thing —she's a fine girl, quiet, dependable, not interested yet in boys, and she's old enough so I know she would never go off with a stranger. She's careful about getting home, too, when she says she will. But if she is ever the least bit late, I think of Avril. What must it be for the mothers of little children, that have to go back and forth to school!

"Because Hashfield isn't the only man like that, there are others around. They'll see how Hashfield got let off and it will encourage them to do the same thing. I don't believe in capital punishment, but you can't help thinking, the man is still here, but the little girl is gone. Of course, we're told he had the mind of a child. But it seems there ought to be a law so that men who have done things like he did before he murdered Avril would be kept in jail, not let go."

The Boonville man in the street would have been more impressed by the concern of the law for Hashfield's constitutional rights, I gathered, if the same solicitude were shown for persons who commit less appalling crimes. "Suppose *I* killed somebody," one man expressed it. "Just shot somebody, maybe, while I was robbing a bank. I would have to settle for second or third best when it came to lawyers, because I would have to pay for my defense and that would be all I could afford. Hashfield gets the very best, and *I* have to help pay for it!"

A number believed that in the end, Hashfield would be released, and a few with whom I talked even thought it had been planned that way. "It will drag on and on until people get tired of it and forget. Even if he is sent to a prison or a mental hospital, they'll turn him loose after everyone has forgotten."

One woman summed up what seemed to be the general feeling. "It looks as if the law was meant to protect men like Hashfield. Who is there to protect our children?"

I have dealt with the Hashfield case at some length, because of the lessons it holds for all of us whose state laws and procedures do not recognize the nature of sex sickness and do not adequately protect the community against sexually sick men.

First, that what happened to bright, pretty, 11-year-old Avril Terry, carefully reared, carefully watched over, carefully warned, in a peaceful midwestern town, can happen to any child, even to one very dear to you and me, so long as these men are released from custody, untreated and uncured.

Second, that the legal aftermath of such a murder can be repeated in any state where adequate provision has not been made for medical handling of these men, when they first come to official attention, and where the law offers the death penalty and the M'Naghten Rule for determining legal sanity in criminal cases—that is to say, in most of our fifty states.

I was told that some Warrick County people had criticized Prosecutor Mock, though no criticism was expressed to me, on the ground that he could have avoided the long legal battle by reducing the charge against Hashfield to second-degree murder, which does not carry the death penalty. For it was to save their client from the electric chair that Defense Attorneys Samper and Broadfield had employed their many legal devices, as Mr. Samper made plain in his summation to the jury. But it was also acknowledged by my informants that if Prosecutor Mock had reduced the charge against Hashfield, he "would have had to leave town," as one man expressed it.

It was not so clearly understood by Warrick County citizens that the defense counsel was only doing its duty by its client, under the law, in the strenuous effort to get Hashfield freed of the charges lodged against him. A lawyer friend explained it to me. "The nature of the crime has nothing to do with the case. The dead child cannot be brought back to life. The defense attorney has a responsibility, under the law, to free the accused man if he can, using every loophole and stratagem the law affords."

Once the sexually sick man has been allowed to proceed to unspeakably savage and degenerate murder, the attorneys on both sides and the judges as well must play out the comi-tragedy of due process to the end.

What effect have Avril Terry's murder and the Hashfield case had on the Indiana system for handling sexually sick men? Soon after Avril's dismembered body was found, the Indiana Legislature, by executive order, rushed through a bill requiring periodic psychiatric examinations of sex offenders who are released on parole. That is good as far as it goes, but far from the complete revamping of an outmoded system called for by Paul M. Doherty in the *Indianapolis Star* in August, 1960, and by Defense Attorney Ferdinand Samper in his summation to the Hashfield jury in November, 1962. Wisconsin's example, just next door, of thorough examination and intensive treatment when the sickness first shows itself and careful examination *before* releasing sex offenders on parole, still has gone unregarded by Indiana citizens and officials as far as I could tell.

Indiana is by no means an underprivileged, illiterate state. It boasts illustrious authors. Bloomington, where the Hashfield trial was held, is the seat of the University of Indiana, which has world-renowned scholars on its faculty and the world-famous Institute for Sex Research, founded by Dr. Kinsey, on its campus. Actually, Indiana's laws and system for handling serious sex offenders are no worse than those of most of the other forty-nine states.

How many more sacrifices of lovely children will it take, how many more legal fiascos like the Hashfield case, for the citizens in all our states to understand?

# 7

# The victims who survive

Yet general failure to understand the problem may be hardest in some instances on the victims who survive. Let us look at the situation confronting adult victims of unprovoked rape attacks.

"Men don't put much faith in rape charges," was the blunt statement of an old friend, a veteran newspaperman, when I told him the subject of my present book.

Former New York City Magistrate Morris Ploscowe indicates in his own excellent book, *Sex and the Law,* that this view is shared by a considerable proportion of those who administer the laws. Many experts in the field of legal medicine believe that "rape cannot be perpetrated by one man alone on an adult woman of good health and vigor," he writes. "Medico-legal experts therefore tend to regard all accusations of rape made under such circumstances as false."

He quotes another authority to the same effect, with the added proviso, "unless there are some very extraordinary circumstances. For a woman always possesses sufficient power, by drawing back her legs and by the force of her hands, to prevent the insertion of the penis while she can keep her resolution entire."

Different states have set up different standards for establishing whether a rape had been consummated, and whether it was a rape at all. Some go so far as to set the exact amount of penetration—in inches—which determines whether it was rape or only attempted rape.

In New York and some other states, according to Judge Ploscowe, there must be signs or marks of a struggle, physical evidence of sexual intercourse, proof of outcry, proof of immediate complaint and of the defendant's presence on the scene, or flight from it. The statutes of many states say no conviction can be made for rape or defilement upon the female on the woman's testimony alone, unsupported by other evidence.

Some states insist that the victim shall have resisted throughout to the fullest extent of her powers. Some others, however, including California, require only that the resistance be proportioned to the outrage and depend upon circumstances, such as the relative strength of the parties, age and condition of the victim, uselessness of resistance, and the degree of force manifested by the attacker. Hence if a woman is slated to be the object of a forcible rape, it can make a considerable difference to her what state she is in when it takes place.

An example of the legal mind at work in this area was presented by a New York City case not many years ago. An actress claimed that she was both raped and sodomized by a Negro entertainer in the home of a woman friend who, she said, had held her hands and kissed her while the assault was carried out. At the trial, the defense attorney introduced proof that, some years before this, the complainant had been arrested when a night club where she was a member of the audience was raided. One assumes this was the most damaging thing the defense counsel could find in her record, for if there had been anything worse he would surely have brought it up. But according to the newspaper clipping sent me by a friend, that was enough for the judge. He dismissed the rape charge on the spot but took the sodomy charge under advisement. It was as if to say that the mere fact that a woman had happened to be in a place of public entertainment when it was raided by the police made her legal prey for any man who wished to use her sexually, against her will, in so-called natural ways; but that so-called unnatural use might be something else again. This line of reasoning was probably clear to the presiding judge, but I find it confusing.

I agree fully with a statement of Judge Ploscowe's that, just as it is no defense under the law for an attacker to plead that he was drunk, a woman should not be permitted to claim rape, when she is sober, if she has been drinking with the man to the point of intoxication. But it might also be taken into account that many rapist deviates—this has been found true of around half in the studies that have been made— are triggered to sex violence by drink. For the protection of other women, it might well be determined by psychiatric and psychological examination whether or not the accused man is a sex deviate, before turning him loose, if there is reason to think rape has occurred.

(I do not want to imply here that Judge Ploscowe is prejudiced against the adult victim. I found his discussion of the problem to be very fair and his statement of the views of other authorities is helpful.)

People have said to me, "Doesn't your experience *prove* that a woman can't be raped by one man, against her will?"

It proves nothing of the sort, and this misconception is terribly unjust to many women. I believe that the experts and the men on the street who hold it are thinking in terms of the normal man, whose instincts forbid him to beat up a woman or to force one whom he finds to be genuinely unwilling. Even very rough men who do not have an abnormal hatred of women, as a sex, appear to have an innate respect for decent women and will protect them against other males. Hence there is a rather natural disposition on the part of many persons to think that, if a man rapes a woman, she has in some way invited it or at least has not been completely averse.

On the other hand, there is the consideration that rape is a charge which can be brought against any man, by any woman, out of spite, hysteria, to extricate herself from an embarrassing situation, or under circumstances where it may be to someone's advantage to have the accused man embarrassed in this way (as in the case of a public figure). A rape charge can be a very underhanded woman's weapon and can ruin an innocent man's life. I have seen cases cited where men were given long sentences for rape on the unsupported word of known prostitutes. Negroes have been killed out of hand, and their slayers absolved by local courts, because of a mere word or gesture that some white woman considered insulting.

But the foregoing considerations do not enter into the cases that are my concern, where an attack by a sexually sick man actually takes place. This is a very different matter from dealing with a normal male, and the difference can scarcely be understood fully by anyone who has not gone through the experience.

First of all, there is the element of shock. The moment my assailant threw open my bedroom door and entered, half crouching, the stories I had read and heard about women found dead, ravished and mutilated, flashed through my mind. I did not dream, then, that I would be alive the next morning. No matter how brave or virtuous or determined a woman may be, I don't see how she could help being momentarily paralyzed by the realization of her awful plight, if not completely incapacitated by fear. (I remember a New York City case of many years ago in which a frail woman writer was raped and murdered by a man who had previously delivered something to her apartment. He said after he was arrested that she had kept begging, "Please don't hurt me, please don't hurt me.")

Second, it is almost routine, at least in the Greater New York area, for a rapist to threaten an adult victim, and frequently younger ones, with a weapon, sometimes a gun but usually a knife. And when the sexually sick man does not come armed, it is common practice for him to start things off by hitting his victim with his fists, or by partly strangling her. I was tremendously fortunate in that my attacker did not use his fists or follow through on the gesture he made toward choking me. When my head hit the window sill and I was partially stunned, I knew that if there was to be much more of that it would be the end, for it had required every atom of physical strength and mental quickness that I possessed to escape the rape. (I am not young, but I am healthy and, I believe, as vigorous as the average young woman.) If my assailant had not given up at that point, the story could have been very different. A woman knocked about or choked to near insensibility early in the attack would be seriously handicapped in resisting effectively. I have wondered, in fact, if the preliminary choking is not done to prevent the "outcry" which some state laws demand as a proof of the victim's unwillingness.

I have been repeatedly impressed by the size of many of the men arrested, or being hunted, for rape attacks. A number have been reported as being over six feet tall and weighing 200 pounds or more.

(My assailant, a young, powerful man only a year older than my own son, outweighed me by forty pounds.) Even if a woman is young, healthy and vigorous, she would have small chance against a man mountain, if she had only her bare hands to defend herself with. Most of the women who have escaped the consummation of a rape under such circumstances have done so through sheer luck, as in my case, or because the man had been frightened away before he could complete the attack.

In his book, *Sex and the Law,* Judge Ploscowe gives a description of the body of a woman who was murdered in the course of a rape attack.

> Her lips were swollen and split and had bled freely. Her jaw was swollen and one tooth had been knocked out and another on the side had been loosened. . . . Her hands were swollen, abraded, discolored and contused. [Perhaps the result of her attempt to defeat the rape with her hands?] There were many abrasions on her arms and others on her legs, which were consistent with her legs having been spread apart forcibly. [Something the medico-legal experts preferred to believe cannot be done by one man alone. Death had been caused by repeated blows on the jaw.]

No doubt the foregoing would rate as "extraordinary" circumstances. But such circumstances are in fact quite ordinary ones, and the small number of men incarcerated for rape, compared with the number charged with the crime, indicates that somewhere along the line of due process, the "extraordinary" features have been passed over.

Women reared in typical American homes are not trained in the techniques of fighting off physical assaults by big, strong men. I have been asked why I didn't do thus and so, involving various barroom tactics. And I am told that women whose work takes them into dangerous areas are instructed in ways of attacking the male in his most tender, vulnerable places. Such a thing never entered my mind. My way of life has not required that I should fit myself with techniques of this kind, and the idea is abhorrent to me. I imagine most women would be in the same case. And I would doubt that a man driven by hatred for the female sex, rather than sex desire, would fall for the other type of technique that has been suggested to me where a woman pretends to welcome the man's advances and escapes on the pretext of freshening up, making herself pretty, so as to be worthy of him.

Some of the restrictions and standards set up by the laws of many states are not very realistic in view of the situation in which the victim of unprovoked sex attack may find herself. While consummation or failure to consummate the rape is extremely important to the victim, it should make little difference in the eyes of the law. There should be only two questions at issue. First, did the accused man in fact attempt to force sex relations on the complainant, against her will? Second, if he did, are his motivations and personality such as to indicate that he will repeat his offense (this to be determined by psychiatric and psychological examination)?

If the case boils down to the unsupported word of the victim against the unsupported word of the accused man, I would suggest psychiatric and psychological examination of both, the reports to be entered as part of the court proceedings.

Leaving all to the haphazard workings of a law based on misconceptions, and administered by persons who are ruled by prejudices of one kind or another, fails to protect the victim, the community and the sexually sick man, in a real sense. For it is no kindness to a sick man to let him run free and commit more and more serious crimes, until he arrives at the ultimate one. Judge Ploscowe has. said that a man who will forcibly rape a woman unknown to him will also commit murder, and the record would appear to bear him out in this.

To date, however, more concern and attention have been accorded the accused man, whether guilty or not guilty, than the victim. In all my reading, I have come upon only one writer who has dealt with the emotional burden laid upon the woman who has been the object of a forcible sex attack. Several studies have been made of child victims of sex offenders, but mainly from the standpoint of trying to learn to what extent the child had invited, or had been an active collaborator, in the offense.

There has seemed to be little interest in finding out what the effects are for the unwilling victim who has been attacked without warning, subjected to an unutterably nasty, horrifying, degrading ordeal against her will and through no fault of her own, and left alive.

"But it is horrible for a woman or child to be crippled or killed by an automobile," protested a kindly faced man when I spoke of the special horror of a sex attack by an unknown man.

Of course, any death or crippling accident that could be avoided is tragic. But I know of nothing that could conceivably happen to a woman or child in the United States today which carries the same horror as to find oneself in the embrace of a man whose urge to degrade, hurt, perhaps to destroy, has taken over. Once my husband and I were held up at pistol point by a masked bandit, as we walked along a residential street at night. We did shiver a bit when we learned a 15-year-old had held the pistol, but at the time we looked upon the experience as an exciting break in our lives. Several times I have thought I was facing death on the highway and was aware merely of a sense of inevitability. Such things come up so quickly, in fact, and are so quickly decided, one way or the other, that there is little time for emotion of any kind. Besides, they are impersonal, they present no threat to one's integrity and self-respect.

I myself would prefer any kind of quick, clean death—and I say this advisedly, because I thought I was going to die at the hands of a rapist, and it was not death I feared—to going through another sordid struggle with a sex deviate, even though I were to emerge as fortunately as I did the first time. And there are effects that have lingered on.

May I have the reader's indulgence to explain, at this point, that I am not a timorous woman by nature. My immediate family was just one generation removed from the pioneers who settled the middle west, and the pioneer tradition of hardihood had lingered on.

My two older brothers managed to find an amazing amount of adventure in the college community where we grew up and learned a new respect for my professor father when he disarmed a mentally disturbed man who had threatened him with a revolver. I have never known anyone with more courage than my gentle little mother. She would have marched into a fiery furnace or a lion's cage, if so extraordinary an action had ever been required of her, without so much as the flicker of an eyelash.

Thanks to this family background, I grew up free of the needless and irrational fears which plague and handicap many women. All of my adult life I have gone wherever I wanted or needed to go at any time of the day or night, have never thought about locking doors or worried about living in isolated places. In the middle west, where I spent the greater part of my life, people are friendly and glad to help strangers. My children had hitch-hiked during their college years and had received much kindness from their temporary hosts. I felt obligated to return the kindness when I saw nice-looking young folk standing by the road and never had cause to regret it. On the few occasions when I have felt some apprehensions, I concealed them, and everything turned out all right. My whole life experience up to the time of my encounter with Jack Smith had taught me that to be cool and calm and unafraid will carry one through any situation that is likely to arise. I cannot remember having known actual fear of a human being until that night in my house.

I did not let that experience interfere with my style of life. I have continued to live in my house, which I own and which suits me very well, though I take certain precautions that I would have scorned before and still feel a little silly about. But it happened once; I cannot allow myself to be caught unaware another time. I don't pick up hitch-hikers any more, but that is not so much because I am afraid to as that I realize if I should have a bad experience again, in any way made possible through some act of my own, people would think I was asking for it.

That is the way things are, on the conscious level. But for at least a year after the attack, an unaccustomed noise would make me jump as if at an electric shock, my heart would pump furiously, the blood would pound in my ears until it drowned out all other sounds. This reaction is not so violent now, but it still recurs when, lying in my bed at night, I hear a sound outside. I leap up then, switch on the floodlights I have had installed, and look out of every window, not because

I think someone is there, but because I ignored warning signals once and feel I must never do so again.

And there are nights when, sitting quietly in my house, sewing or reading, suddenly a cold fear comes over me for no reason at all. At those times I get the revolver I bought after the attack and carry it with me as I move about the house, laying it ready to my hand while I perform any task, for I imagine being trapped in one of the rooms and must not be defenseless.

I know that I shall carry these fears as long as I live, even though my conscious, daytime mind is as free and serene as it ever was. For my nerves, my internal organs, the very cells of my body will never forget that stealthy entry, the helplessness of a woman against a powerful man. It is a fear unlike other fears and far worse, believe me, than the threat of death.

Perhaps it is partly a deep, primordial fear of an unnatural phenomenon, as of being confronted by a wild beast in the shape of a human being, a werewolf in reverse, so to speak. On a more conscious level, it is a fear of being at the mercy of a man who is bereft of his humanity yet has a power to degrade and defile the female possessed only by the human male. When I hear the old saw, "If you are going to be raped, you may as well relax and enjoy it," I do not find it amusing.

Yet I was one of the lucky ones. I suffered no important physical harm, and the emotional turmoil subsided when Jack Smith's case was settled, finally, in as satisfactory a way as was possible under the law.

What of the women who have been subjected to the ultimate indignity, a consummated rape, possibly attended by sodomy, and must continue to live with *that?*

In all the medical meetings I have attended over the years, I have only once heard the subject discussed, and that was out of scientific curiosity as to whether a baby conceived in rape might show physical or mental signs of the mother's traumatic experience. What it would mean to a woman or girl to have to bear a child conceived in this way was not touched upon.

The one authority I have found so far who has addressed himself to the victim's problem is Dr. Seymour L. Halleck of Madison, Wisconsin, formerly head of the Psychiatric Service for the Division of Corrections of the Wisconsin State Department of Welfare and now chief consultant for this Division. His article, "The Physician's Role in Management of Victims of Sex Offenders," printed in the April 28, 1962, issue of the *Journal of the American Medical Association* (Vol. 180, pp. 273-78), is designed to help general practitioners understand the victim's plight. For it is generally the family physician who is called in when a sex attack takes place.

"The embarrassing, shameful qualities surrounding sexual assault tend to produce attitudes of protecting the victim, shielding her from publicity, and avoiding psychiatric examinations," Dr. Halleck says, and for this reason, psychiatrists see few sex attack victims soon after the event. But he adds that the psychiatrist often gets them as patients many years later, after they have developed chronic personality disturbances as a result of the experience.

This does not mean that every victim of a sex assault will necessarily require psychiatric treatment. The amount of permanent damage done will depend upon the victim's own personality and the circumstances under which the rape occurred.

The victim may seek the services of the family doctor for medical care, or to establish legally that a sex attack has occurred, or for help with nervous symptoms that may result. Dr. Halleck feels that this gives the general practitioner an opportunity in many cases to prevent serious lasting damage, and his article contains guidance for dealing with the different classes of victims of violent sexual offenders.

Dr. Halleck feels it is difficult to conceive of any woman going through this experience without developing some symptoms.

A woman who has been sexually assaulted has undergone an experience in which she is aware of overwhelming, angry feelings toward her attacker but is helpless to do anything about it. She repeatedly searches her own motivations to discover if there was anything she could have done to prevent the attack. Often she blames herself for having neglected some minor defensive effort that she feels might have protected her. She is uncertain as to her role as a woman, which appears to her at the moment as a degraded and helpless one. She wonders if she is ever going to be attracted to men again or interested in normal sexual relations.

Dr. Halleck advises that the doctor should encourage the woman to talk about the experience she has undergone—"ventilate" is the psychiatric term for what the layman calls getting one's feelings off one's chest. People are inclined to stay away from the topic, in order to avoid embarrassing the victim further. While admitting that psychiatrists have had very little experience with rape victims soon after the event, Dr. Halleck says that everything else known about persons who have undergone a traumatic experience indicates that avoiding the subject is not the best approach. "The immediate ventilation of painful experiences, together with the appreciation of the empathic reaction of another person to feelings of suppressed rage and humiliation, are the most helpful therapies available to the patient."

I think the foregoing advice should be taken to heart by family and friends, as well as by doctors. Some people I knew very well never mentioned the attack to me, though they must have heard of it. The ones who called immediately to offer their sympathy and allowed me to "ventilate" were perhaps more helpful than they realized. Even though the circumstances are such that one has no need to feel personal guilt or responsibility, nevertheless one feels vulnerable to public opinion. When people carefully stay away from the topic, does this indicate that in their minds the victim has cause for shame? That is the sort of thing one thinks about.

The matter of guilt should be handled most delicately, Dr. Halleck says. "Masochistic fantasies are not uncommon and are perhaps experienced by every woman at some time in her life. The victim then may feel that she might have willingly invited or provoked the attacker." This would be particularly true, I should think, if there had been any previous association, as in a case where the attacker has done work about one's home or has delivered something there. The sex deviate, contrary to the normal man, needs no invitation. But Dr. Halleck says that nevertheless many victims, surrendering to their guilt feelings, may assume responsibility for something of which they are totally innocent.

By discussion of what actually happened, he believes that the patient may be brought to realize how helpless she actually was, and it is important that this should be made clear. For in some cases the guilt feelings may become so intense as to cause depression and other debilitating symptoms. Severe depression in a sex-assault victim calls for immediate referral to a psychiatrist.

An accidental victim who was well adjusted, prior to the attack, and had no personality disturbance, should be free of most symptoms and functioning adequately in a few months or even weeks. If neurotic symptoms linger after several months, psychiatric help is indicated. The patient should not be given an alarming idea of her condition, however. The family doctor should point out that even the healthiest personalities are temporarily disorganized after serious traumatic experiences, and there is no reason to think that the disturbance will be permanent.

But when the victim has in fact provoked the attack by imprudent or seductive actions, it is important to determine if she has a personality pattern which predisposes her to this type of behavior. "A single instance of a provoked sexual assault may represent little more than a transient, injudicious lapse on her part. On the other hand, this type of victim may have serious emotional problems which require psychiatric treatment," Dr. Halleck says.

It is undeniable that a proportion of rape victims have contributed in some way to the attack. One of the solved rape murders in my files was that of a social worker, in her fifties, who struck up an acquaintance with a youth in his early twenties in a tavern and took him home with her. He confessed that he had forced the woman to submit by holding a knife on her, then had stabbed her to death. This woman may have had innocent motives in carrying on an association which began in a tavern, but she became an accessory before the fact to her own murder in so doing. Dr. Halleck makes it clear that chronic sex recklessness on a woman's part should be as much a cause for concern as a tendency toward sex violence on a man's part.

There are women who claim to have been subjected to a sexual attack but whose stories raise doubts in the physician's mind that the attack actually occurred. They may invent this kind of story in order to solve disturbing emotional problems, or to shock the physician, or to give themselves a feeling of importance. These women are almost always disturbed persons, according to Dr. Halleck, and, like the woman who has contributed to a real sex attack, may need psychiatric treatment.

And Dr. Halleck mentions women who come to their doctors so full of shame and guilt feelings that they have not confided a genuine case of molestation to husband or family. Such a patient, Dr. Halleck advises, should be urged to break her silence. Sharing the burden, with few exceptions, makes it less painful, and an understanding, sympathetic attitude on the part of the husband or parents may be all that is needed to banish the victim's symptoms. Dr. Halleck suggests that the doctor might spend some time with family members, encouraging them to adopt a realistic, helpful attitude.

Whatever the woman's personality and history, the right kind of help and attention at the time of the attack may avert serious results later on. If she does not receive adequate help, the results may take a variety of forms. Women who have less stable personalities to begin with may develop anxieties, phobias, depression, or become hypochondriacs. Less commonly they may fall prey to alcoholism or promiscuity, if the early symptoms are neglected.

With child victims—he has set an arbitrary upper age limit of 14 for these—Dr. Halleck finds, as have other investigators, that a considerable proportion have offered little resistance or have actively invited the attentions of the offending adult. Often the victim is well acquainted with his or her violator or seducer. But Dr. Halleck does not feel that the child can be held responsible.

> Even though these children may be quite aggressive sexually [Dr. Halleck mentions that many are charming and behave in a very seductive way toward adults], all except a handful of them must be considered as victims. . . . The adult who becomes involved in sexual play with a child, even a seductive child, takes advantage of an individual who is in no way capable of maturely

judging her actions. He is also allowing himself and the child to participate in an immature and abnormal sexual act.

The child victim may be either a boy or a girl, and the emotional impact on a boy of homosexual assault or seduction may be as serious as heterosexual exploitation of a girl. (Cases of women involved sexually with little girls are very rare.)

In a number of the case histories of sexual offenders, early homosexual rape or seduction had played a part. Dr. Halleck says that even though a boy has come from a very deprived background and may have sought the attentions of an adult male, he may still have strong feelings of guilt and shame. "Such feelings may produce psychological and somatic [physical] symptoms. Any type of emotional disturbance in children also tends to interfere with optimum achievement in social and educational areas."

Homosexual contacts with boys of their own age, or even with adults, are not uncommon male experiences in growing up, and Dr. Halleck says it is often difficult to trace any lasting effect from such contacts made in boyhood or adolescence. "On the other hand, the psychiatrist also sees many patients who are severely traumatized by these events. Most often it is the child who is already emotionally disturbed who becomes permanently damaged." The circumstances of the child's life at the time he was seduced have a great deal to do with whether or not he will become fixated at the homosexual level.

If a child was experiencing emotional deprivation and parental neglect at the time of the act, it tended to take on an aura of comfort and satisfaction. This type of behavior was then difficult to relinquish later in life. If it took place when the child's relationship with the parents and his emotional development were satisfactory, deviant sexual patterns did not develop during adult years.

The foregoing applies equally to girl victims of adult males. Dr. Halleck says it is by no means uncommon for girls who grow up in a city environment to encounter an exhibitionist, and the great majority of a group of girl students studied at the University of California who had had this experience reported that it had not interfered seriously with their adjustment to life. Actual molestation is a different matter, however, and one may get an idea of the number of girl children victimized by adult males, far in excess of the number of men convicted for this type of crime, from the fact that 35 per cent of the girls in this same study had at some time been subjected to handling or other form of sexual molestation by adult males. "Many of these girls, particularly those threatened with rape, reported that they had encountered subsequent problems in the sexual area."

Dr. Halleck believes that with girls, as with boys, the amount and permanence of damage done depends upon the child's previous personality development and the family situation at the time the sexual violation was experienced.

> In working with large populations of promiscuous, adolescent girls, it is possible to trace back histories of sexual seduction during latency or puberty. Most of these girls come from seriously disturbed homes . . . a surprisingly large number have had prepubertal sexual experiences. If the sexual event takes place at a time in the child's life when she is deprived, isolated, or upset, it may take on a particular significance. Promiscuity may then appear as a neurotic compulsion.

Dr. Halleck has noted that most promiscuous adolescent girls report that they do not actually enjoy sexual intercourse but that they are interested rather in receiving love, attention and affection.

With the girl who is a willing participant, the same investigation is suggested into the child's previous history and the family climate at the time of the attack as was suggested for the boy who collaborates with his seducer, to determine whether or not she should be referred to a psychiatrist. Where there have been only one or two sexual incidents, and the family relationship is good, psychiatric care may not be needed. But if there have been repeated sexual incidents or behavior problems or school difficulties, and the family situation is disturbed, the girl should have immediate psychiatric help.

Treatment of the young accidental victims, who have been entirely innocent, should proceed along much the same lines as that recommended for the accidental, unwilling, adult victim. The boy should be encouraged to talk about the experience and reassured as to his masculinity. It may be necessary to explain the incident and to give further sex information. It is essential that the boy be given an opportunity to express some anger and that there should be a realistic discussion of guilt feelings.

The parents must also be made aware of the possibility that the event will have a profound impact on the child. When there is evidence that the child has been neglected in recent months, the parents should be urged to remedy the situation. They, too, may need opportunities to express their feelings, particularly when there is intense guilt.

The little girl who has been an accidental victim will experience the same feelings of rage and helplessness and doubts about herself as the unwilling adult victim, and these will probably be accentuated by the fact that the child does not understand much that has happened. "She may feel permanently injured," says Dr. Halleck, "and indeed, serious physical trauma may actually have taken place." Or she may have experienced a vague excitement and have guilt feelings on that account. As a result, the unwilling little girl victim may pay with a seriously dislocated sex life, ranging anywhere from frigidity to an aimless kind of promiscuity or, in some cases, to lesbianism.

It is important for the doctor to make the child understand that she is not permanently injured and that what happened to her has nothing to do with the expression of sex between a man and woman who love each other. The parents, too, may need help to avoid communicating their own anxieties and shamed feelings to the child. They should treat the matter openly and calmly and answer the child's questions freely.

In incest cases—Dr. Halleck believes these are more numerous than is generally realized—the physician may find that the affected daughter, the guilty father and the mother are all seriously disturbed persons, needing expert treatment. The girl should be removed, at least temporarily, from such a damaging environment, and the doctor, whenever possible, should enlist the help of community agencies to deal with the general family situation.

Dr. Halleck shows us that sexual sickness is not a self-limiting disease. Like a highly contagious physical ailment, it causes distressing symptoms temporarily in all those it touches. If the victim be of a susceptible nature or has been rendered susceptible by outside circumstances at the time of exposure, it may be permanently contaminating.

Dr. Halleck has made one of the most valuable contributions of all to the problem by pointing out how much of this tragic waste can be avoided. Many boy victims can be saved from becoming victimizers themselves; many girls from becoming man-haters, working out their hostilities and disturbed sex feelings on their sons, and thus producing more molesters of women and children. Many women can be saved from neuroses, invalidism, or worse, when the people about them understand.

# TWO
# Causes of sex violence

# 8

# What is this sickness?

What is "the type of mental problem or block on which the devil plays to turn a man into some kind of animal," in the phrase of the attacker of the young Long Island housewife?

Nearly every authority who has discussed sex offenders has begun by saying that not much is known about the sex deviate or psychopath —the person who obtains sexual gratification in ways considered abnormal or antisocial. The late Dr. Benjamin Karpman called attention to the fact that every year perpetrators of rape or rape murder are being executed or sentenced to terms in prison. "Those who have been executed have carried the secret of their illness with them to the grave, those who are imprisoned are not being studied." He asked how far medicine would have advanced if, in similar fashion, pathologists had never been given an opportunity to learn the nature and structure of physical disease.

Undoubtedly, there should be a great deal more investigation of sexual sickness. But I find that, beginning with about 1920, many sex offenders have been studied, and a vast literature has collected on the subject. The vacuum lies in authoritative information about treatment. Many writers stray back and forth between the nonviolent sex deviates—exhibitionists, Peeping Toms and the like—and the men whose sickness leads them to prey on children or to rape or murder. In the quite laudable effort to show that the nonviolent ones merely offend our sensibilities without being dangerous, they tend to fog the problem of the ones who are a real and dreadful menace.

Dr. Manfred S. Guttmacher is one of the foremost authorities on the sex offender. Since 1930 he has headed the psychiatric clinic attached to the Baltimore courts, except for a few years' leave of absence spent with the Armed Services in World War II and acting as a psychiatric consultant to the World Health Organization. Thousands of sex offenders have been studied psychiatrically in the Baltimore court clinic during the decades he has spent there.

Dr. Guttmacher points out in his book, *Sex Offenses: The Problem, Causes and Prevention,* that there are individuals who commit isolated or very infrequent sex offenses who are not real sex deviates. Through lack of strong personality integration, their defenses may break down as a result of undue strain. Usually the offenses they commit are the ones we consider minor. Confused adolescents may engage in isolated, minor sex deviations, in what Dr. Guttmacher describes as a kind of instinctual groping. If the act is not repeated by the adult, or if the adolescent outgrows his tendency to deviate, neither is a sex offender in the true sense.

> On the other hand, if a crime is of sufficient magnitude, the single act marks the offender as a criminal. A man need only hold up a bank once to be branded as seriously antisocial. And rightly enough, a man need commit only one forced rape to be considered a serious sexual criminal.

The minor, nonviolent sexual aberrations are called paraphilias. Homosexuality is rated as a paraphilia when practised only with other consenting adults, and children are not debauched or violated. Voyeurism—the Peeping Tom—is another, along with exhibitionism, although all these are against the law. Fetishism, inability to gain sexual satisfaction without having at hand some female garment or other object of erotic interest, is still another paraphilia. The test is that a paraphilia does not endanger or morally damage any innocent and unwilling person.

Psychoanalysts believe that paraphilias result when the orderly development of a child's personality has been interfered with. Freud, and students of child psychology following his lead, long ago made us aware that certain sex manifestations are normal at certain stages of development. It may be worthwhile to recapitulate briefly the kind of normal behavior which has a bearing on paraphilias that may show up later on.

First of all comes the awareness of the pleasurable sensations connected with the genital region, as the baby's explorations of its own body extend this far. It is also natural and normal for tiny children to be interested in the products of their own bodies, as they become aware of these. Babies will play with their feces, if given the opportunity. Every mother of a boy knows the innocent pride the little fellow takes in his male organs somewhere around age 2 to 3, the curiosity children of both sexes have about other people's sex organs, and such things as where babies come from.

Also around age 3 it is normal for the child's love to be fixed on the parent of the opposite sex, in the case of a boy, his mother. Wishing to possess all her love, he looks upon his father as a rival and may go through a period of displaying hostility toward the kindliest and most loving father. At the same time, psychoanalysts tell us, he fears his father, thinking his father must have the same hostile feelings toward him and will punish him by castrating him (the famous Oedipus complex). There are several periods in early childhood when nearly all little boys, and many little girls, may do some masturbating. Dr. George E. Gardner has said that the 9-year-old boy may quite normally have aggressive destructive impulses from which he derives pleasure.

Children outgrow these types of behavior, provided they have not been subjected to too painful and damaging punishments or threats in connection with them. The 9-year-old can be expected gradually to gain control of his aggressive impulses and to replace the pleasure he has found in them by socially useful reactions. The aggressive, destructive sexual deviate, however, enters puberty deriving equal pleasure from killing, mutilating impulses and sexual impulses.

Many parents, through ignorance or unconsciously motivated by guilt feelings because of things they have done at an earlier age, still threaten the child with dire consequences, as that the aggressive 9-year-old will wind up in jail, the masturbator in an insane asylum. I myself once heard a physician tell a group of mothers that when a child was referred to him for masturbating, he would take a scalpel, draw an imaginary line around the genitals, and say that he would cut out the organs if the child didn't stop his practice.

Dr. Benjamin Karpman wrote, "No one can at present say exactly how many cases of sexual aberration would have been prevented by a rational sex education early in life, but it seems certain that the number would be considerable."

Most children outgrow childish practices, even when the parents have not handled the matter wisely but, nevertheless, have done whatever they have done out of a genuine love and concern for the child's welfare. But when the parents overreact out of their own disturbed sexual emotions or out of hostility to the child, punishing, frustrating, in a threatening, angry way, the pain and the fear remain, although fear, as of castration, will be forced below the conscious level. However, as serious conflicts arise, neuroses or character disorders may develop, and under emotional stress the individual may regress—revert to an earlier stage of development.

There have been isolated cases of exhibitionism in men of fine character and high attainment, who have regressed to the small-boy exhibitionist stage as a result of overwork or emotional strain. These men are unutterably shocked when they learn what they have done. Mentally sick persons may regress to so infantile a level that they begin to play with their bodily excretions. Adults usually considered normal may revert on occasion to other developmental stages—tantrums, for instance.

Mental sickness is thought to develop when the individual's personality has become fixed, in some respect, at one of these early development stages, though in some types of mental or emotional disturbance there is a growing tendency to search for physical causes also. A study made by Dr. Guttmacher showed, for instance, that twice as many sex offenders who have gone through his clinic had suffered head injuries, when young, as had non-sex offenders. It is now known that unborn babies may suffer brain damage as the result of infections incurred by their mothers during pregnancy, and many conditions are being discovered which may affect mental processes after a baby has been born.

Dr. Winfred Overholser, former superintendent of St. Elizabeth's Hospital in Washington, D.C., and a past president of the American Psychiatric Association, has pointed out that the mind does not exist in a vacuum. There are many causes of brain damage—for example, toxic substances in the blood stream, and the degenerative changes due to advancing years—and these can bring about changes, temporary or permanent, in the individual's personality.

Research into the possibility of physical causes for mental disorders has lagged far behind research into other types of disease, and particularly so in sexual sickness. The tranquilizing drugs have brought about improvement in many cases, as in other types of mental illness. But there must be much more research and experimentation before we can hope for a cure through medication.

As for the way emotions can affect mental states, the mechanism is very involved, but it is enough for our purposes to say that, as we grow up, inevitably conflicts arise between our instincts and desires and the authority of parents or the demands of society. Such conflicts give rise to guilt feelings which cause us to become depressed and anxious and to look about for someone else we can blame for our shortcomings. Some people develop neuroses. They may have compulsions and psychosomatic symptoms, but it will usually be found that their symptoms serve some useful purpose in their lives, whether or not they are aware of it. Thus the hypochondriac gets more attention, the exaggerated aches and pains give the individual an excuse not to work. But when the mechanism operates to the point that the individual loses touch with reality, and his imaginings become the true world to him, he is psychotic or, to use the lay term, insane. The extreme form of holding others responsible for our own failings is found in the paranoid psychotic, who has delusions that he is plotted against and persecuted.

The largest number of psychotics suffer from schizophrenia, or dementia praecox. This disease appears fundamentally to be a regression toward an earlier, less mature mode of thinking and feeling, with the substitution of fantasy for reality, along with delusions and hallucinations. In some instances the schizophrenic may panic and act violently, in others he may become tense and rigid. The marked changes in behavior that may take place are in fact the reason why schizophrenia has been known as the disease of split personality.

Dr. Overholser believes that probably most sex deviates are neurotics and represent a fixation at an earlier level of psychosexual development. They have found a form of behavior that suits their needs, hence the compulsive exhibitionist, Peeping Tom, homosexual and so forth will continue his practices unless he can be cured of his neurosis.

Few psychiatrists today attribute all emotional disturbance to sex conflicts, though they are a common cause, inasmuch as the sex drive is so strong and our society places so many taboos around it. In most of the cases of sex offenders that have been studied, there have been contributing factors such as poor parent-child relationships, unhappy home backgrounds, frustrations because of poverty, or inability to adapt to society.

A study made of the hospital records of 280 men committed to California institutions as sexual psychopaths showed that their intelligence did not differ signally from that of the general population. The same was true of their education, judged by the number of grades completed in school. They came largely from the ranks of unskilled labor.

Two thirds had histories of previous sex offenses; some admitted they had committed acts as many as twenty times prior to their arrests. Most had used children. About one third were either chronic alcoholics or heavy periodic drinkers. Nearly one third were intoxicated when they committed the offense for which they had been committed. The majority were white, born in this country.

A study made in Baltimore by Dr. Guttmacher of 172 sex offenders, compared with 172 non-sex offenders, revealed many interesting facts about sex offenders in general. The sex crimes committed were both minor and serious. First of all, his study showed that Negroes are not primarily sex offenders, a finding that has been confirmed by studies in other places. While the crime rate among Negroes in slum sections is often high, for understandable reasons, many more are arrested for general offenses than for sex offenses.

There was a comparatively low rate of both sex and general crime among the foreign born. The highest incidence of sex crime was found among native white men, as in California.

In the Baltimore clinic, the average age of the general group was 26, while in the sex group it was 32 years and 10 months. One third of the general group fell in ages 16 to 20, as against only one sixth of the sex group; less than 10 per cent of the general group were over 40, more than one fourth of the sex group were over 40. These figures have been closely approximated by studies made in other clinics.

Nearly half the sex group were married or had been married, indicating that early marriage is not the solution to all sex problems, as has been suggested by some psychiatrists. A little more than one third of both groups had wet the bed beyond the age of 5 and had been nail-biters, many still continuing the habit.

The sex offenders rated somewhat lower on both I.Q.'s and amount of education than the general ones. All but 10 per cent of both groups said they had some religious training in childhood. The sex offenders as a group reported they had begun masturbation and heterosexual relations at a later age than the non-sex offenders. Sex offenders were nearly twice as likely to insist on their innocence, in spite of a guilty verdict, as the general offenders.

Sharp differences, however, appeared among the sex offenders, according to their offense. The child molesters, the exhibitionists, and those who had committed incest or statutory rape were considerably older than the forcible rapists, and their responses to the Rorschach test were very different.

Those of the exhibitionists, for instance, tended to be vague, undifferentiated. They did not analyze, organize, create, look for things, but merely responded to the impact the blots made on them.

> These exhibitionists, then [says Dr. Guttmacher], are shown by the Rorschach to be unproductive people who do not relate actively to the environment, whose basic orientation is a passive-receptive one, and who lack the sense that they can produce what they need, but feel that someone should give it to them. . . .
>
> As to their social attitudes, most of them have no feeling that they can win someone, influence someone, relate to someone. In

sexual as in other contacts they are not capable of building up a satisfactory relationship with another person. [The foregoing, of course, refers to the habitual exhibitionist, not to the isolated case.]

Similar responses are found among the practitioners of other forms of paraphilia and among the molesters of children who do not hurt their victims. These men are so lacking in confidence in themselves as sexual beings that they do not have the courage to approach mature women. Dr. Guttmacher says that a depersonalized form of sexual expression, such as peeping at or touching or exhibiting the genitals, seems more possible and congenial to them than a relation in which the partner has to be treated as a human being. They are, in fact, emotional cripples, their spirits having been so crushed by episodes in childhood that they are unable to have a satisfying sex relationship on a mature basis. Edward J. Glover has stated that sexual disorders of adolescents and adults are not simply chance disturbances of normal function but, paradoxically, are attempts to cure earlier disordered functions.

Dr. Guttmacher has found that many young pedophiliacs, men who choose children as sexual objects, are similarly passive, immature individuals who lack the courage to make sexual contacts with contemporaries. In his experience, those who prey on little boys exclusively are hardest of all to cure.

Then there is the senile group, ever growing larger because of our society's increasing longevity, who indulge in various forms of sex play with children. Entering their second childhood, they tend to revert to childhood activities. Many of them have begun to experience potency difficulties and hence seek unsophisticated sexual partners. There are others who have retained their potency but whose wives have died or have lost interest in marital relations. It is very difficult for these aging men to find a receptive adult female, unless they are financially able to dispense substantial gifts in return for sex favors.

With the forcible rapist, the sadist, and the sex murderer, however, the story is quite different.

# 9

# Men who hate

It is not hard to understand why a boy or man whose normal sexual development has been halted at some infantile level should be unable to work out a sex life on a mature basis. But this does not account for the forcible, aggressive sex criminals. The rapists in Dr. Guttmacher's study reported that they had begun masturbating at 13, and more than half had begun having intercourse regularly at the age of 15. Of forcible rapists, in general, it has been found that the majority marry young and have children. They are not deprived of normal sex, as is true of many practitioners of the various paraphilias.

Dr. Benjamin Karpman stated the puzzle very well when he asked:

*Why* should a man violate a woman, then abuse her physically, inflicting all sorts of physical injury, occasionally even killing her? Above all, *why* should any normal man wish to secure sexual outlet through the use of force, when society provides more than fair opportunities for release of sexual tensions through marriage, clandestine relations and prostitution? [Italics mine.]

Why should a young man—most rapists arrested and convicted are in their late teens, twenties, or early thirties—choose as a victim a woman in her fifties or sixties or even seventies, as many do? I remarked to the troopers when we were hunting a clue to my assailant that he was a personable young man who could have found plenty of sexual partners among younger women, and without having to use force. Why should he have gone to much trouble, as well as incurring the danger of a prison sentence, to attack a woman old enough to be his mother?

Why should the young, vigorous rapist so often beat, choke, kick, stab a woman whom he could easily overpower without this needless brutality? And going through cases cited in books, newspapers and reports of the two Sing Sing studies, I was impressed with the number of times that sodomy was charged, in addition to beating and forced intercourse. Sodomy in the New York statutes covers a variety of "unnatural" offenses, so one could not know just what had been done to the unfortunate victim. Nevertheless there had been an evident urge on the part of the assailant to debase and degrade an unknown woman who had never harmed him in any way, even beyond the forcing of sexual intercourse upon her.

It began to appear that some of these men, at least, are motivated by something other than sex desire, and this is in fact the case in the majority of unprovoked sexual assaults.

Dr. Guttmacher tells us that there are at least three types of rapists. There is the one whose assault is the explosive expression of a pent-up sexual impulse. He is a true sex offender, inasmuch as his crime is motivated by sex desire only.

The sadistic rapists comprise a second group. They are motivated by an impulse to punish and hurt the victim, rather than by sex desire, or else obtain sexual satisfaction through the suffering they inflict.

Then there is a third type of rapist, the aggressive criminal who is out to pillage and rob, like the soldier of a conquering army. "We have had cases of apparently sexually well-adjusted youthful offenders who have, in one night, committed a series of burglaries and, in the course of one of them, committed rape—apparently just as another act of plunder."

And finally, there are offenses which appear entirely dissociated from the sex impulse but which, in actuality, are in the nature of symbolic sex acts, according to Dr. Guttmacher.

For instance, he has found female kleptomaniacs to be sexually unsatisfied women with tremendous hostility. (Men kleptomaniacs are rare, perhaps because males discharge their sex hostilities in other ways.) Stealing frequently is used to alleviate sex tensions, by youngsters who have been taught that an overt expression of sex feelings through masturbation or intercourse is a worse crime than robbery. Dr. Guttmacher speculates that certain instances of car theft, a prevalent form of youthful crime, may be attempts on the part of the youths involved to resolve early sexual conflicts.

Dr. Walter Bromberg has listed still another group, whom he calls "lust-murderers." Lust murder, according to Clifford Allen, is characterized by periodic outbreaks, due to recurring compulsion or paroxysmal sexual desire. There is nearly always cutting or stabbing, particularly of the breasts or genitals, and frequently the maddened man sucks or licks the wounds he has made, bites the victim's skin, and sometimes has a desire to drink the blood and eat the flesh. Sexual violation of the victim may follow, but often it does not. Jack the Ripper was a lust murderer, though the newspapers of the day failed to grasp the sexual significance of the Ripper's mutilating or removing parts of a victim's reproductive system. (This was before Freud's work had become generally known.)

Even today the significance of murderous, unmotivated attacks on strangers, when not accompanied by sexual abuse, is often missed. "Cases of pure sadism, in which aggression is discharged for its own sake and pain is inflicted as an end in itself—and its inverse behavioral pattern, masochism—rarely come into court because of offenses that are obviously sexual," Dr. Guttmacher says. He believes that depth probing would frequently reveal their covert sexual basis.

Dr. Bromberg says that, in true lust murders, mental disease is usually present and is often of the schizoid type, or withdrawal from reality.

The Rorschach test responses of forcible rapists and others who express their sex conflicts in violent ways are markedly different from those of the timid and crippled souls who shy away from sex on a mature level. They reveal a great deal of conflict and inner disharmony, beneath a rigidly controlled surface. These men tend if anything to be over-controlled. "Unlike the exhibitionists, who generally release their impulses with relatively little inhibition, these people allow steam to accumulate to an explosive degree," Dr. Guttmacher says. The sudden breaking through of the dammed-up impulses when controls are weakened, perhaps under the effects of alcohol, leads to the explosive and violent behavior of this group.

"Intense conflict and frustration are sometimes indicated. An extreme degree of social isolation is also evident in these cases. They seem to be without resources in forming satisfying contacts with others." I am reminded of Jack Smith's statement to me that he had never been able to figure out what society expected of him.

"In record after record [of the Rorschach tests], the theme of violent penetration appears," Dr. Guttmacher writes. "A brick wall is broken through, worms bore into a rabbit's face, something shoots up through a tube and breaks through water at the top."

One offender saw "the window of a church" in one of the ink blots and added spontaneously:

"If you come to one of *those* windows, you got to break it to look through it. It's thick glass. You don't try to break it with your hand. . . . But don't try to break in no churches—you don't get much out of it. Break into some of those people that's always screwing you." . . . In some records, an unmistakable sadistic quality is present.

Dr. Benjamin Karpman has stated that all the rapists who had come under his care had been profoundly abnormal. But it is not in most instances a kind of abnormality that fits the usual classifications of insanity or mental disease. In a study made of sex offenders at the New Jersey State Diagnostic Center, only about 25 per cent were found to be actually psychotic, borderline psychotic, mentally deficient, or impaired by brain diseases. About 35 per cent were severely neurotic, while around 40 per cent were found to be normal, from a psychiatric standpoint, or merely mildly neurotic. (This study included sex offenders of all types, but other studies confirm that most of the ones who commit sex crimes of violence are not insane by the usual definitions.)

The illness of the otherwise normal men who force sex relations on women unknown to them and maul, sometimes kill, is a sickness of hate—hate of the female. Their sex instincts have become twisted and perverted by this hatred to such a degree that the protectiveness toward the self-respecting female which is inherent in decent, civilized men has turned to a desire to ravish and degrade, not for the sake of sex gratification—many derive no sex satisfaction from these forced relations—but from a desire to avenge themselves on the female sex.

Numerous studies have shown this. Dr. Walter Bromberg says, "To the sexual pervert, belittlement of the sexual partner is a source of unconscious gratification because it satisfies hostile impulses directed toward women."

Dr. Benjamin Karpman bears out the other authorities quoted in telling us that sexual hostility is the motive for other types of aggression than sexual assault, listing aggravated assault and battery, assault with a dangerous weapon, and murder. Often the assaulter obtains sexual release by his action.

A young boy stabs a totally strange girl with a knife. Analysis reveals that . . . his mind is constantly occupied with fantasies of the most cruel, sadistic torture. A man slashes the throats of young girls. On arrest, it is found that his underwear is bespattered with semen. To this group also belong the men who cut off women's hair, the acid-throwers, the fur coat and dress slashers, the Jack the Rippers, and the like. There are many pyromaniacs whose desire for an orgasm constitutes the sole reason for setting fires that have cost the lives of many people.

This appears to explain the crimes of William Heirens, one of the most sensational sexless sex murderers of our day. Heirens was the University of Chicago student who wrote on a mirror, using the lipstick of his latest victim, "Catch me before I kill again. I cannot help myself."

A youngster who had never experienced a close, confidential relationship with anyone, least of all with his own parents, Heirens began his aberrant career as a fetishist. When only 9 years old, he stole women's undergarments, first from clotheslines, then from basements and later by entering the houses of strangers when he found a door ajar. At quite an early age he started to have orgasms when he put on the stolen garments. When he was around 12, he began entering houses through windows in order to obtain these objects, and presently the "thrill" of entering through the window produced orgasm. As time went on, however, it took several window enterings to produce this effect.

Heirens was sent to a reform school for burglary when he was 13. When he was caught entering a house two months after his release, he was sent, by request of his parents, to a boarding school. He appeared to adjust well in both places and frequently took Holy Communion. Entering the University of Chicago at the age of 16½, he had been a student there for a year before he was arrested for the three murders he committed during this time—those of two women and a 6-year-old girl whom he had kidnaped, killed and dismembered. In no case did he molest a victim sexually. He had had a few dates and had kissed several girls but maintained that it was because they wanted him to. Actually, heterosexual intimacies were repugnant to him. The psychiatrists who studied him believed the murders had been committed for the same reason as the 500 burglaries to which he owned up—to achieve orgasm.

He had fought hard against the impulse toward ever more bizarre ways to gain sex satisfaction, going so far sometimes as to lock up his clothes and hide the key. But he always yielded in the end.

"The sexual offense is not a substitute for normal sexual intercourse," Dr. Karpman says, "and cases are known where neither excessive intercourse nor abstinence stopped it. It is a form of sexual activity all its own, satisfying some very specific needs of the individual that normal sexual activity cannot give." He points out that when the sexually twisted person has found a way by which he can attain sex satisfaction, it is difficult to divert him from it, as Heirens exemplified.

This last is true of all types of sex deviates, whether they practice one or more of the paraphilias, degrade women by making them objects of lust, or kill and mutilate women or children without molesting them sexually. But it is the one who acts aggressively and dangerously, out of a consuming sex hatred, with whom we are concerned here, and, as with the harmless paraphiliac, the roots of his disorder lie in childhood experiences.

Many violent sex criminals who have been studied had histories of sickening abuse and brutality as children. Many had been introduced to sex practices in the "reformatories" to which they had been sent to "be straightened out"—in more cases than one, forced by a member of the staff of the institution or else by older boys. They would victimize younger boys in their turn. As one reads these cases, one understands how little chance a child born into such surroundings would have to become anything but antisocial and sexually perverted.

But why the hatred of females, as such? Whence comes the need to fight fears and inferiority feelings by abasing and abusing some member of the opposite sex whom the attacker has never seen before and against whom he has no shred of a personal grievance? This is the crux of the problem of the sexually sick man who has a bent toward violence. It deserves thorough understanding.

# 10

# The part families play

All the authorities who have studied sex offenders have found the genesis of the difficulties of the majority to lie in the kind of parents and home backgrounds they drew in the lottery of life. The same thing, it's true, can be said about most general offenders and about the great majority of persons who fail to make a satisfactory adjustment to society and adult responsibilities.

But with the aggressive sex criminal, there is a difference. In his case, resentment and hatred have somehow been engendered deeply in him at an early age, along with distorted concepts of sex. Not that this has been done purposely. Sex crime is not hereditary; the parents of the serious sex offenders seldom have been convicted of serious sex crimes. They often suffer, however, from emotional maladjustments and conflicts, the result of their own faulty upbringing.

"Sexual maladjustment would not occur if children were exposed to proper adult attitudes," Philip Riker states, going on to say that if the youngster has learned to be an active part of the life about him, has not had his curiosity and his capacity for being interested in things excessively thwarted, and has been allowed to feel that it is not wrong to act out some of his impulses within reasonable limits, he is likely to have available to him a variety of methods for sublimating his primitive sexual drives.

The aggressive sex criminal not only has grown up with distorted ideas about sex. In most cases he has not had a father from whom he could learn proper masculine attitudes, nor has he had warm, self-sacrificing maternal love. Nearly all who have been studied have suffered severe emotional deprivation in childhood. A frequent family constellation was a masculine, dominating mother, mated with an ineffectual father, or a neurotic, ineffectual, or overprotective mother, mated with a tyrannical father. Many of the offenders had been exposed to sex experiences at an early age or to perverted behavior by older companions.

Still another element is often present in the background of the sex deviate who reacts violently—an unwholesome tinge in the relationship with the mother during the offender's childhood and adolescence.

I have been asked, "Are women ever sex criminals?"

In the nature of things, women cannot overpower males and rape them, and women do not murder unknown men out of sex fury, though a woman may murder a man against whom she has a grievance. Incest between mother and son, or overt use or perversion of a child by a woman, happens sometimes, but rarely. About the only overt sex crime of which women are guilty to any extent is prostitution. But it is a well-established psychiatric fact that some woman is at the root of the sexual hostility of the aggressive, violent sex criminal.

As we have seen earlier, there is probably something of an incestuous element in the feeling of every small boy toward his mother, but in a wholesome atmosphere this is outgrown. In the case of aggressive sex criminals who have been studied, it has been found that a large proportion of the mothers behaved toward them in a seductive manner, thus fostering and strengthening the natural incestuous feelings of the child. The seduction is seldom overt, the mother may not be aware of what she is doing, but out of her own emotional needs she behaves toward the child in a way that is calculated to arouse sex feelings. As the late Dr. Robert Lindner wrote in *The Fifty-Minute Hour:*

With such mothers the child is conceived of as a lover, and to all her actions toward him she imparts an aura of sexuality. This stems from the fact that the mothers of psychopaths are usually unrequited in their feelings for their husbands—who are regularly strong, brutal, aggressive and domineering persons—or otherwise starved for love. The child is thus the recipient of mixed and forbidden feelings and desires, a stand-in or substitute for a lover.

In an atmosphere of this kind, the incestuous feelings remain. They engender a terrific conflict in the boy, for in the male world the ultimate, the unforgivable, and unimaginable sin is to have sex relations with one's mother. There is an unpleasant epithet for this, and Dr. Lindner had seen men in prison killed for using it.

Investigation soon disclosed that the power of this invective lay in that it touched a chord in psychopaths particularly, that for them it was true; in other words, that the expression gave voice to a basic fact which many of the psychopath's actions were aimed to keep hidden, and for the disclosure of which he was prepared to kill.

Emotional disturbances stemming from such conflicts were found by Dr. Benjamin Apfelberg in the backgrounds of fourteen men he studied at Bellevue Hospital, in New York City, all of whom had murdered women close to them, a wife in twelve cases, a mistress and a sister in the other two. Dr. Apfelberg found that all fourteen murders had their genesis in sexual fears and hostilities engendered by father-mother relationships in the murderers' childhoods. In one group, the men had had hostile fathers, whom they feared. Dr. Apfelberg conjectured that they had responded to conflict with the father by increased dependence on the mother, and that they had anticipated unending affection and unfailing protection from her. When, inevitably, she failed to fulfill their demands, she, not the father, was held responsible for their frustration and impotence.

While they felt a conflict with authority growing out of the conflict with the father, on the conscious level they admired and loved the mother; the hostility toward her was unconscious. The "positive" elements of this ambivalent attitude made it possible for them to enter into a marriage relationship which effectively duplicated the relationship with the mother. But unconscious motivations forced them to make the marriage relationship a duplication also of the one that they thought had disappointed them and endangered them.

The marriage relationship, however, had differences from the one with the mother which, to the disturbed men, offered a justification for revenge. (In most of this group of cases, the men had brought themselves to believe that the wife or mistress was unfaithful and trying to kill them, which justified them in killing her instead.) Their seriously disturbed personalities made it possible for them to commit murder, but it was their mother fixation which caused them to kill the woman who had taken the mother's place in their lives.

Where it was possible to trace out interrelationships, the woman killed was revealed to be a prototype of the murderer's mother, though the man himself was not aware of this. Dr. Frederic Wertham has said that excessive attachment to the mother can be transferred directly into a violent hostility against her. Dr. Apfelberg adds that the murderer of women has no quarrel with society and only a shadowy one, if any, with his victim. "The murderer's real quarrel is with himself."

Very occasionally, the hatred is vented upon the mother who, at least in the disturbed man's mind, brought it into being. One of the rapists studied at Sing Sing had chosen his mother as his victim. He resented the fact that she had not protected him against his brutal father, and on the eve of his own wedding he had taken his mother back to the house where he had suffered the mistreatment and, telling her that since he could not marry her they would "have to do it this way," had raped and sodomized her.

In the great majority of cases, however, the sex rages are vented upon persons who had nothing to do with inspiring them, and hostility that has been repressed for years may suddenly break out in the form of violence. At a medical convention, I heard a psychiatrist describe a case in which a man in his forties, seemingly well adjusted, had come for help because of an urge he had developed to strangle elderly women who had sweet, motherly faces. The urge would come upon him when he saw such a woman, a complete stranger to him, in an elevator, for instance. But it was strongest toward sweet-faced, motherly women in his own office who had been especially kind to him.

Analysis revealed that, in his childhood, a woman of this type had used him to serve her sexual desires. The incident had been forgotten, but the shame and guilt and resentment he had felt had lingered on and, after decades, had asserted itself against guiltless women of the same facial type as his early seducer.

The mechanism by which sex fury can be inculcated in a boy to such an extent that he murders, in a particularly horrible way, a stranger against whom he has nothing at all, was graphically mapped by Dr. Robert Lindner in his story of Charles in his widely read book *The Fifty-Minute Hour.*

Charles was not yet 18 when a young woman, representing a religious group, called at the apartment of Charles' mother, where he was alone. Charles had never seen her before. He picked up a hammer and hit her on the head with it until she fell to the floor. Then he stabbed her sixty-nine times with an ice pick, mostly in the breast region, and violated and mutilated her sexually after she was dead.

In many psychiatric interviews, Dr. Lindner elicited from Charles a story of childhood neglect, rejection and brutalization almost beyond belief. His parents having separated when he was 2, his mother placed him in an orphanage, where he was subjected to abuse and sexual degradation, and kept him there in spite of his pleas to be allowed to live with her. The mother would appear now and then at the orphanage, beautiful and beautifully dressed, seeming a fairy princess to her son. On the rare occasions when he was allowed to visit her daintily furnished apartment, it was like going from hell into heaven, but he was never permitted to remain; she always sent him back to the institutional hell. When he was 9, Charles was ousted from his mother's bed, where he slept during his visits, to make way for a man. After that he was a demon at the orphanage. Dr. Lindner said that by the time Charles was 10, "he had become perverted in every way to the roots of his being—already his soul had been twisted into that of a murderer." He became worse still when, at the age of 13, he learned that his father was living instead of dead, as his mother told him, and that his father, too, had not cared what happened to his son.

So far as the crime itself was concerned, [Dr. Lindner wrote] it was obvious that the intended (psychologically, the real) victim of murder was not the unhappy girl Charles killed. She was but the substitute, the unfortunate innocent bystander in a drama of incest and matricide whose origins were removed almost two decades from the time the last scene was played.

Before you condemn the "unknown sex fiend" as innately an inhuman monster, not deserving of pity or help, read the full account of Charles' upbringing in the chapter "Songs My Mother Taught Me" in Dr. Lindner's book, *The Fifty-Minute Hour.*

How much nonsexual juvenile delinquency is due basically to sex conflicts? A most interesting study in this connection was made at the Worcester, Massachusetts, Youth Guidance Center and was reported on at the 1958 annual meeting of the American Orthopsychiatric Association, by Drs. Howard Lee Wylie and Rafael A. Delgado.

In the backgrounds of many serious offenders, both sexual and nonsexual, are brutal or indifferent or weak fathers. What is the effect when the father is not present at all? The clinic studied twenty boys who had been referred to them because of aggressive, antisocial behavior. Seven of them had already appeared in juvenile court; most of the others were obviously headed in that direction. The twenty were selected because they were being reared by mothers alone, the fathers either being dead or absent through divorce or separation.

Most of the boys were doing poorly in school and were behavior problems in school and at home; none was in trouble because of sex offenses. One half were bed-wetters, and one fourth were still soiling themselves. Nearly all had been sent to the clinic because of pressure from the school or the court. It was felt that their mothers, though deeply annoyed or worried about the son's behavior, would not have asked for help of their own accord.

In every case an erotic element in the boys' relationship with their mothers was found to be at the root of the aggressive, antisocial behavior of the youngsters. Consciously or unconsciously, the mothers had tried to have the sons replace the husbands. They allocated to the boy the duties a man customarily assumes in a household, which is not bad in itself. But they also had a semi-sexual relationship with the boy, stopping just short of actual incest. Half slept in the same room with the son and often in the same bed, though the son was an adolescent. Those who did not share a bed with their sons managed to have a great deal of physical contact with them, through such things as wrestling or, in one case, physical fights which to the investigators had a decidedly erotic tinge.

"It seems to us that a good part of the overt behavior difficulties of these boys was directly related to this aspect of their lives," said Drs. Wylie and Delgado. "It was occasionally possible to induce the mothers to force their sons to sleep alone, and to witness a rather marked decrease in the intensity of some of the boys' symptoms."

Mingled with the sexual stimulation of the boys, in the cases where the husband and father was living but absent, was the mothers' hatred of their former mates. They abused the father constantly to the son and kept telling him that he was just like his father and would come to the same bad end his father had. In several cases, the investigators felt that the mother actually wanted to see her son land behind bars, expressed as a fear that the boy would get into trouble and be locked up. "In one form or another, this need to get rid of the boys was present in most of the cases; and in half of them there had been actual separations, either placements by the mother or incarcerations by the law."

The hate felt for the husband was sometimes transferred openly to the boy. One mother told how her son had fallen to his knees, pleading and crying, when she brought out "the rawhide." "He asked me how I could beat someone who was on his knees. I told him I would like to see him crawl on his belly like his father did and I would still do it, and I would drive him out of the house then like I did his father too."

The mothers whose husbands had died tended, on the other hand, to give the boy an overidealized picture of the father, while trying to have him do the tasks the father had done about the home and take his father's place in the mother's bed. The incestuous overtones were even stronger in these cases.

It must be kept in mind that the sons in this study were boys who were problems in school and in the community. Countless women, deprived of husbands through death or separation, have reared fine sons. The mothers involved in the Worcester study were themselves emotionally crippled persons. Most of them had a hostility toward men not unlike the hate of women characteristic of the sexually disturbed, aggressive male, and, as with these men, the roots of hostility were established in early childhood. These women could not form satisfying relationships with men. They always picked the same kind of man for a husband or lover, mostly men of a passive, dependent nature whom they could order around and despise. They also had a very poor opinion of themselves, feeling that they were no good, worthless.

After the husband was dispensed with or had taken himself off, the mother used the son both to work out her spiteful attitudes toward the male world and her sexual feelings. The hostility and sexual aspects counted equally, the investigators told me when I visited the Worcester Clinic, and the problem of the boy was a mixture of the two. The mother did not want overt sex relations with the son, but as the boy progressed into adolescence both the mother and the son were deathly afraid that the sex play they engaged in would turn into overt relations. Nevertheless the dominance over the boy and the semi-lover role he played in her life filled such a strong need in the mother that most of the women in the study either rejected outright the offer of treatment or withdrew after a very few visits. One mother did announce triumphantly that she had stopped having her teen-age son sleep in her bed. It developed that she had solved her problem by getting into his bed instead! In only one case did the investigators feel that there had been any lasting improvement.

"There are several factors which might contribute to our poor therapeutic results," said Drs. Wylie and Delgado. "First, these are often quite severely disturbed people, and the degree of their sickness might be expected to limit their response. Second, most of them were poorly motivated for therapy, since they came in at a time of crisis and under external pressure. It is common experience that people coming to a clinic under such circumstances often withdraw quickly or are hard to work with.

"A third factor is the great difficulty these women have in giving up their sons as their sexual objects. The boys, too, struggle to maintain the situation and view the treatment as a threat to this source of pleasurable gratification."

Not all the boys who exhibit this type of behavior are fatherless, and not all boys from backgrounds of this kind get into trouble. There were other sons in the twenty families studied by the Worcester Clinic who did not display the same symptoms as their brothers who were problems.

"In these cases, the forces which determine the pattern would appear to stem from the mother's conflicts about her own role as a woman and a mother, her conflicts with her own parents, and her attitudes toward men. The boys in our group would then be the ones who were, for some reason, selected by the mother to be used in her attempts to solve these conflicts."

Where the father had died and the mother had attempted to have a son replace him in her life, the relationship "became highly sexualized and loaded with accompanying guilt and hostility. . . . In these cases, most of the boys' symptoms seemed to be directly related to incest conflict." (However, there were indications that this might represent a period of adjustment and be transient, especially if the mother remarried.)

I happened to be present at the meeting of the Orthopsychiatric Society when this paper was read. It touched off an extremely lively response from the floor. Psychiatrists and psychiatric social workers rose to report similar cases and to agree about the difficulty of reaching mothers whose own needs impel them to use their sons as sexual objects. It is evident that much delinquent behavior that does not appear on the surface to be sexual stems from this factor.

Other investigators bear this out. A study of delinquency by Sheldon and Eleanor Glueck of the Harvard Law School shows that 33 per cent of the delinquents had this same type of background. A particularly fine section on sexually disturbed children in the Michigan *Governor's Study Commission on the Deviated Criminal Sex Offender,* contributed by Ralph D. Rabinovitch, mentioned both the children who have been used sexually by some adult, establishing a compulsive need through repeated experience, and the children affected by unconsciously seductive attitudes of the father or mother. On the other hand, Dr. Rabinovitch found that overly restrictive home climates, which indicate that parents have not come to terms with their own sex natures, accounted for more cases of sexually disturbed youngsters than the unwittingly seductive parents. In some cases the child had been severely punished, when under a year old, for the body explorations normal to babies. There were other cases where verbal admonitions and prohibitions were combined with physical stimulation of the child by one parent or another.

An important contribution is a study made at the Section of Psychiatry of the Mayo Clinic and reported by Drs. Adelaide M. Johnson and David B. Robinson in the *Journal of the American Medical Association*. They state in the issue for August 3, 1957 (Vol. 164, no. 14 pp. 1559-65) that the patients studied included all social and economic levels, that hostile seduction by parental figures underlies all the sexual deviation they studied, and that the deviations originate in either permissiveness or actual coercion by adults. Petting and manipulation, they say, are much more common than is suspected, and along with hostility toward the child, usually unconscious, is an equally unconscious drive to destroy the child's developing personality.

According to Drs. Johnson and Robinson, the taking of a case history reveals the following elements:

(1) The child is born into, and grows, in a climate of confusion and frustration resulting from a poorly integrated marriage of parents who never even approximate a mature or gratifying marital relationship.

(2) One parent unduly stimulates the child by behavior of a sexual coloration.

(3) The stimulation is aborted short of genital contact between parent and child. Hence the relationship is heavily burdened with frustration.

(4) The parent deflects the child toward unnatural behavior of an immature nature, which does not threaten the parent. "The child senses that he is expected to misbehave sexually. . . . Unconsciously the parents gradually maneuver the child into adolescent sexual acting-out."

Merely eliciting the factors which had caused the sex abnormality had not been found sufficient to effect a cure. Therapy has proved to be "a formidable undertaking." It was futile in patients who showed "no compelling motivation for treatment."

Every once in a while a woman or child is murdered by a stranger, without being sexually violated or mutilated, as by the lust-murderers mentioned in Chapter 9. Dr. Manfred Guttmacher has described a case which came before a Baltimore court, where a Negro youth had stabbed five white girls without attempting to molest them. The fourth and fifth stabbings, both of 11-year-old girls, were fatal. Dr. Guttmacher instances Eugene as the type of individual from whom society must be protected, but who is allowed to proceed to murder because of society's laxness.

Eugene had been sent to reform school when he was 13, for persistent truancy, and again when he was 15, for assaulting two young white girls but without sexually molesting them. Released after a year, he next came to the attention of the law after unmotivated knife attacks on three young white women, still with no sexual molestation, and was sentenced to ten years in the penitentiary.

He behaved so well in prison that he was released after six years and returned to his mother's home. At no time had he been given a psychiatric examination.

Less than four months after Eugene's release, three brutal crimes took place in or near Baltimore. First a white woman was raped—the only time the sex motif became obvious in Eugene's crimes—then an 11-year-old girl was killed in Washington, D.C. The third crime, and the one for which Eugene was hanged, was the fatal stabbing of another 11-year-old girl in Baltimore. In classic "unknown sex fiend" style, Eugene had leaped out of a thicket and plunged his knife into the child as she rode by on a bicycle, then jumped back into the bushes again. When asked why he had stabbed the girl and whether he had intended to rape her, he replied, "I don't know why I done it. Raping her was not in my mind at all."

Eugene's parents were not divorced, but his father lived much of the time down the street with a male neighbor, leaving the mother to care for Eugene and his four sisters. Both parents were strict with

Eugene, and the mother, a neat, pleasant-appearing woman, disciplined by whipping with a razor strop. Eugene's sisters appeared to be well adjusted, but the lone boy had been a problem from babyhood on. He said he had had a lot of trouble with all women, whether white or colored. "I know I don't like no woman boss. If I have one of them dizzy headaches and a woman is near me, I hit her, I surely do hit her." There was no report of mother-seductiveness here; mother-dominance appeared to be a factor in the hostility Eugene had toward females.

Dr. Frederic Wertham had the unique opportunity of studying Robert Irwin, the triple murderer whose farcical trial was referred to in Chapter 5, years before Irwin killed his kindly former landlady, Mrs. Gedeon, her daughter, Ronnie, who had been his good friend, and their boarder, Mr. Byrnes, whom he did not know at all. Hence we are able to have a full picture of the factors which shaped one of the most complex and fascinating personalities among the unmotivated murderers of our day.

Irwin, a sculptor and former theological student, was not a lust murderer. He did not kill for a sex thrill, and the idea that he might have offered any sexual indignity to the women he killed was abhorrent to him. He was not a sadist, for he derived no pleasure from the hurt he inflicted on his murder victims. Yet his crimes were caused by sex disturbance, and the roots lay in his relationship with his mother.

Dr. Wertham tells this story also in his book, *The Show of Violence,* and its intensely dramatic features—the homicidal bent in an appealing and inoffensive-seeming young man—have inspired several particularly blood-curdling works of fiction.

The childhood of Bob, as Dr. Wertham calls him in his account, was marked by poverty and deprivation. The father, an evangelist, had been absent from the time Bob was 3; the mother was a religious fanatic. Bob had looked up to his father, a big, handsome man, until his mother told him, when he was 12, that the man had been anything but godly and had deserted his wife and three sons. Bob's two older brothers reacted to their home situation by becoming delinquents, graduating from reformatories into jails and penitentiaries. Bob appears to have been the one chosen by his mother, in the pattern of the Worcester Study mothers, to take the place of the husband who had deserted her. He adored his mother and did his best to help her. His mother loved him but, according to Dr. Wertham, expressed her love mainly in terms of a fanatical religious education.

> Like a red thread, the three themes of mother, religion, and sex were early woven into the fabric of his life. He loved and hated all three with the full intensity of his tremendous temperament. He rationalized his attachment to his mother by glorifying her devotion, brooding over the fact that she had to wash floors to support her children . . . and comparing his own sensitive make-up and personality to hers. His deep antagonism toward her he rationalized by the feeling that she made him more like her instead of his father, by his loathing of her narrow-minded emotional religiosity.

Bob, unlike his two brothers, as a youth never did anything illegal or wrong, but when he was 18 his mother placed him in a reformatory just so that he might have enough to eat. In the reformatory he became interested in sculpture and, after leaving there, worked with a sculptor for a while. He read philosophy and evolved a theory about art which he called "visualization," involving a good deal of mental concentration rather than actual practice. Dr. Wertham states that his fixation on his mother-image was unmistakable. On several occasions he became attached to women older than himself and had sex relations with one of his landladies, an older woman, feeling shamed and guilty afterwards. He told Dr. Wertham that at one time he was living with a nice old lady in Brooklyn who "was just like a mother to me. . . . I was so miserable and so sick that I thought I would commit suicide. But I wasn't going to kill myself. I thought I would kill her and go to the electric chair."

Bob's "misery" and suicidal impulses stemmed from the fact that when he came out of the institution the Great Depression was at its depth and jobs were all but unobtainable. He worked at anything he could get but was constantly being laid off.

The young man first came to Dr. Wertham's attention when he applied to a hospital surgery after an attempt to emasculate himself. His reasoning was that if he did away with his sex urges he would have more energy to apply to sculpture and his theory of visualization. After his wound was dressed he was sent on to the psychiatric division of the hospital, where Dr. Wertham examined him and held him in the hospital much longer than his injury called for, in order to observe and study him.

Dr. Wertham finally succeeded in convincing Bob that emasculation was not the answer to his problems but could not sway him from his "visualization" theory, which had been keeping him from actual achievement. Bob consented to being committed to a state hospital, where his mental illness was diagnosed as dementia praecox, hebephrenic type. Dementia praecox is another name for schizophrenia. The term hebephrenia is applied when deterioration is rapid and is marked by hallucinations and absurd delusions. Dr. Wertham calls the diagnosis about the most serious that can be made of a young mental patient.

The referral was made in March of 1933. During the next five years, Bob several times was released from the hospital but persuaded to return by Dr. Wertham, who could see no change in Bob's obsession with visualization and his search for a "way out." One night Bob showed up at the Wertham home just as the doctor was setting out for a meeting of fellow psychiatrists. He took Bob along, and Bob willingly answered the questions put to him by Dr. Wertham's colleagues. Some of them considered the young man's case hopeless—this was several years before the murders. Dr. Wertham, though considering that the pattern of violence in Bob, against himself or others, that he had previously discerned was still there, believed there was hope of recovery if Bob were given active and prolonged psychoanalytical therapy.

The last time Bob returned to the hospital at Dr. Wertham's urging he stayed two years, then followed the suggestion of an attendant at the hospital and entered a theological school. The studies seemed to present no difficulty, in spite of the fact that Bob had not gone to high school, but he was dogged again by his old enemy, lack of money. He cut lawns, delivered papers, and taught classes in sculpture—he charged children only 25 cents per lesson—and managed to stay in school until a university student broke some figures the children had made. Bob got into a violent fight with the student, which ended in his expulsion.

He went to New York City and hunted up the widowed Mrs. Gedeon, one of several landladies who had been kind to him in a motherly way. When he had lived in the Gedeon home he had become very good friends with one of Mrs. Gedeon's two beautiful daughters, Ronnie, a model, and had been attracted to the other daughter, Ethel, though Ethel soon wearied of him and his theory of visualization.

Back again on the city streets, with no job, his schooling ignominiously ended, and once more despairing, he walked past the Gedeons' house and on down to the East River pier at 53rd Street, intending to drown himself. Brooding as he waited for the dark, so that he would not be rescued, he decided that, instead of drowning himself, he would kill Ethel Gedeon and die in the electric chair. He knew Ethel had married but had an erroneous impression that she had left her husband and was living again with her mother and sister.

Instead, that night he strangled Mrs. Gedeon, when Ethel had not appeared and her mother had told Bob she wanted to go to bed and he must leave. He pushed the body under Mrs. Gedeon's bed in an adjoining room. Her little dog crawled under the bed, and Bob thought of killing it too, to keep Ethel from discovering her mother's corpse, but could not bring himself to hurt an animal. When Ronnie came home, he held her on the bed in the darkened room, a prisoner for two hours—she never knew her mother's body was beneath them—until she called his name and told him he would get into trouble. Then he strangled her. He was hurt by her natural assumption that he intended to rape her and insisted afterwards that he had had no sexual thoughts about her. He said that after he had choked her he had turned on the light and ripped off her nightgown. (He had stayed hidden while she prepared herself for bed.)

He left her "on top of the bed, her mother's body lying underneath. At that moment she was the most repulsive thing I ever knew."

Bob completed his night's work by stabbing Mr. Byrnes, the boarder, asleep upstairs, seven times on the head with the ice pick he had brought along for Ethel's murder. Mr. Byrnes was slightly deaf and had not heard the commotion. Bob said the man had lain twitching after the first blow; he had kept stabbing him to put an end to his pain. It was light by this time. Bob left the house, after searching it and finding no trace of Ethel, and went eventually to Cleveland. Identified by a fellow employee in a hotel where he had found work, he went to Chicago and gave himself up to the Hearst newspapers, making a contract with them to tell his story of the murders and his life for $5,000, most of which was to go to his brothers, who were in penitentiaries.

As was noted in Chapter 5, through Dr. Wertham's intervention Bob was charged with second-degree murder, which did not carry the death penalty, but was found by the jury to be sane and guilty of that charge, then quickly diagnosed as insane by the psychiatrists at Sing Sing, when he was sent there, and referred to a hospital for the criminally insane, where he still is as this is written.

In Doctor Wertham's explanation of Bob's crime and the irrational acts that had preceded it, the psychiatrist focuses on the abnormal attachment Bob had had for his mother from early childhood on.

The mother-image, distorted in his mind and loved and hated at the same time, prevented him from making a normal love adjustment to other women without leading to a dominant homosexual pattern. He acted as if he wished to keep indefinitely an overwhelming pure love for his mother. He renounced the mother-image and sought it at the same time. While not even writing his mother, whom he had helped financially when he was making only fifteen dollars a week, he repeatedly showed friendliness for older women who were like mothers to him. He would leave these mother-substitutes as abruptly as he had left his mother. His unconscious striving to escape the overpowering influence of the image of the mother led to the development of hostility toward her and her substitutes. The opposite of love is not hate, but indifference. He never could be indifferent to his mother. . . . His whole life was a flight from his mother.

The victims of the murder night were not so "accidental" as they seemed to him. . . . Symbolically the two overt violent acts [the attempt at self-emasculation and the murders] are the expression of the components of the ambivalent feelings toward his mother-image: self-castration as punishment activated by guilt feelings arising from his libidinal fixation on her; murder as an expression of his hostility against her.

There were of course other factors involved as well in Bob Irwin's case. The hardships of his childhood and his difficulties in finding work as an adult contributed greatly to his depression and in the end precipitated his plan to commit suicide by killing someone else and being put to death by society.

But the mother-image can be very disturbing where these factors are not present. Dr. Ralph Brancale, Director of the New Jersey State Diagnostic Center, told me that boys from good, comfortable and self-respecting homes are showing an increasing tendency to express their problems through patterns of delinquent behavior. Many of these offenses involve acute acts of violence which, while they appear senseless on the surface, are found to be rooted in complex sexual conflicts.

"The observation of increasing delinquency in the suburbs is creating some concern," Dr. Brancale said. "For example—in a recent study, out of one hundred such cases reviewed, half the delinquents came from privileged homes. This strengthens the concept that delinquency in a real sense is an expression of deeper needs which are not met and complex conflicts which are not resolved. The juvenile meets these problems through acquisitive offenses—arson, assault, homosexuality, etc." Violence with rape is not too common, but Dr. Brancale believes that crimes of violence which mask sexual problems are on the increase.

"Analysis of such cases often shows an overpowering, protective mother," Dr. Brancale continued. "A child enjoys her protectiveness and is dependent on her. On the other hand, he resents this dependency. His need for masculinity intensifies because he cannot express resentment openly against a mother who is so good to him. As resentment builts up, often triggered by some other incident, the aggression is openly expressed against some other person than the mother against whom he has these hostilities. Such cases are outwardly passive and their dangerous potentiality is not easily detected. In training schools, they often make model inmates and on the surface appear good subjects for parole. Such cases obviously require extremely close and studious clinical attention. When there is no psychiatric observation at all or the psychiatric staff is overworked or lax, such pathological types with propensity for episodes of violence may have better than an average chance for being released without proper safeguards."

It is particularly characteristic of the forcible rapist to adjust well to life in a prison or mental institution. He is temporarily relieved of the need to fight his impulses of violence toward women or children, since none are present. He can relax. When there is "no psychiatric observation at all or the psychiatric staff is overworked or lax," the sexually disturbed man with a propensity for violence has a particularly good chance to convince a lay parole board that he is cured of his bad ways.

Yale University investigators have recently reported a similar situation in countries all over the world where there is a trend toward matriarchy. There was a high rate of theft and personal crime where young boys had little contact with their fathers and home and family life centered about the mothers, who "fed them, nursed them, clothed them and shared their beds with them."

The investigators found the crime in these mother-centered societies to be an expression of revolt against femininity. "For the boys, it was an attempt to become masculine. Since they did not have the father to imitate, they were virtually forced to turn against their mothers' standards of goodness in order to feel masculine" (*New York Times,* July, 1963).

There are many ways in which a young soul can become twisted. The great pity lies in the fact that a 4-year-old Edith Kiecarius, an 11-year-old Avril Terry or Grace Budd, a young housewife or a grandmother in her sixties or seventies may be called upon to pay the penalty for parental failings or blindness.

But let us remember that a child, whose greatest need is for warm, unselfish love and whose whole instinct is to respond with love, must suffer very terrible hurts to be transformed into a hating, destroying monster. Is there not reason for pity in this, as well?

# 11

# The two
# Sing Sing studies

The first really comprehensive and searching investigations of sexually sick men who commit acts of violence were the two Sing Sing studies, referred to in earlier chapters, which were conducted in New York State's famous prison.

In 1947 the New York State Legislature passed a bill providing that sexual psychopaths might be confined indefinitely, until such time as they were considered no longer to be sexual psychopaths and no longer dangerous (the indeterminate sentence). Thomas E. Dewey, governor at this time, very rightly vetoed the bill, because it failed to recognize differences in the types of sex offenses committed, and to provide safeguards for the civil rights of the accused men. It has been mentioned that similar laws passed around that time in other states have seldom been invoked by county attorneys and judges. The very term "sexual psychopath" is misleading, in the opinion of many psychiatrists, because it has never been satisfactorily defined and is so vague that almost anyone who strays from the conventional path by the narrowest margin might be considered a sexual psychopath.

After vetoing the bill, Mr. Dewey in 1948 recommended that the New York Legislature call for a study of sexual offenders, to be made under the auspices of the State Commissioners of Correction and of Mental Hygiene. He suggested that its purpose be "the development of information as to the underlying causes of sex crimes and the development of treatment for persons committing such crimes." The Governor's recommendation was adopted by the Legislature, and the first study of serious sex offenders in Sing Sing was undertaken by the New York State Psychiatric Institute, with a research staff headed by Dr. David Abrahamsen of Columbia University.

(In this same period, California, Wisconsin, Massachusetts and Michigan undertook investigations as a prelude to wise sex legislation, undoubtedly a reason why these states are leaders in attempts at more intelligent and enlightened handling of the problem under the law. However, though all of these investigations were helpful and developed much valuable information, none was as intensive as the two made in New York State.)

The average intelligence quotient of the 102 men studied compared favorably with that of the general population, and one of the rapists had an I.Q. of 152, which placed him in the very superior or "genius" class. It was conjectured that more mental defectives would have been found in a larger sampling, but the 102 studied had not committed their crimes because they didn't know any better. Often their crimes were committed in a way which indicated the offender wanted to be caught—one of the rapists gave his name and address to his middle-aged victim, who had never seen him before and had no idea of his identity. But the guilt feelings from which some of the men suffered—many expressed no feeling of guilt—were not necessarily connected with the crimes they had committed. Quite commonly they stemmed from events which had happened long before, possibly from unexpressed hostility in childhood toward a parent, or sex experiences undergone and worried about as a child, or strong resentment the men had felt at rejections.

This could help explain why the sex offender repeats his crime over and over again, the report said.

> When emotional conflicts are left unresolved in childhood and youth, they continually seek expression, or an outlet, later on. A person suffering from emotional conflicts unconsciously goes through life creating situations whereby he can act out his early unexpressed feelings. This becomes the pattern of his life. Thus he lives not in terms of adult reactions to these situations, but rather tries continually to find satisfaction for early frustrations through his immature and unrealistic attitudes.

This pattern will continue until, or unless, the offender can be freed from being mastered by emotions he cannot understand; develop a social life that is satisfactory both to him and to society; be enabled to work effectively but not compulsively [many throw themselves into work to an inordinate extent to keep down their aberrant impulses]; and be helped to overcome his sexual immaturity, so that he can function on an adult level.

Every one of the 102 men in this first Sing Sing survey was found to have some type of mental or emotional disorder, though usually it was not sufficiently pronounced to meet the legal definition of mental illness, and there were many cases where the behavior pattern could not be fitted into any clear-cut classification. The fact that all the 102 men studied at this time had been convicted of felonies—serious sex crimes involving forcible violation of women or physical molestation of children—may explain why the incidence of mental disease was found to be higher than in clinics where sex offenders of all types are studied.

The investigators concluded that there is no type of mental disorder which predisposes to sex crimes. Three of the subjects, however, were found to be actively psychotic—insane, in lay terms—at the time of the study, and 9 had been committed at some time to mental hospitals, several having served terms in Matteawan, one of the New York State hospitals for the criminally insane. The 99 men who were not insane were all found to be suffering from neuroses.

Almost all the men had had unusually unfortunate childhoods, with severe emotional deprivation, although with some of the men the deprivation had taken the form of being constantly overindulged and overprotected, which is a sign of parental selfishness rather than of love. "Pampering fathers and mothers dominate their children by bribing them and in this way try to possess them completely." The child who is allowed to have and to do anything he wants is brought up to follow his impulses and passions without regard for the law or the rights of others. At the same time, he may resent the fact that he was deprived of his individuality by his parents' indulgent dominance, it was explained.

Fourteen of the 102 had been considered "model boys" as children, and at least 32 others had appeared to be good boys. A young man who had brutally raped and sodomized a woman old enough to be his mother, a stranger to him, had been extremely well behaved as a child, was always neatly dressed, and "looked like an angel." Actually, this abnormally good behavior was a defense mechanism. The "good" and "model" boys had been submissive as children because they were afraid to assert themselves. The offenses they committed later were an expression of their long-suppressed resentment and rebellion against the authority of parents with whom, for one reason or another, they had never had a satisfactory relationship. Many displayed, to a potentially or actually dangerous degree, a hatred and resentment against authority and persons representing authority.

Also, as a result of early home conditions, most of the 102 sex offenders had been confused about their sexual role and had not developed a normal sexual concept. They were not oversexed, as one might imagine. Rather, they proved as a group to be immature and underdeveloped, sexually as well as emotionally, a reason why a number sought out small children as objects of sexual attention.

Alcoholism was found to be an associated and precipitating factor in the sex crimes of over half the 102 men. "The extensive consumption so often found among offenders is a means of release from intense anxiety and is a vicarious gratification of other, deeper needs." Many of the sexually disturbed men were able to keep their aberrant impulses in check while sober but would lose control when they had had too much to drink. Deterioration as a result of drink is an important factor in many cases of older men who begin to abuse children, the investigators reported. This may well have been the case with Fred Thompson, the slayer of little Edith Kiecarius.

Since the serious sex offenders were impelled by forces beyond their control, the researchers did not believe that the punitive atmosphere of a penal institution would do them any good. Most, in fact, had been incarcerated at least once before and, if anything, had been made worse by their experiences in reformatories or prisons. What they needed was psychiatric help, and efforts made by the research team to treat a number of the 102 convinced the investigators that a prison was a poor place for that.

They believed that 52 of the 102 they studied might be cured if given intensive treatment and, as an instance of a hopeful case, cited a sex offender who had had the bad fortune to be born to drunken parents, who themselves were the offspring of drunkards. The family history was fully documented, because the parents had been brought frequently to the attention of social agencies from the time of the offender's birth. The young man's own childhood history was of periods spent with various drunken relatives, who abused him, interspersed with periods in institutions. He had sex relations with a girl in an orphanage when he was 13, but previous to that he had sodomized younger boys in the orphanage. His teen years were spent in homes for delinquents and reformatories. When he was 17 he was released on parole and a month later was arrested for offenses against small children, both girls and boys. "He said he saw nothing wrong in that. He had no pangs of conscience about that kind of act. . . ."

Yet this chap was not insane, he had simply been behaving according to a neurotic pattern that had been laid down for him by his early experiences. He was responding to treatment, and it was believed that if the treatment could be continued he had a good chance to make a decent, adult adjustment to society. This was not very likely, however, if he were to be freed into society, his rehabilitation not completed, when his sentence expired.

"The faulty emotional adjustments which caused this man's offenses cannot be corrected by the usual prison routine," the report said. "Under this procedure he would go out from prison, in his midtwenties, still neurotic and still a danger to little children."

But the appalling part of the report was the conclusion of the psychiatrists that not only were 50 of the 102 men studied incurable by any then known methods but that of these 50 all but three murderers were due to be released within a short time, either on parole or because their sentences would have expired. A number had already been released before the report appeared; 47 had been released years before this book was written.

A considerable proportion of the 50 incurables were men who had committed incest; there were many rapists and men who had made carnal use of little girls or little boys. Eighteen were found to be predisposed to violence. Five of this group had been convicted of incest. One had had sex relations for years with an older daughter, by whom he had had two children, then had transferred his attentions to a younger daughter. A second had used his 12-year-old daughter sexually from the time she was 5 years old and had also been intimate with two other daughters, whom he had threatened to kill if they told. A third had forced sex relations on his young daughter when his wife was in the hospital giving birth to their tenth child.

Among the remaining 13 found to be both incurable and predisposed to violence, one had gained entry to the apartment of a woman he did not know, on the pretext of checking the electric lights, and had forced sex relations on her at knife point. A second had forced sex relations at knife point on a young married woman, six months pregnant, whom he had never seen before. A third had approached a strange woman old enough to be his mother, had forced her into a hallway, beaten her brutally and threatened to kill her, then had both raped and sodomized her. A fourth had stabbed a woman thirteen times with an ice pick when he was 22 and had committed bodily assaults on other persons. He was in Sing Sing because he had choked his mistress to death. A fifth was the man, previously referred to, who had both raped and sodomized his mother on the evening before his wedding day. The offenses committed by the other 32 considered untreatable ran along much the same lines, with a high proportion of incest, rape and sexual abuse of children, both boys and girls.

The sentences imposed for these crimes by various judges are interesting in themselves as an indication of the haphazard workings of the law. The man who raped the pregnant young woman at knife point was sentenced to from one and a half to two and a half years, while a man who bound a woman and raped her received thirty to forty years. The man who beat, threatened, raped and sodomized the woman his mother's age was sentenced to two and a half to five years.

The investigators' assessments were based not on the nature of the crime or on past criminal history but upon the personality and character traits exhibited by the offenders, under psychiatric examination.

The 50 considered untreatable as of 1948-1949 exhibited no sense of guilt or remorse, and their maladjustments were so deep that they could not be reached by therapy.

And yet the "assaultive" despoiler of two of his daughters and the "dangerous" attacker of the young pregnant woman were both released in 1949. A man who had murdered his pregnant mistress "because of a welling up of unconscious forces" was due to be released in 1952; an alcoholic and aggressive run-of-the-mill rapist, who hadn't murdered anybody—yet—in 1951. The man who had strangled his mistress after many attacks on other persons was due for release in 1957. It was the belief of the investigators that these men would repeat their crimes or perhaps commit worse ones. Whether they have or not cannot be known, because the identities of all the offenders were carefully concealed.

Governor Thomas E. Dewey mentioned in the foreword he wrote for this report that it emphasized the need for more understanding of, and better attempts at, rehabilitation of offenders. "But it also faces the grim findings of the research workers that many of these men will probably continue to be dangerous when their maximum sentences expire, and that many of them suffer from maladjustments that cannot be cured or treated by any methods now known."

The conclusion of the Abrahamsen group was that the problem of the sex offender cannot be solved by the passage of any laws or by any sudden panacea whatsoever. "It is necessary to extend mental health and psychiatric activities beyond the mental hospitals and into closer contact with the people through clinics, general hospitals and general medical practice."

Specific recommendations were made, however, for improving New York State's handling of serious sex offenders, and a psychiatric approach was strongly urged. It was acknowledged that psychiatric treatment is expensive, time-consuming and uncertain in results. Without such treatment, however, many of the 102 at Sing Sing—and, they might have added, thousands more in other prisons over the country—would continue to commit offenses, would be returned to prison, and would spend most of their lives in state institutions. "That process also has proved expensive, time-consuming and unsatisfactory in results."

They pointed out that it cost $2,000 to keep a man in prison for one year (that was in 1950; the latest figure is $3,500), that the product of two generations of drunken parents who was responding to treatment had been a public charge all his life, "and with normal life expectancy, he is likely to be a great public expense before he dies— unless his treatment should be effective. That amount of money would pay for a great deal of psychiatry in prisons and the institutions for juveniles where the young man started his criminal career." The report added that psychiatric examination of all men convicted of the more serious sex crimes is the only way in which the dangerous ones can be recognized.

A hospital atmosphere would be much more beneficial than a civil prison for handling these men, it was suggested. Those administering psychiatric treatment should be free to experiment and to alter an individual patient's environment to fit his needs, as treatment progressed. The researchers suggested setting up a special place for sex offenders between prison and parole, as an experiment, with a limited number of offenders.

"Such experimentation might lead to a new type of institution in which mentally maladjusted offenders of all types, not just sex offenders, might be truly rehabilitated." The researchers also suggested an unlimited sentence, but with proper legal safeguards and with psychiatric treatment during the time of confinement, for serious sex offenders whose mental or emotional aberrations predispose them to repeat their crimes against women or children. "Such offenders as pose a threat to personal safety should be in a different category from those whose variant sex conduct is only offensive to public morals and decency."

In 1950, the New York State Legislature amended the laws governing sex crimes in accordance with many of the suggestions made in the report of the first Sing Sing study. At the discretion of the judge, an indeterminate sentence, ranging from one day to life, can now be imposed (except in the case of murder), but only if a psychiatric examination has first been made of the convicted man and a full written report submitted to the judge for his consideration. Periodic review of such cases is also mandatory.

The Department of Correction was directed to set up psychiatric clinics in the various prisons, to be staffed by personnel supplied by the Department of Mental Hygiene. The statutes also empowered the Department of Mental Hygiene to establish training courses for personnel to man the clinics and to conduct research into the nature and causes of criminal behavior and methods of treatment for such behavior.

However, when men on indeterminate sentences began arriving at the New York State prisons after the laws were revised in 1950, the staffs found themselves too busy administering treatment to do any research. Soon dissatisfaction arose with the results of the therapy. The rate of repeaters among the sex offenders was disquieting, as was the fact that many committed new and sometimes more serious sex crimes soon after their release from prison. It was felt that more information was needed about the personality and environment factors which may produce serious sex offenders.

A very considerable proportion of the men who commit felonies of any description—robberies, hold-ups, muggings—come from home backgrounds that are deprived in some respect. What were the factors which impelled an emotionally disturbed or maladjusted man to assault women, despoil children, possibly to kill and mutilate persons unknown to him, rather than to carry out an armed robbery, for instance?

The legislature appropriated money for research to find answers to this question, and the second Sing Sing study was begun in 1952, this one under the direction of Dr. Bernard C. Glueck, Jr., the psychiatrist son of the man who had set up the first psychiatric clinic at Sing Sing.

The second investigation involved 170 serious sex offenders and a control group of non-sex offenders, matched as closely as possible with the sex offenders with regard to life histories, intelligence quotients, family backgrounds and similar matters. Wives and families of both groups were interviewed, wherever this was possible, and all previous records of the men in both groups were studied, in addition to psychiatric interviews with the men and batteries of psychological tests.

Many significant differences were found between the two groups, of value to psychiatrists who treat both sex and non-sex offenders in a prison setting. Serious students of the sex crime problem will want to read the entire report. There is space here for only a few of the numerous comparisons made by Dr. Glueck's research staff.

The sex offenders, by and large, had a better record for carrying family responsibilities and as workers than the controls, but a much worse record as drinkers. Alcohol had figured in only 16 per cent of the crimes of the control group, as against 44 per cent of the sex offender group as a whole and 70 per cent in the rape and incest cases.

The sex offender group had a higher incidence of mental illness, and 80 per cent of the group as a whole were impaired in their ability to relate to others, in particular to empathize with others. (The rapists were the exception here, having a better record than the rest of the sex offenders for friendships and heterosexual relationships.) The general failure of the sex offenders to adjust socially was believed by the investigators to be an important element in the constellation of factors that made their offenses possible.

One of the marked differences between the two groups was in their concepts of sex. In contrast to the general offenders, the sex offenders as a group were extremely naïve about sexual matters, felt inferior, had suffered in childhood from anxiety and fears about sex, such as castration, and had lacked accurate sex instruction during their formative years.

The sex offenders also had suffered much more severely than the control group from domestic unhappiness and parental indifference or hostility. The ages at which both groups had married was about the same, but all the wives of the sex offender group showed signs of disturbance, while nearly one third of the control group wives (29 per cent) showed no such signs. Mental illness, chronic physical illness, alcoholism, economic irresponsibility, nagging and sexual promiscuity were frequent findings among the sex offender wives.

However, Dr. Glueck does not believe the husbands had become sex offenders because of unhappy marriages. "These men hate women so much," he told me, "that they are incapable of making good marriage choices."

Parental attitudes toward the sex offenders presented almost as dismal a picture. Only about one fourth of the sex offenders had been accepted by their fathers, and one third of the fathers had been actively hostile toward their sons. Slightly *less* than one fourth of the mothers had been accepting, with the rapist group having been least accepted of all. Thirteen per cent of the rapists' mothers had been actively hostile. At the same time, 44 per cent of the rapists had slept in the same bed with their mothers, either frequently or occasionally, as against 25 per cent for the whole sex group and 18 per cent for the controls. Sixty-seven per cent of the rapists showed continued Oedipal desires for the mothers, as against 28 per cent of the controls, and two thirds of the controls thus affected had arrived at a healthy solution, as against only 27 per cent of the rapists.

In the entire group of sex offenders, the investigators failed to find a single man with an adequately restraining, yet sufficiently flexible, conscience mechanism. These men appeared to be operating at the childhood level of fear of detection and punishment as the main mechanism of restraint, which helps to explain the commonly reported "good behavior" of sex offenders in prisons, where control is tight. Many exhibited the rigid overcontrol noted by Dr. Manfred Guttmacher in the rapists he studied, which is often a defense against loss of control. In the serious sex crime, there was usually a precipitating factor, most often alcohol, which broke down such control as the man had been able to maintain.

The second Sing Sing study confirmed and reinforced the general conclusions of Dr. Abrahamsen's group and discussed castration, frequently advanced by laymen as a remedy for sex crimes. The investigators doubted it would be any help, since it would make real the concern about symbolic castration that was prominent in the sex offenders studied and, in fact, might make the emasculated man even more hostile and violent. The fact that the sexual offense is frequently an expression of a motive other than sexual gratification also made the investigators doubt the efficacy of castration.

Making sex more available, as through earlier marriage, suggested by some authorities, or legalizing prostitution, suggested by others, would not answer the problem since, as has been repeatedly stated, many child molesters are incapable of approaching an adult female, and the availability of a wife or other sexual partner does not seem to have affected the pattern of offenses of the rapists or incestuous fathers.

The report closed with personality profiles of the different major classes of serious sex offenders and explained why each had turned to that particular form of antisocial sex expression.

Personality Profile of Men Who Commit Sexual Assaults on an Adult Female (From the second Sing Sing study). In general personality, these men were closest to the controls.

They showed a more aggressive, outgoing, impulsive type of personality than the other sexual offenders and were somewhat better integrated into community activities because of this. They were the youngest in the group, which may explain their poorer employment records . . . they showed less fear of approaching an adult female but showed much greater difficulty with their unresolved sexual feelings toward their mothers [and] a great deal of hostility toward generally rejecting, hostile, yet seductive mothers. The sexual assault would appear to be a hostile expression of their unresolved incestuous wishes for sexual relations with the mother and frequently happens when control is diminished by alcohol or by a combination of sexual frustration and temptation. Under these circumstances, the rage response overcomes the restraining conscience, and an aggressive outburst occurs.

The Men Who Approach Pubertal or Early Adolescent Girls. These are closest to the rapists, among the sex offender group, and next closest to the controls, after the rapists, in their general adjustment.

They tend to be fairly well integrated but on an adolescent, or childish, level of performance. They show the least degree of traumatic exposure in the area of sexual development and have very little apprehension over heterosexual activity. The main cause of the offense in this group appears to be the rather marked disturbance in judgment caused by the large number of schizoadaptive patterns found . . . so that the adolescent girl becomes a suitable object for the sexual approach, either in the absence of an adult female, or when the man has been rejected by his usual sexual partner.

Eleven out of the twenty-three incest cases in the second study were in this group.

The Men Who Prey on Little Girls. These were among the best adjusted in the socio-economic areas.

They tended to be somewhat older than the other groups and had generally made some attempt at a sexual adjustment with an adult female. This relationship was usually characterized by a great deal of tension and overt hostility, with little or no pleasure coming from the sexual relationship. They show a great deal of fear of any kind of sexual activity, and appear to have been traumatized to a greater degree [than the other groups] in childhood, by a sister or other female close to their own age. They show an arrest of psychosexual development at a childhood or early adolescent level and appear to be more comfortable with children than with adults. They also show a great deal of disturbance in their reality perception, which is kept under fair control most of the time, by a greater degree of rigid, obsessive-compulsive behavior than any of the other groups, but which comes out readily when alcohol is used.

Men Who Debauch Adolescent Boys.

The men in this group showed marked disturbances in their psychosexual development, with a great deal of traumatic sexual experience in childhood. This is related to a greater degree of sexual curiosity than the other groups seemed to show. The fathers of the men in this group were more rejecting and hostile and were generally less adequate than the mothers, who tended to be the dominant figures in the family constellation. They (the mothers) were usually rather hostile, threatening people, without the evidence of seduction of the boy found in the rapist group. There was somewhat more exposure to sexual contact with brothers in this group, which may have been a conditioning experience. The psychosexual age of these men is at the early adolescent level, with evidence of considerable impairment in their capacity for interpersonal relationships and with some, but not marked, distortion of their reality perception and judgment.

Men Who Prey on Little Boys.

The men in this group show the greatest amount of disturbance of all the groups. They have the least satisfactory socio-economic adjustment, even though [as a group] they tend to have more education and have held better jobs. Their ability to relate to the people around them is seriously impaired at all levels, and they show evidence of marked impairment of reasoning and judgment, as well as of perceptive ability. This impairment of function is directly related to the serious nature of the [illness] found in these men, with 79 per cent of the group being diagnosed as psychotic. The early sexual traumatic experiences frequently involve seduction by an older man, which may be an important conditioning influence. They are also caught in a marked conflict between a passive, rejecting father and a dominant, hostile, aggressive mother, who frequently uses the boy as an object of her rage and frustration over the failure of her husband to perform as she would like. The only individuals with whom these men can successfully relate are boys, who are sexually nonthreatening, and who are on the same level of psychological development as the offender. The sexual activity in this group frequently seems to be an accidental, and relatively insignificant, part of the total relationship with the boy who is the sexual object.

(The foregoing does not take into account the men like Albert Fish who torture and even murder the little boys and girls who are their sexual objects. However, it explains Dr. Guttmacher's finding that sex offenders in this group are the most difficult to treat of all.)

Men Who Commit Incest.  The Sing Sing investigators did not consider the perpetrators of incest to constitute a group in themselves but placed them in the other groups, considering such men to be primarily rapists, for example, who had also happened to commit incest. They did not find that incest as such has any special characteristics, the motivations being as described in the other groups, except that the illness is at its maximum when a man commits a sex offense with his mother or daughter. From this standpoint, the men who had committed incest were deemed the sickest of all the sex offenders, even though they may have made a fairly good adjustment at some time in the past.

Unfortunately, after this admirable start, New York State did not carry through. There are now psychiatric clinics in all of the state correctional institutions, but the treatment institution or facility suggested in the report of the first Sing Sing study has not been provided to date. Evidently, many court officials do not consider that the treatment measures available are sufficient.

The indeterminate sentence for sexual psychopaths went into effect in New York State in 1950. Only 272 persons had been committed under it by November of 1962, and at that time only 138 men sentenced under it remained in the state's correctional institutions. Readers may be interested to compare these figures for New York State, population around 17,000,000, with those for Wisconsin, population around 4,000,000, since its Sex Crimes Law was adopted in 1951; and with California, where a special institution for rehabilitating sex offenders was opened in 1954. Statistics for these states will be found in Chapters 15 and 16.

Since 1950, a great many dangerous men must have gone out from New York's reformatories and prisons after serving their one and a half or two and a half year sentences for rape or child molesting. We can figure on a high incidence of sex crime as long as this is the case.

# THREE
# What's to be done about it?

# 12

# "Well, lady,
# what do you want?"

You may remember that when I asked one of the country's leading psychiatrists if there was something I could do about the Jack Smith case he replied, "They would just say to you, 'Well, lady, what do you want?' "

The research and personal investigation I have done since then have convinced me that there are no quick, ready-made solutions to the sex crime problem. The Sing Sing reports indicate the ineffectiveness of prison sentences, emasculation, earlier marriage, and more readily available sex. These conclusions are concurred in by the many experts I have talked with.

There are two other commonly encountered approaches to the problem that I deeply deplore. One is the contention of some persons, noted in Chapter 3, that violent sex offenders constitute so small a percentage of the criminal population that there is no need to do anything about them. To me, this is tantamount to arguing that because the population of lions and tigers in this country is infinitesimal as compared with that of domestic tabbies, we should periodically release the big, dangerous cats from their cages and allow them to run loose until they have killed or mauled.

Besides, it isn't true. Men convicted of serious sex crimes form anywhere from 10 per cent to 25 per cent of the population in civil prisons, and those convicted are a small proportion of the number charged with such crimes; the majority are either tried for lesser crimes or never brought to trial at all. Our daily newspapers show us that many rapists repeat, and sex murderers, too, when they are left free to do so.

The other approach, the one usually seen in articles on sex offenders in popular magazines, is to lay the burden of prevention upon the possible victims. Women are advised to keep doors locked and either to have chains on them, as well, or peepholes through which they can survey a caller before unlocking the door. Parents are advised to warn their children against going off with strangers or getting into cars with people they don't know.

We should by all means take such precautions. My own blithe disregard of elementary safety measures was foolhardy, and due to my ignorance of the kind of threat posed by the sexually sick man. I am very careful about outside doors now, and the strong bolt on my bedroom door is a great comfort, supplemented as it is by a telephone beside my bed. For I know that a determined person could get into almost any house, but the bolted bedroom door would give me time to telephone and to get away through a window, if I had to. It is only sensible for every woman who lives alone, or who at times is left alone at night, to have a protection-plus-escape plan worked out, in case it should ever prove necessary. In the same way, parents must warn their children against going off with strangers. But let us not delude ourselves that such things will truly protect, so long as men who have shown themselves to be sexually sick are allowed at large.

Women can't hide behind locks and chains all the time; we must venture forth occasionally, and again the newspapers show us that there is no place, however public, where a member of our sex can be safe from a sex-maddened man.

It is very difficult to teach a small child never to go with a friendly seeming stranger, and older ones can be tricked. Few mothers have the time to watch youngsters every minute when they are out of doors, and in any event, constant, anxious hovering by an adult does not provide a healthy atmosphere for a child to grow up in. Several psychiatrists have reported anxiety neuroses in little girls, induced by their mothers' very desire to protect them.

Yet in any given case, a single unguarded moment can be fatal. Little Edith Kiecarius was left unguarded, in front of a relative's apartment, for only ten minutes. It was in those ten minutes that Fred Thompson came by, looking for a victim. There could not have been many minutes that Avril Terry was not under someone's observation as she walked along the Courthouse Square in Boonville, Indiana. It was during that span of time, however brief it was, that her encounter with a known offender against children took place, and he managed to spirit her away without being seen. Against such contingencies as these, and they occur almost daily in the United States, warnings and locks are no more protection than they would be against a bolt of lightning, if we happen to be in the spot where it strikes.

Doesn't it make better sense to attack the problem at its source—to find more enlightened ways of handling the sex offenders, themselves, when they show the first evidences of their sickness? I believe the time will come when society will look back on the present custom, in most of our states, of releasing known sex offenders while still uncured, with the same incredulity and horror we of today have for the bedlams of a bygone age. How could people have been so blind, so uncomprehending? our critics of the future will ask.

It is, of course, because so few have understood the peculiar nature of sexual sickness. We have not tried to understand, because we have seen no reason why we should do so. The sex attack, the sadistic murder, are things that happen to other people, not to us or to those we love. When they happen, the law will take care of them; they are no concern of ours.

I plead guilty to the foregoing indictment. The sex crimes I had read and heard about had made no lasting impact, because, frankly, no one could have convinced me that such a thing could happen to someone like me. I had not the faintest idea of the inadequacies of the laws and procedures for handling these cases. As I have said before, even my lawyer friends, concerned mainly with the civil law, were as shocked as I was to learn how they are conducted, at least in some instances. I never would have known if I had not myself been subjected to a sex attack and had my eyes opened to the way sex crime can actually be fostered by unenlightened legal processes.

We must first of all realize that no individual woman, no individual child, whether male or female, is exempt from the danger presented by the sexually sick man or boy. In many cases, it is a matter entirely of being the first one to catch the attention of the prowler, while he is in the grip of his dreadful obsession. Let me repeat—*no woman, no child, can be truly safe as long as we release dangerous men from jails or prisons, untreated and uncured.*

Second, we must realize the special nature of the menace presented by the sexually sick man. A sex attack *is* a very different matter from being robbed, or struck by an automobile, or even from being mowed down by a gun in the hands of a lunatic or gangster. Such things are deplorable; we should do what we can to prevent their happening. But compare these with the pictures that must be in the minds of parents whose child has been sexually abused and tortured to death. It *could* happen that way to your child or my grandchild, and we would have to share the blame, as long as we are content with the present slipshod system.

Dr. Manfred Guttmacher has said, "The first step to prevention is knowledge," and he considers the subject vast enough and important enough to justify one of our great foundations in establishing an institute for the study of sexual behavior in connection with one of the universities, where psychologists, sociologists, criminologists, biochemists and psychiatrists could "jointly explore this great and fascinating domain." (The Institute for Sex Research at the University of Indiana has made a study of sex offenders which will be reported on in the future, but only from the standpoint of comparing their rate of sex activity with that of nonoffenders.)

I have wondered myself that the National Institute of Mental Health of the U.S. Public Health Service has not applied itself to this problem. While helping a number of research projects which will presumably shed light on one phase or another of sexual sickness, it has no program of its own, so I am informed, for studying this form of illness.

That a great deal more study is needed cannot be denied. But the studies of sexually sick men and boys that have been made and the experiments conducted in treatment during the past forty years present us with a body of information more than sufficient for a hopeful start toward a solution. Let us pause a moment to sum up what is already known.

(1) There is some disagreement among authorities as to the proportion of sex offenders who are "sexual psychopaths," or "deviated," or "mentally disordered," to use terms applied in different states to the men who are our concern: that is to say, men who commit violent sex crimes because of subconscious hatred and guilt feelings which on occasion they are unable to control.

You will recall that the Sing Sing investigators found some degree of mental illness in all the sex offenders they studied there, and that Dr. Benjamin Karpman reported that all the rapists he had studied had been sick men. On the other hand, Wisconsin experts, who have observed and examined since 1951 all the men convicted of serious sex crimes in Wisconsin courts, have found a little more than half to be "deviated," in the Wisconsin terminology.

On the basis of the foregoing, we are certainly justified in assuming that at least half the men convicted of serious sex offenses are governed by uncontrollable impulses and cannot be expected to change their ways without expert treatment.

(2) The first Sing Sing study reported that, of the 102 serious sex offenders they studied, 50, or nearly one half, were not only sick but were incurable by any method of treatment then known.

This finding has been confirmed in California. Beginning with 1954, observation and psychiatric studies have been made of all the men convicted of serious sex crimes—rape, incest, child molestation—whom the presiding judge considered to have a potential for danger. Around one half of the thousands of men studied under this law have been found to be incurable by present methods, the same proportion reported in the first Sing Sing study. (More will be said about the California system in later chapters.)

We may therefore assume that half of the men convicted of serious sex offenses are at present incurable, even by the best psychiatric treatment obtainable. Obviously, they should not be released unless, or until, better treatment methods are developed.

There is, however, another and brighter side. Wisconsin and California, which have led all the other states in applying the intensive medical treatment so many experts have called for, find that a goodly proportion of these men can and do respond and can return to society as useful citizens, no longer dangerous. To deny *them* the opportunity to be rehabilitated and take their place in society again is both inhumane and uneconomical.

The crux is that *only by thorough, careful study and testing, by experts, can it be determined in many instances which of these men have a potential for danger and which of them have reached a point where it is both safe and desirable to give them a trial in the community.*

A great problem is the failure of the law, in most of our states, to recognize the special nature of sex sickness. Due process excludes from the courtroom much material essential for understanding the case and for assessing the accused man's potential for danger. The lack of an impartial tribunal for determining the medical aspects opens the way to the purely punitive approach, which has proven so ineffective and which protects the community only during the time a dangerous man is incarcerated. Saddest of all, legal farces like those of the Fish and Hashfield cases simply delay an attack on the root of dreadful sex crimes and the instituting of measures calculated to prevent them.

When a plea is entered of not guilty by reason of insanity, the M'Naghten Rule can make a hollow mockery of the elaborate show of protecting, in what appear to the layman to be trivial technicalities, the constitutional rights of an accused man while denying him the fundamental right to a neutral, scientific mental evaluation.

To the layman, it looks as though the M'Naghten Rule can be twisted to suit any purpose. I have read many cases in which the prosecutor has cited some attempt by the defendant to conceal his crime as proof that he knew right from wrong. But lack of any attempt at concealment is not necessarily taken as proof that the defendant did *not* know right from wrong.

In a sensational New York City case of 1964, Winston Moseley stabbed to death and sexually molested a woman within full view of thirty-eight of her neighbors, watching from upper-story windows.

Pleading not guilty by reason of insanity, the man confessed in open court to the sex murders of another woman and a young girl—all three of his victims were unknown to him—out of an uncontrollable urge to kill as well as to rape. Two psychiatrists testified for the defense that Moseley was a schizophrenic with catatonic reactions beyond his control (I saw Jack Smith in a catatonic phase and knew he had lost control) and incapable of stopping himself once he got the urge to kill "and thus was unable to distinguish right from wrong" (the M'Naghten Rule as stated in 1843). A psychiatrist for the State testified that Moseley had shown logic in carrying out his murderous impulses.

The presiding judge, a justice of the New York State Supreme Court, instructed the jury that legal sanity means a person must be held criminally responsible for his conduct unless he has such a *defect of reason* that he cannot distinguish right from wrong, and that "the fact that he may be mentally ill or have an uncontrollable impulse to kill has no bearing on this case" (*New York Times* for June 12, 1964). The jury, thus instructed, found Moseley guilty as charged and, under a New York State law, sentenced him to die, a sentence confirmed by the presiding judge.

Jack Ruby shot the man arrested for President Kennedy's murder before a television audience of millions in addition to the immediate presence of one hundred police officers and newsmen, and three nationally known medical authorities testified that he was mentally unbalanced. A jury found him legally sane and convicted him just the same. These examples will not prevent the State in future cases from citing any attempt at evasion or concealment on the part of the accused man as proving he knew right from wrong.

Dr. Manfred Guttmacher has pointed out that it is only in criminal trials that all this fuss is made over mental status in "What Can the Psychiatrist Contribute to the Issue of Criminal Responsibility?" (*Journal of Nervous and Mental Disease* for February, 1963). A judge in Maryland, for instance, can order an accused man to be confined in a state psychiatric hospital for observation with no formalities whatsoever.

His fitness or unfitness to stand trial is arrived at by psychiatrists without a hearing or trial. To guide them there is no formula decreed by legislative enactment or appellate court pronouncement. In many jurisdictions the defendant declared not guilty by reason of insanity at time of trial is released from the hospital upon recovery, solely as the result of a letter to that effect from the superintendent.

In murder cases, Dr. Guttmacher finds that insanity verdicts are in large measure dependent upon the temper of the public and the psychological reactions in the jury room. "Moral issues in a trial often take precedence over law. . . . Doubtless this is one of the major reasons that legislators have hesitated to abandon the M'Naghten Rule, phrased in terms of right and wrong and good and evil."

This may be cold comfort for a stricken community when a defense attorney, foreseeing that medical testimony will get him nowhere, chooses to employ the full armory of legal weapons that due process places at his disposal.

But leading psychiatrists do not believe the solution lies in turning the whole matter over to the medical profession. Dr. Guttmacher describes the difficulty, from a psychiatric standpoint, of determining to what degree an individual was responsible for his conduct at a given time, able to distinguish right from wrong and to govern himself accordingly. One of three psychiatrist advisers to the committee of the American Law Institute engaged in formulating the Model Penal Code, Dr. Guttmacher wrote that he felt the psychiatrist could best assist the court if he were not required to express an opinion as to the defendant's responsibility but merely required to state:

(1) whether the defendant was suffering from a definite and generally recognized mental disorder and how and why this conclusion was reached;

(2) the name, the chief characteristics and symptoms of the disorder with particular emphasis on its effect on the judgment, social behavior and self-control of the affected individual;

(3) the way and degree to which the malady has affected the defendant's behavior, especially in regard to his judgment, social behavior and self-control;

(4) whether the alleged act could be considered symptomatic of the disorder.

Dr. Frederic Wertham agrees with Dr. Guttmacher in his reluctance to leave the disposition of sexually sick men entirely in the hands of psychiatry.

It is true that a relatively small number of offenders suffer from some definite mental disease. They do belong entirely to the province of the doctor. . . . But we must learn to realize that the largest number of these offenders belong to a group *between* crime and disease. If we treat them merely according to medicine or merely according to criminal law, we treat them as something they are not, and that can help neither them nor us.

Thus Dr. Wertham expressed himself in an article, "Psychiatry and the Prevention of Sex Crimes," published in the *Journal of Criminal Law and Criminology*. He urged that the matter is neither a psychiatric question alone nor purely a question of law and penology, and that psychiatry and the law should work together.

Obviously many sex crimes are preventable. But the fault lies with the lack of co-ordination and of mutual constructive critique and supervision of existing agencies. The social responsibility in the prevention of sex crimes is so diffuse that it is actually absent. Is it not reasonable to believe that the road to a constructive program should start from this point? . . . It is not more and more research that is needed before we act. What we need, now, is an attempt to co-ordinate and interweave the agencies we *have* and the facts we *know*.

That was Dr. Wertham's view in 1938; he tells me that it represents his thinking today. His solution for sex crimes is more intelligent handling of disturbed males when the pattern first shows itself.

Dr. Guttmacher remarks that, to psychiatrists, "the extraordinary emphasis placed on deciding whether a man is guilty or not guilty by reason of insanity is puzzling. . . . They would far rather have the tremendous power of the law focused on the rehabilitation of the treatable and the prolonged incarceration of the untreatable."

Not only psychiatrists but jurists have urged that special institutions should be set up for serious sex offenders, where their illness can be studied and different methods of treatment experimented with. Judge Morris Ploscowe has called for a specialized institution in each state, with the characteristics of both a hospital and prison, for the custody and treatment of sexual offenders. "It must be a center of research on sex offenders. There can be tested the many conflicting theories of causation for the various types of sex abnormalities. There programs of community action for the prevention of sex offenses can be formulated, men can be helped to attain standards of socially acceptable sexual behavior."

Judge Ploscowe emphasizes that it is against the relatively small number of dangerous offenders that the laws must be directed. "Here is the group that must be submitted to intensive treatment at specialized institutions. If treatment fails of its purpose, then these offenders must be incarcerated for life, if necessary." Like the Sing Sing investigators, he very properly stresses that we must not make the mistake of confusing the smaller dangerous group with the much larger group of minor sex offenders for whom incarceration up to life is not warranted. The reader will be interested to see how this distinction is made in Wisconsin and California.

Judge Ploscowe's proposal involves not merely a revision of existing laws but the setting up of a special system, designed to single out the men and boys who present a very personal and dreadful threat to the innocent and then to give them the kind of treatment their individual condition requires.

The system must be "two-pronged," in the phrase of officials who administer the Wisconsin system for handling serious sex offenders. The primary consideration must be protection of the community. But treatment and rehabilitation of those males coming within its jurisdiction who can be rehabilitated must also be provided for.

The system must provide for incarceration so long as an offender remains dangerous—for life, if necessary—but must also be flexible enough to permit his release when or if he ceases to be dangerous. At all points the civil rights of accused individuals must be safeguarded;

they must be assured of fair trial, of unprejudiced, objective and thoroughly expert medical diagnosis, and of the right of appeal.

I agree with Judge Ploscowe that the place to start is with men and boys who come to the attention of the courts because of crimes of violence they allegedly have committed. At the present time, we do not begin to have the facilities for searching out and treating all the males —young, middle-aged and elderly—who harbor smoldering hatreds, like explosives buried in a mine field, waiting to be triggered into violence. But every state now lagging in its treatment of sex offenders can begin at once to improve vastly its handling of those who come into the hands of the law. The number of offenders who have repeated rape attacks, or gone on to savage murder after incarceration for serious sex offenses, indicates what a great step this would be toward solving the problem.

To do this requires a special body of laws which take cognizance of the special nature of sex illness and are implemented by diagnostic and treatment facilities. The spadework in this field has already been done. I find that many brilliant legal, medical and medico-legal minds have addressed themselves to it, as will be seen from the Bibliography at the end of this book.

The late Roscoe Pound suggested in his introduction to Judge Ploscowe's valuable book, *Sex and the Law,* that the fifty states might well adopt uniform statutes in matters concerning marriage, divorce, legitimacy and sex crimes, and it seems to me that this would be especially desirable in the field of sex crimes. It can be a source of embarrassment to be living in sin in some states, while properly married in others. It can be a severe hardship to have been born out of wedlock in a state which considers illegitimacy as permanent, and a bar to inheriting the parents' property, even though they have subsequently married each other. But inadequate management of sex crime in one state can spell death for innocents in other states that try earnestly to protect their women and children.

Uniform statutes—good ones—are certainly a goal to work toward. But I would not have the citizens of the many states with inadequate procedures wait for that day to come. In the Appendix you will find synopses, beginning on page 330, of the laws of the fifty states regarding psychiatric examination and treatment of serious sex offenders. Check your own state laws. Where there is no mandatory psychiatric examination of men or boys charged with serious sex offenses; where the M'Naghten Rule is the gauge of the offenders' mental state if he pleads insanity; where no facilities are provided for treatment of those convicted of serious sex crimes; and where psychiatric examination is not mandatory before their release into the community, you can know that you and the other citizens of your state had better start doing something.

The new territory is not unexplored; it has its pioneers, whose experience we can draw upon. Beginning with 1951, a handful of states not only passed special laws but set up facilities for diagnosing and treating the persons committed under these laws. As we saw in Chapter 4, the facilities range from special wards in mental hospitals, through a special facility in a maximum security prison, to separate and special institutions, the last-named being the ideal solution for larger states in the light of present knowledge. The experience of states using the different types of facility can be drawn upon by citizens of other states in formulating a system which best meets their particular needs. A Model Law approved by the American Law Institute and complete with legal phraseology can be obtained from the American Law Institute, 133 South 36th Street, Philadelphia. I shall therefore only call attention here to statutes which, from my special vantage point, have struck me as being particularly worth noting.

Several states now have a law which requires that, after release from a mental hospital or other institution, a serious sex offender should undergo psychiatric examination at intervals for a period of time. Dr. Manfred S. Guttmacher considers this a necessary precaution and states that men who have shown dangerous tendencies should be seen by a psychiatrist at least once a month, in some cases oftener, after they are released into the community. "One difficulty about the serious sex offender is a tendency for him to be released from an institution and then lost sight of," he told me. "A psychiatrist who knows his business can usually see the storm beginning to rise and can send the man back to the institution."

A law which, as a result of my own experience, has struck me as particularly just, humane and sensible is a Michigan statute which provides that persons diagnosed before trial as criminal sexual psychopaths, and hence subjects for medical treatment rather than legal punishment, may not thereafter be tried or sentenced for the offense originally charged.

The custom in most states is that when a man has been found mentally incompetent and sent to a hospital for the criminally insane or other institution without a trial, he is returned to the community for trial and sentencing on the original charges if he recovers and is discharged from the hospital.

If it is acknowledged that the man presumably was not responsible when he committed his crime, is it right that he should be punished for it after he has recovered? The issue before the courts in such a case should be: Is it truly safe for this man to be discharged from treatment and released into the community?

That brings us to another law, on the books of several states, which empowers a court to decide whether a man who has committed a sex crime while insane may be released into the community from a mental hospital, upon a statement of the hospital authorities that he is cured and ready for release. Under this law, the judge may recommit the offender to the hospital for further treatment, if he considers it advisable. I shall discuss this point in the next chapter. I shall only say here that, again as a result of my own experience, I consider this a highly desirable provision.

Iowa and several other states have a law which is aimed at solving dilemmas similar to those of my friend's daughter, Sue, and the doctor's daughter—a specific threat of violence, about which the police can do nothing as long as it is not carried out. This law permits any person to go to the local prosecutor and allege that someone in the community is a sexual psychopath. If the prosecutor, upon investigation, feels there is a basis for the charge, the alleged psychopath can be summoned to court and if, after observation and testing, he is deemed to be dangerous, he may be committed for treatment. The Iowa law (described in the Appendix) provides ample safeguards for the rights of the accused person, including the right of appeal from the decision of the court and examining doctors. The Supreme Court has found this law constitutional, while pointing out the necessity to exercise extreme caution in administering it. It offers recourse for persons who are told in most states that they must wait until the psychopath strikes, before the law can step in.

In the summer of 1963, Governor Mark O. Hatfield of Oregon signed a series of bills passed by the legislature, directed toward a goal both of more effective detection and apprehension of the criminal who preys on children and of the criminal's rehabilitation, if it is possible. Among the provisions is one permitting the civil commitment of any person found to be "sexually dangerous to children," in order to meet the difficulties inherent in having children testify in a court of law. The different bills include psychiatric examination and transfer jurisdiction to circuit courts of all criminal cases involving children as victims. Safeguards are provided in hearings before the court and in the ability to appeal. Committal under this process will be for an indefinite period, but with the right of the offender to periodic examination.

Included among the new provisions is one for co-ordinating city, county and state efforts at identifying and apprehending persons suspected of sex crimes, through prompt reporting of all sex offenses to a central state police bureau. It is hoped to offset in this way the peculiar difficulties of running down attackers who have had no previous connection with their victims.

Along with the bills, the Oregon legislature passed an appropriation for construction of facilities, at Oregon State Hospital, exclusively for persons committed under the act. Heretofore Oregon has had no special facilities for treating sex offenders, and this will be the first one in the United States designed to deal primarily with offenders against children.

And now, what about the handling of hideous, sadistic sex murder, which under traditional processes can lay such a heavy added burden upon the family and community that have suffered so heavily from the crime itself? It is rather late in the day to be very much concerned over what happens to an Emmett Hashfield, except on general principle. But what can happen to the bereaved family and to the local community which must bear the cost of the defense should concern us, whatever our views on capital punishment. Not the least of our concerns should be the breaking down of respect for the law and confidence in its power and intention to protect the community.

Such situations could be done away with, as they have been done away with in a few states, by abolishing the death penalty and permitting objective, neutral scientists to use their own judgment as to whether an accused man is mentally sick. When the question at issue boils down to a decision as to whether the man, if convicted of the crime, belongs in a prison or in a hospital for the criminally insane, there is no need to call in the opposing teams of "trained seals," as one lawyer has designated the state and defense experts. But experience has shown that this can be done only over the dead bodies of a certain segment of the population. It may not be due to a desire for vengeance alone. There may be a perfectly legitimate fear that deadly dangerous men will at some future time be released, still dangerous, from life sentences to prison or from commitment to hospitals for the criminally insane. Such things have happened.

If we are going to continue that process, though, why not be honest about it? Why not decree, in the law, that a sadistic sex murderer shall be put to death if found guilty, regardless of his sanity or insanity? That at least would eliminate the legally and medically degrading spectacle of state psychiatrists always finding the man sane, defense psychiatrists always finding him insane. The only point at issue then would be whether or not the accused man had actually committed the murder.

It is still not a solution. The Warren Commission, reporting on President Kennedy's assassination, stressed the difficulty of providing a fair, unprejudiced trial in a local court for a man accused of such a crime. It recommended that the assassination of a president be made a federal offense, the accused to be tried in a federal court. Experience has shown how difficult it is for a man accused of revolting, inhuman sex murder to get a fair, unprejudiced trial in a local court. Why not make sex murder a federal offense? That would remove it from the prejudices the local community can hardly help entertaining.

But I would go farther. The penalty for those found guilty should be life imprisonment, and a federal facility should be provided to which they would be committed for intensive expert study and the trying out of experimental treatment methods. There should be no possibility of parole or discharge—unless of course it should develop later that the convicted man was innocent.

Very few sex murderers have been studied by psychiatrists; the great majority have either been executed or have been buried in the back wards of state hospitals for the criminally insane. In Wisconsin, murderers are barred from the sex offender program, and under the California law, only those considered to be capable of rehabilitation must be accepted by California's special treatment institution for sex offenders.

I would doubt very much that an Emmett Hashfield, at the stage his malady had reached, would be considered capable of rehabilitation. But study of men like him, as well as of those in less advanced stages, might furnish clues to early symptoms in men and boys who have not as yet seriously injured anyone.

A number of psychiatrists have deplored society's practice of jettisoning this rich source of information about mental disease in its most virulent form. The above proposal offers a way to stop this waste and at the same time quiet the fears of the public. It would remove the burden from the local community, where it does not properly belong. And these men could be allowed to be of some benefit to society, in reparation for the harm they have done.

None of the aforementioned measures should be allowed to replace the purely research project into sexual illness as such proposed by Dr. Guttmacher. At the various facilities I have visited, where scientific diagnosis or treatment, or both, are carried on, the experts have been too busy to do very much research or to analyze the material they have, and there is little prospect of any change in this. Just as the law and medicine must work together to arrive at effective solutions, treatment must be supplemented and speeded up by research. Then we will be on the right track.

Also, the statutes drawn up now must be subject to review and changed as medicine grows more expert in this new field. Conceivably, treatments might be devised in time so effective as to warrant an experimental release of men on parole, even from the federal facility for sex murderers that I have suggested. At the present time, I believe the public should have the assurance that women and children will be safe from those particular men for the foreseeable future.

# 13

# When law and medicine
# work together

Now let us see how medicine can be brought into the deliberations at the court level, to the advantage of us all.

Here, too, the way has been prepared. I have mentioned the court-connected clinics in nearly a dozen of our big cities and the statewide clinic facilities open to courts in Massachusetts. These clinics can be studied by anyone interested in having a clinic of this kind in his or her own city.

We also have at our disposal a blueprint drawn up by Dr. Manfred S. Guttmacher for the World Health Organization, for a court-connected clinic which would afford the legal officials neutral, object-tive, scientific data in a number of areas. It grows out of Dr. Gutt-macher's experience of more than thirty years as the chief medical officer of Baltimore's court-connected psychiatric clinic. While it is designed to improve the handling of sex offenders at court level the world over, it can be adapted to any American city or civic entity. Among many other virtues, it affords an opportunity to detect, in men and boys brought into court for any type of offense, those who may have a potential for sex crimes of violence, *before* they have committed serious crimes and before their illness has become incurable.

The essence of Dr. Guttmacher's plan is that a scientific legal insti-tute should be established in conjunction with a city court or courts. Its purpose should be the "social, psychological, and medical study of the juvenile and adult offender." There should be similar agencies conducted by the country or state to serve smaller populations.

*Scientific legal institute.* This scientific legal institute should have three divisions: A social division directed by a sociologist or a professionally trained social worker, a psychiatric division directed by a psychiatrist who has had training and experience in criminal psychiatry, and a medical division directed by a physician who has sound clinical and pathological knowledge. These divisions should be administered by men whose intellectual attainments, professional training, and personal stature are equivalent to those of men of the legal profession who become judges, and they should be compensated accordingly.

*Social division.* The social division, in addition to making recommendations in regard to the granting of probation and being responsible for individuals placed on probation, should have as one of its major duties the obtaining of full and accurate socio-medical case-histories in a high proportion of cases. These socio-medical investigative studies must be completed within a limited time but should be sufficiently broad in scope to serve all of the agencies making use of them. They should be made a part of the permanent record and be filed and made accessible to the proper authorities. They should be kept current by contemporary notes and reinvestigations. Such investigations and current records would not only be of the greatest assistance to the court in sentencing, but would also serve as the basis for probation and parole work. They would, furthermore, be of the greatest value to the penal authorities in rehabilitation and proper prison administration.

All juvenile court cases, except those considered trivial by the evaluating authority, should have a socio-medical investigation prior to hearing. Such investigations can determine better than a court hearing on a specific charge whether the child is potentially a serious delinquent and can best indicate the direction that treatment should take. They should also ascertain which cases are in need of referral to the psychiatrist for examination.

It is highly desirable that a full socio-medical investigation and report should be made on all offenders who plead guilty or who have been found guilty in criminal courts.

In order to function most efficiently, the scientific legal institute should reach down to the magistrate or police court level for its base. Whenever possible, a specially trained psychiatric social worker representing the social division should be present at the sessions of these courts to spot psychiatric problems and to advise the magistrates in psychiatric matters. Furthermore, one can visualize such a social worker as an official agent, working informally in the cause of criminal justice by advising parents concerning predelinquent children, aiding individuals involved in serious marital discord, and giving advice in regard to the handling of suspected cases of mental disorder. *This service should act as a powerful force in the prevention of crime.* [I have italicized the preceding sentence because the service offers such an excellent opportunity for early detection of mental illness or delinquency before it has become firmly established.]

*Psychiatric division.* The psychiatric division of the institute would be staffed by one or more psychiatrists, psychiatric social workers, and clinical psychologists. This division should have its own psychiatric ward or ready access to psychiatric hospital beds for the observation of the more psychiatrically difficult cases among both juveniles and adults. Psychiatric examination of offenders should not be made before the socio-medical investigation has been completed by the social division.

The psychiatric division could not and should not examine all individuals charged with crime. Such routine examinations, even if practical, would have little value except from a research point of view. [This squares with the experience of New Hampshire scientists who felt, after experience with mandatory examination of all juvenile offenders of certain types, that these were not necessary in all cases and in some cases were actually harmful to the youngster.] In juvenile cases, no radical treatment plan, such as commitment to an institution or to a boarding home, should be made without a medical and psychiatric examination. It is also believed highly desirable that a psychiatric examination be made before granting probation or parole to an adult.

These facilities would be available for evaluating any offender, either prior to trial or after conviction, at the request of the court or grand jury, prosecutor or defense attorney, with the consent of the court and the medical and social divisions. But Dr. Guttmacher would have socio-medical and psychiatric examination made routinely before trial of individuals charged with crimes which indicate a strong possibility of mental illness. Those he mentions in this connection are capital crimes, sex offenses, homicide, arson, bigamy, abandonment of and cruelty to children, assault on wife, turning in of false fire alarms, and third-time repetition of the same crime of whatever nature. This measure hence would not only provide for psychiatric examination in all sex crimes but in a number that have been found in many cases to arise out of disturbed sex emotions.

In the adult cases examined prior to trial [Dr. Guttmacher continues] a preliminary report should be made to the court . . . confined to two issues: whether the individual is competent to stand trial, and whether he appears to be a responsible individual. After trial and conviction of such individuals, the full diagnostic and advisory report should be sent to the court.

The psychiatric examinations made prior to trial should be made available to the defense and the prosecution as well as to the court. These examinations, carried out by the professional staff of the psychiatric division of the institute, would in large measure eliminate ex parte testimony and the resultant "battles of experts," spectacles that have so long redounded to the obloquy of both medicine and the law.

In juvenile cases, the psychiatric examination should always be made prior to trial and the full report sent to the court, since such courts are not administered under the criminal rules of evidence.

The foregoing offers a way for an objective evaluation of persons whose behavior indicates they may be sick, and of full use of this evaluation by officials, including the defense attorney, as a guide in the handling of each case. It offers a way to detect harmful conditions and situations before they have become incurable. It offers a way to do away with the disgraceful spectacle of embattled psychiatrists, without depriving the accused man of his constitutional rights.

Think how much time, grief and expense would have been saved in the Emmett Hashfield case by a measure of this kind!

Dr. Guttmacher suggests that the psychiatric division of the institute should provide treatment facilities for certain selected probationers and parolees.

Moreover, in co-operation with the other divisions, it should serve as a powerful educative and inspirational force for the staffs of the penal institutions and the probation and parole offices by advising workers in regard to specific cases, holding case conferences, giving lecture courses, etc.

In American cities, he would have the medical division of the scientific legal institute serve as an official neutral medical agency, advising the court and its agents on all problems that fall within the province of medicine. His reason is:

In the USA, and in Europe also, the police frequently consider themselves solely as prosecuting agents. As a consequence, their scientific work may have an unscientific basis. Instances have been known where evidence obtained by police department laboratories has been suppressed, when it has proved favourable to the cause of the defendant.

The present writer is therefore of the opinion that an impartial agency of the courts performing medical investigations, and serving equally the judges, defence counsels, prosecutors, and police, would have great socio-legal value.

He gives as examples of the type of examination which should be conducted by the neutral medical agency, among others:

the examination of injuries of complainants in assault, rape cases, etc.;

presence of venereal infection in putative sex offenders, prostitutes, et al.;

blood-alcohol determination in traffic offenders, murder suspects, et al.;

blood-grouping in bastardy cases, in criminal identification problems, etc.;

analysis of stains for blood, semen, etc.

(Medical science has reached a point where semen can be typed, as blood groups are typed. There have been cases where rape-murder suspects were cleared by the fact that their semen was not of the type found on the victim. This technique of course would be no protection if an innocent suspect happened to have the same semen type as the murderer; nor, if the semen type matches that found on the victim, should this be considered as conclusive evidence of guilt.)

After conviction, but prior to sentence, Dr. Guttmacher would have all three divisions give definite recommendations regarding disposition in their reports to the court.

These advisory reports should be made matters of record but would, of course, not be binding nor mandatory upon the court.

One of the chiefs of the three divisions of the scientific legal institute would act as the general director. He would, along with other duties, abstract and, if necessary, translate for the court the technical findings and recommendations of the divisions.

In order to furnish personnel needed to carry out the system of examinations and reports, Dr. Guttmacher suggests that university fellowships be provided by government funds in order to train individuals in this field.

The foregoing plan represents an ideal which, as far as I know, is not yet carried out in full in any American city. But it was my privilege to sit in on a staff meeting of Dr. Guttmacher's court-connected clinic in Baltimore and see for myself how a neutral, scientific appraisal of offenders can protect both the community and the inherent right we all have to treatment, rather than punishment, if a mental condition should render us unable to meet the requirements of our society.

Present were the clinic psychiatrists, psychologists and psychiatric social workers, who had studied the persons whose cases were under review. In several of the cases, the victims had been interviewed as well as family members of the accused men.

Two cases were particularly interesting and enlightening as to the value to the individual offender of this kind of assessment. Both were men of more than ordinary education and considerable achievement. Yet one had deliberately made a homosexual solicitation of a member of the vice squad—thereby incurring arrest, the loss of his excellent job, and disgrace for himself and his family.

The other man held a position of unique trust, which he would not have been given unless he had proved himself to be stable and responsible in the highest degree, as well as alert and intelligent. This man had shot the woman he loved, though not fatally, an act completely out of character. How either of these men could have behaved so recklessly and foolishly was the question before the staff.

The psychologist contributed a very significant clue. On the intelligence tests given them at the clinic, one had scored 90, the other 92, which is below the average intelligence quotient of 100. Yet in order to have gained the advanced college degrees they held, and to have attained the positions they had sacrificed by their crimes, they would have had to have intelligence quotients at least in the 130's and possibly much higher. "They were honestly trying, too," the psychologist insisted.

The psychiatrist and psychiatric social worker, from their talks with the men and visits with their families—and with the victim, in the one case—were able to supply a story of long-continued physical and emotional strain which eventually had led to impairment of mental functions, even though neither man could be considered insane.

In another case, the weird images the offender had detected in the Rorschach test had indicated an extremely disturbed fantasy life—"In one blot, he saw a bat flying around, with a rabbit sticking out of its rectum!" the psychologist exclaimed—and in still another, a man convicted of a not very serious sex crime was found by the tests and examinations to have a highly dangerous potential which had not been indicated by his record to date. For the safety of the community, the clinic staff felt, the two latter offenders should not be released unless they improved very markedly after treatment. But there were other cases in which the staff members could see no reason why the offenders should not be handled under the usual legal processes.

Cases are referred to the Baltimore clinic by judges, the state's attorney, the defense counsel, the Probation Department and the jail physician. Its reports are made available to all the parties officially interested in a case and are frequently, by consent of both sides, admitted in evidence. "The most important function of the office is not the determination of the sanity or insanity of the accused," says Dr. Guttmacher, "but that of providing the sentencing judge with an evaluation of the personality of the offender, founded upon a psychological and psychiatric examination. Special attention is paid to estimating the strength of the antisocial impulses, recommending methods of disposition, and estimating their likelihood of success."

Dr. Guttmacher assured me that the cost of such a court clinic, even with a full staff of psychiatrists, psychologists and social workers, is an inconsequential matter in an over-all court budget. "Since it increases the usefulness of probation, it abundantly pays for itself in dollars and cents as well as in lives salvaged."

Final decision in the cases referred to the clinic rests with the court, the judge being free to accept or reject the clinic's recommendation as he sees fit. But in making his decision, he has at his disposal much scientific data and factual information which would not be brought out in a trial. Also, the various court officials who use a court clinic are being educated in psychiatric methods.

In his ideal court plan, Dr. Guttmacher recommends that final decision be left with the court, and this is the course followed in the states which to date have approached the problem of the sex offender from an enlightened standpoint. The scientists are unhampered in carrying on their work in the way they consider best and in the recommendations they submit. The court decides, after studying the medical as well as the legal aspects of the case.

I believe this is as it should be. The court, after all, is responsible for the safety of the community; it cannot discharge its duty if it is deprived of the power of decision in the cases which hold the worst threat to the community.

A feature of the Jack Smith case which had particularly impressed me was the powerlessness of our excellent and conscientious judge— until Jack's plea was changed to guilty, on a charge which would permit a longer sentence than those originally lodged against him—to protect the community as he obviously wished to do. This was because a quirk of the New York State law had left the power of decision entirely in medical hands.

Several years previously, a law had been passed requiring observation, in a state hospital, of persons found not guilty of a crime because of insanity. They may be committed to the hospital if diagnosed as insane. But Jack Smith had been committed to a mental hospital before he was tried, and apparently his discharge as recovered blocked returning him there, if he had been found not guilty by reason of insanity. At the same time, he had been in custody as long as the highest sentence that could be imposed for the offenses with which he was originally charged. Hence he would have had to be released if the jury found him sane and guilty.

The psychiatrists who made these decisions, I gathered, were not accountable to anyone. The law, in protecting the privacy of the patient, also protects his doctors from examination as to the thoroughness of their treatment and the grounds on which they base their belief that it is safe for the patient to be returned to the community. The court, and we of the local community, had no way even of knowing how much the psychiatrists who discharged Jack knew about the circumstances of the attack. I had asked to be allowed to talk with the state psychiatrists who had examined Jack, partly to learn, if possible, what had impelled him to seek *me* out, and the likelihood of his seeking me out again, in the event that he was discharged, or escaped, as he had escaped once from a mental hospital. The law, however, forbids consultation with state psychiatrists unless they grant permission, and in my case they did not.

"Oh, they wouldn't talk to you," the eminent psychiatrist to whom I had gone in my distress assured me. "They would rely on the reports from the institutions the man had been in previously and from the grand jury record." But I had suppressed, before the grand jury, material which might have interested his doctors, because it had no part in a purely legal proceeding.

Dr. Frederic Wertham has long maintained that psychiatry is an exact science and that a potential for danger can be detected. He has proved his own ability in this direction many times over, notably in the Bob Irwin case, in which he had several times persuaded Bob to return to hospitals which had discharged him as recovered. In 1964, Dr. Wertham figured in the release from a hospital for the criminally insane of a man who had been shamming insanity for many years in order to escape prison. Dr. Wertham had examined the man at the time of his trial and detected the imposture, but the man was committed to the hospital. When at length he wished to be discharged, Dr. Wertham's testimony that he had never been insane was an important factor in gaining his release. (The man had long since served any sentence that could have been imposed for his crime.)

Nevertheless, in both cases the psychiatrists who treated these men in the mental hospitals had been deceived, in the Bob Irwin case in thinking he had recovered, in the other that the man was insane. This is more likely to happen when no investigation is made into backgrounds and circumstances. There have been cases within my own knowledge where psychiatrists have been seriously misled as to the true nature of a home situation when they have relied on the unsupported word of a mental patient. One must wonder whether this has happened when gruesome, senseless murders are committed by individuals only recently released from mental hospitals.

I recognize that the psychiatrists in most state institutions labor under great handicaps—there are never enough of them, and they never have sufficient staff to do the kind of job I am sure they would like to do. We of the public do not appreciate as we should what a thankless task they have, and I am reluctant to criticize. But I believe the special danger presented by the sex offender calls for special precautions before such men are released into the community, and the psychiatrists and psychologists with whom I have discussed this matter welcome a check of their own findings by officials of the law.

Dr. Guttmacher's plan offers a way to obtain the thorough examination, at court level, of persons who may pose a threat to the public, while leaving final decision in the hands of the law.

And now I should like to make an appeal, to both the law and medicine, for more attention to the situation of the victim of sex violence. This should not be a matter for statutes but of recognition on humanitarian grounds of the state of anxiety in which the victim of a sex attack is left, anxiety not just for herself but for the other unsuspecting women, young girls and children who may be victimized.

The worst feature of my own experience was my inability to establish any contact with the county officials and state doctors who had Jack Smith under their jurisdiction. I couldn't even find out when the trials that were contemplated at different times were to be held. It was sheer accident that I was not in California when the grand jury considered Jack's case, because of the deep silence that prevailed at the county seat after his arrest. What the result would have been if the principal and only witness to the crime had been three thousand miles away when the grand jury met, I am unable to say.

I do not suggest that officials should hover protectingly about the rape attack victim. I merely want to point out how it adds to her fearfulness, bewilderment and frustration to be treated as though she didn't exist. The woman who reports a sex attack and stands ready to co-operate with officials for the safety of the community is performing a most unpleasant duty of citizenship. I myself would have been saved a world of fret and worry if someone at our courthouse had merely thought to advise me, by letter or telephone, of developments which deeply concerned me. I believe that, on occasion, the victim who survives may have a contribution to make. Won't you gentlemen of the law and medicine at least give her a chance to make it?

# 14
# Whose job is it?

Let's suppose now that you are one of the many millions of Americans living in states whose laws and procedures regarding sex crime need improving. Whose is the responsibility for setting up a new and better system?

*It is the job of the citizens of these states, people like you and me.*

"Officials won't do it. Psychiatrists won't do it. Lawyers won't do it," I was told wherever I went. However, all these people will help citizens and citizen groups who take the matter in hand. An Association for Mental Health might be an ideal group to start the ball rolling, enlisting other organizations, but this is a game in which anybody can play. A single citizen could interest organization leaders, get a core committee set up, which would then draw in all manner of groups and individuals who could be helpful.

In Wisconsin, women's organizations took a major role in bringing the excellent Wisconsin system into being, as women's groups have brought many social advances into being, and I believe that more enlightened treatment of sex offenders is peculiarly a job for organized women. After all, the goal is our own safety and our children's. Women can exercise a formidable power when they are working for the welfare of children.

Women's organizations such as the Women's Clubs, the League of Women Voters, and the P.T.A., which have had experience in legislative matters, could serve as a focal point, drawing in the men's organizations, the bar, the medical associations, the labor unions, the welfare agencies, experts of many kinds.

There is no law which says that a man, or men's groups, may not initiate such an effort, and if the women of a state do not act, I hope the men will.

A first step might be to learn what the local sex crime situation is. What happens to offenders in local courts and state institutions after they are arrested? What treatment is provided? What is the repeater rate for sex offenders paroled or discharged from your jails and prisons? Then it would be helpful for representatives of your group to visit systems where offenders are being handled and treated in an enlightened manner.

When you have assembled your facts, go to the newspapers. To rouse the general public from its apathy with regard to the problem, some goad may be needed, and the goad can and must come from the press. Merely to print the story of the dreadful rape murder is not enough. The community takes it for granted that the perpetrator, if found, will be properly dealt with. Only through the newspapers can the inadequacies of a faulty system be kept in the limelight.

The press is frequently accused of sensationalism in its handling of sex crimes and is sometimes accused of impelling further ones by publicizing at all the ones that occur. In my surveys and reading of newspapers, I did not feel that this charge held up. The New York papers I reviewed tended to play down sex crimes. The few rapes noted at all usually appeared on inside pages, under one-column headlines. Even a rape murder sometimes rated no more than a few paragraphs. Big play was given only to the occasional particularly shocking crime which engaged the anxious interest of the entire community and, I believe, rightly so.

My criticism of the press is that it does not go as deeply into the sex crime problem as it should. In most cases the story is dropped when an arrest is made or dropped after a day or so when an arrest is not made. Only the most sensational trials are publicized. The release of the run-of-the-mill offender on probation, or the voiding of charges against him, or the acceptance of a guilty plea to a lesser charge, is seldom noted at all. When the rapist or sex murderer is released from prison on parole or discharge, nobody knows about it.

Some reporter might win a Pulitzer prize by taking rape attacks and other sex crimes of violence as his particular bailiwick, following them through the courts, keeping the public informed as to what is being done in its name. From time to time, the score of local sex crimes as yet unsolved might be run. Citizens have a right to some idea as to the number of serious sex offenders at large in their vicinity.

Now and then a paper runs a general story on the sex crime picture in its locality. These stories are helpful; there should be more of them. I applaud the practice generally followed by New York City papers of suppressing the names of rape victims, and I don't feel that men released from prison after serving sentences should be named in all cases. But a paper might report the number of serious sex offenders released from state or local institutions each month, the nature of their crimes, the amount of treatment they have received, and whether or not they had had psychiatric evaluation before being released. The record of the individual repeater is printed after the ghastly crime has been committed, but at that point its publication does little good. A constant reminder of the slipshod nature of their system might just possibly stir citizens into action.

For the newspapers can't do the job alone. Mr. Doherty of the *Indianapolis Star* mercilessly exposed the Indiana system, but, as far as I could learn, the citizens of Indiana did not consider it their business to make the sweeping changes his exposé had shown to be the only solution.

But let us imagine now that the citizens wish to do their part and have joined together in a movement to improve their system. The papers, by reporting their deliberations and interviewing informed members of the citizens' committee, can be educating the public in the scientific aspects of the problem and gaining its support.

I should like to add a note of warning here. A new system must not be sold to the public as a miracle cure which will stop sex crime dead in its tracks. In the beginning we can only hope to cut down materially the number of repeaters—men or boys who have come to the attention of the law because they have committed crimes and have been found, by scientific diagnosis, to hold a potential for danger.

It must be understood that these men in many instances are difficult medical subjects and that the science of treating them, on a general scale, is in its infancy. Much experimenting must be done; inevitably, some mistakes will be made. It seems to me, in fact, that the treatment of serious sex criminals is at much the same stage as the science of obstetrics was in 1900, when every year hundreds, perhaps thousands, of women died in childbirth who would be saved today through techniques available to every physician.

I do not believe we are justified in judging harshly if an occasional mistake should be made under a system like Wisconsin's or California's, where I have seen the careful attention given to sex offenders up for parole or discharge.

The public, however, is entitled to be sure that the experts have gone into every case thoroughly, have made the best decision within their power to make at the present time, and are learning what they can from the mistakes. An important factor in cutting down maternal deaths in hospitals in this country almost to the vanishing point has been the physicians' committee, in many hospitals, which investigates every maternal death occurring there, to see if it might have been prevented. The attending doctor is closely questioned as to the measures he used, and, while the inquiry is directed toward eliciting facts rather than apportioning blame, no doctor wants to have to appear before this committee. For years the *New England Journal of Medicine* has printed reports of such investigations, and any doctor who reads this department can learn what leaders in the obstetrical profession would do in such and such a contingency. In recent years, the *New England Journal of Medicine* has alternated the analyses of maternal deaths with similar analyses of deaths of newborns, since it has been found that many of these, too, could be prevented.

I do not know to what extent this kind of soul-searching takes place in a mental institution when a patient proves to have been released prematurely, or whether it takes place at all, such a mantle of secrecy is thrown about mental illness. But this, too, can be a matter of life or death to someone, maybe to more than one person. While recognizing that no human being can be perfect, I believe we of the public are entitled to know that such incidents are not regarded by the doctors concerned as "just one of those things."

I have faith that progress in the treatment of sexual sickness will be much faster than it was in obstetrics, because medical science has made such tremendous strides since 1900, and new drugs and techniques which hold promise are constantly being made available. We can be sure that, with experience, performance will improve in treatment institutions, and I would hope that the citizens who get the system set up will keep in touch with these institutions, assure themselves that the experts are doing the best job they know how to do, and stand behind those who are giving the best they have to give.

A present difficulty is the shortage of trained personnel, which falls hardest on public institutions, for the psychiatrist today who works in a public institution not only must often do so for less money than he could make in private practice or a private institution but is called on for other sacrifices as well. He feels shut off from his colleagues; there is a tendency to look down on persons who accept these posts, on the part both of the public and members of their own profession.

Much of this prejudice stems from the fact that public institutions too often are mainly dumping grounds for society's unfit. Experts with whom I have discussed this feel that the situation could be remedied to a very great extent if such institutions were provided with sufficient staff and facilities to make them fountainheads of treatment and research, to which the entire medical profession could turn for information. It is not the financial sacrifice as much as the other present aspects which keep many experts out of the public service. They should by all means receive adequate payment. But, more importantly, they should have recognition for the valuable service they render.

When sex sickness is accepted for what it is, the sexually sick man no longer will feel the need to conceal his sickness and deny his crimes. I saw this myself in Wisconsin and California. He can feel free to consult a physician *before* he has done something dreadful, if he can be reasonably sure he will not be met with loathing and dismissed with a moral lecture.

And now let us see what the pioneers in sensible, scientific and humane handling of sex criminals and troubled youngsters are doing.

# 15

# Any state can do this

Eleven men sat at ease about the long conference table in the big, well-lighted room, most of them smoking cigarettes. All were in their early twenties, except for one who appeared to be in his thirties, or possibly early forties, and a man in street clothes who sat at the head of the table, but with his chair pushed back from it, as though to dissociate himself a bit from the others. The young man at the corner, on this man's right, also sat back a little from the table. He was a nice-looking chap, with straw-colored hair and rather innocent blue eyes. He had a special chair, upholstered in green; the rest had regulation conference chairs.

Not one of the men gathered more closely about the table was unattractive; there was nothing in any face that would arouse fear or revulsion. All were clean-shaven, with neatly trimmed hair, and looked well-scrubbed. Except that their shirts were the khaki and their trousers the green cotton of a prison uniform, they might have been a group of very young executives, gathered to discuss a business matter. Their expressions were serious. A stranger entering the room might have thought he had intruded upon solemn and important deliberations, of unusually sober and responsible young men.

The men were, in fact, with the exception of the one in civilian clothes, inmates of the Sex Offender Facility in the Wisconsin State Prison at Waupun. This was one of a number of therapy groups carried on in the Facility. Each of its members had been convicted of a serious sex crime, ranging from forcible rape or attempted forcible rape to impairing the morals of a minor. The man in civilian clothes was the therapist. I sat at his left. The thirtyish man, who was on my other side, had been convicted of incest. The blond young man opposite me, in the green-cushioned chair, had been convicted of having sex relations with girls in their very early teens, some as young as twelve. The group was indeed engaged in an important task—to try to understand what had made each one a sex deviate and to plumb and finally overcome the hostilities which had caused them to vent their inner turmoil on women or children who had never harmed them.

As this is written, only two of our states, California and Massachusetts, have separate institutions for the study and treatment of sexually sick men. Wisconsin has plans for such an institution, to be completed by 1965 or 1966. Meanwhile, men convicted of serious sex crimes and diagnosed as sex deviates are being given treatment in a Sex Offenders' Facility at the state's maximum security prison.

I had come to Wisconsin because the Facility at Waupun, established in 1951, was the first special arrangement set up in this country for the purpose of giving adequate psychiatric treatment to sexually sick men; and because Wisconsin's Sex Crimes Law and system of handling sex offenders was citizen-inspired and gives unprecedented leeway to science in diagnosing and treating these men.

In 1947, Wisconsin, like many other states around this time, passed a "sexual psychopath" law, of the kind Thomas E. Dewey very wisely vetoed in New York State (as discussed in Chapter 11). "The sexual psychopath gets locked up, and that's the end of it," was the terse description of this law given me by Mr. Sanger B. Powers, director of the Division of Corrections in the Wisconsin State Department of Public Welfare, which administers the Wisconsin Sex Crimes Law.

We have seen that the indeterminate sentence has seldom been invoked in states which have not provided intensive treatment for those men sentenced under it. It was never applied in Wisconsin. Instead, a large citizens' committee was formed in 1950 to see if a better way could be devised. The committee contained representatives of organized labor, church groups, P.T.A.'s, women's and community organizations; judges and lawyers; psychiatrists, psychologists, social workers and administrators in the correctional field; faculty members from the University of Wisconsin and Marquette University; and prominent citizens who were interested in welfare matters. After studying the sexual psychopath law and the problem presented by the sex offender, the committee drew up the present Wisconsin Sex Crimes Law and sponsored it through the legislature, where it was passed without a single dissenting vote.

"It was not the product of hysterical reaction to a series of violent crimes, it was more the result of recognizing the futility of past legislation aimed at this particular group of offenders and the desire of the intelligent, enlightened citizenry to take advantage of recent advances made in the medical field in the treatment of mental disorders," says Mr. Matt Coogan, reporting "Wisconsin's Experience in Treating Psychiatrically Deviated Sex Offenders" in the *Journal of Social Therapy* for January, 1955.

The system for diagnosis and therapy went into operation in July of 1951, as soon as the law was passed, being carried out principally at the State Prison at Waupun. At the time of my visit there in June of 1963, the authorities and psychiatric staff had had twelve years of experience in trying to rehabilitate men with a sex disturbance that leads them to violent, aggressive behavior and makes them a menace to the community.

Under the Wisconsin law, the courts *must* commit to the State Department of Public Welfare—I shall refer to it from now on merely as the Department, for simplicity's sake—any man convicted of rape, indecent or improper behavior with a child, or attempts at any of these actions, for a thorough social, physical and mental examination. [must have] Should the investigators decide the man is sexually deviated, the court *must* either place the man on probation, with out-patient or in-patient psychiatric treatment as a condition, or re-commit him to the Department until such time as those responsible for him decide he is no longer dangerous. The investigators' finding is final.

When a man is re-committed to the Department, it has complete jurisdiction as to the way he shall be handled. He may be paroled at any time he is considered to be capable of making an adjustment to society, or held in custody indefinitely, the committing court approving, if the Department scientists are not satisfied with the improvement he has made. The kind of therapy he receives, and the institution where he receives it, are left entirely to the scientists. Because the Department is also held responsible for the safekeeping of the men, to date the fortresslike Waupun Prison has been used principally, though the farm program is occasionally employed, with the deviates there carefully supervised.

Dr. Benjamin Glover of the University of Wisconsin Department of Psychiatry called attention to the "medically interesting features" of the law in an assessment of the Wisconsin system which appeared in the magazine *Federal Probation* for September, 1960.

> First, it removes sex deviation from the realm of simple crime and acknowledges the existence of a motivation for both the deviation and the act committed in a malfunctioning of the personality of the individual. . . . Next, the law extends to the field of medicine the rights of determination of methods of treatment, including use of the ancillary services of psychology and social work, and it does not intrude on the manner, frequency or duration of therapy. Lastly, the law permits the medical man to reach conclusions of his own as to the adequacy of his methods and their effects on the improvement of the convicted and to recommend as to whether he is improved or stabilized sufficiently to return to his community.

Final decisions as to commitment remain with the court, as Dr. Glover believes is right—the Wisconsin authorities agree with him—but determination of the mental status of every serious sex offender rests with the Department scientists, and the law makes mandatory supervision and psychiatric treatment for every person diagnosed as a sex deviate. This is a radical departure from the M'Naghten Rule and the battle of contending psychiatrists, and Dr. Glover warns that it becomes incumbent on medical men "to guard these slowly won steps with careful observation, diagnosis, treatment and disposition of their problem patients."

I was curious to learn how this forward-looking plan had worked out in actual operation. I wanted, if possible, to see and talk with some of the deviates, so that I might get at first hand their own view of their problems and their feeling about being treated as men with a sickness which the psychiatric staff is attempting to cure.

I learned that the Department welcomes as visitors to the Facility lawyers and others with a special interest in the system, and that male visitors had sat in on the group therapy sessions. So far, however, no woman had been permitted such a privilege. I knew I was asking a great deal and would have felt no resentment if my request to observe the treatment and to talk with some of the men in the Facility had been denied.

However, everything was thrown open to me, the sole proviso being that the deviates must consent to my presence at their group deliberations, and to private interviews, and that they must not be identifiable to their home communities. I was the first woman ever admitted inside the prison proper, with the exception of one social worker. I was urged to express my impressions frankly. "We know we're not perfect. We would welcome your criticism."

Before going to Waupun, I was briefed on the system by Mr. Powers, the Corrections Division Director mentioned before, who is in direct charge of the program; Dr. Asher R. Pacht, Chief of the Clinical Services in the Division of Corrections—comprising psychiatrists, psychologists and clinical service workers—and Dr. Thomas Bassett, Chief Psychologist. I got further fill-ins from Dr. Pacht and Dr. Bassett on the fifty-mile drive from Madison to Waupun and back, from the therapists at the prison, and in a final session with Dr. Pacht after I had had my interviews.

The law bars murderers from participation in the program, and I was told that Wisconsin has a very small proportion of shocking, sadistic sex crime. "Ours is largely a rural and homogeneous population. We have hardly any of the depressed slum conditions which are more likely to produce brutality and savagery, though we do have men who commit violent crimes out of sex hostility and who might murder in time if nothing is done about them. What we try to do is to institute treatment before men have reached that point, and the law allows us to keep them confined as long as their hostile, aggressive impulses are uncontrolled."

(Not that Wisconsin has never had a sadistic, inhuman murder, but the state does not have the death penalty, and examining psychiatrists are not bound by the M'Naghten Rule. The few men who have murdered for sex thrills or out of sex hostilities have landed in Wisconsin's Central State Hospital for the Criminally Insane, without a costly and farcical court battle.)

It appeared to me to be an advantage that the entire machinery for handling the sex deviates is concentrated in the Department of Public Welfare, from diagnosis through parole or probation, up to the time when a deviate is finally discharged. Its corps of trained workers contributes materially to the thoroughness of the investigation—social, physical, mental—the law commands for every man found guilty of a serious sex offense. Clinical psychologists and psychiatrists are used interchangeably—Dr. Pacht, the head of the Clinical Services, holds his degree in psychology.

When a man is convicted in the courts of a serious sex crime, the usual procedure is to place him in a separate unit at Waupun Prison for the sixty-day observation period allowed by the law. During this time he wears a blue band on his sleeve, to differentiate those undergoing diagnosis from the other inmates.

"We don't like the blue band too well," Dr. Pacht admitted. "It is used only during the sixty-day period when the convicted men are sent for observation and diagnosis and is employed because custody is close during this period, and the blue band identifies these individuals instantly to the staff. The feature we don't like is that it labels the wearer as a sex offender to other inmates with whom he will be associating if he is returned to the institution under either the Sex Crimes Law or the Criminal Code." In the separate institution contemplated, this factor would be of no importance, since all the men committed would be sex offenders.

The man tells his own story of his crime and his life up to this point, undergoes physical and psychiatric examination and psychological testing. Meanwhile, Department field workers are investigating his background, getting his previous criminal record, if any, from the police, interviewing his parents, wife, and other family members and, if possible, his victim or victims, and making note of his habits with regard to health, activities, recreation, religion, work record. Then a member of the staff at the prison goes over the same ground with the man himself.

This investigation is a far cry indeed from the quickie psychiatric examination given in many states in a jail. I scanned some of the thick files of the Wisconsin offenders and could see what a help all this background material would be, for diagnosis and for evaluating the information a man gives about himself.

As has been found in other places, most come from families on lower socio-economic levels. "Sons of well-to-do families rarely land in court for any sex crime short of murder," I was told. "Their families usually settle with the victim out of court. If they are too dangerous to be running loose, they are cared for in private institutions."

Wisconsin's experience confirms the researches reported in earlier chapters. Nearly all the deviates had suffered severely from abuse and emotional deprivation in early childhood. The majority of the aggressive, violent men had mothers who were both rejecting and seductive or both dominating and seductive, combinations, as we have seen, which are peculiarly productive of hatred for the female sex and of violence in the sons. Dr. Pacht, however, refuses to place all the blame on the mothers. It is his experience that the sex offender rather is the product of a family constellation in which the different personalities react upon each other in a certain way, and the child reacts to all.

An unusual opportunity to study this phenomenon intensively was presented to the Wisconsin scientists when three men convicted of incest were in the Facility at Waupun and their wives and the daughters they had preyed upon were in other Wisconsin institutions. Fathers, mothers and daughters alike were found to be exceedingly dependent individuals with no inner resources, looking to others to provide them with their satisfactions and pleasures. The relationship between husband and wife in every case was bad; the wives were promiscuous. They knew of the father's relationship with the daughter, and in one case the mother had actually welcomed it as freeing her to give all her attentions to outsiders. The husbands were weak individuals who had accepted this state of affairs. They had turned to the daughters for the satisfactions denied them by their wives and to bolster their egos. The daughters, already promiscuous at an early age, felt contempt for their fathers but were sorry for them too. They had consented to the incest out of pity.

Approximately 40 per cent of the offenders have previous records, and many others have been wards of the state. (One young man whom I saw at Waupun told me, with a trace of pride, that he had been in seven different institutions in seven years.)

"Our experience indicates that sex deviates, as a group, function in the world as inadequate individuals. They are impulse-ridden, demonstrate poor controls in most areas of their lives, and have considerable difficulty in experiencing the possibility that they have some role in their own destinies." So Drs. Pacht, Halleck and Ehrmann, all of the Wisconsin scientific staff, reported in a paper presented at the 1961 meeting of The American Psychiatric Association.

The impact of arrest on the sex deviate leads to feelings of shame and humiliation . . . he becomes even more helpless. He often rationalizes that he was seduced by sexually aggressive, precocious young boys or girls. Some sex offenders presumptuously dismiss their deviant behavior as being entirely the product of alcohol. Another common defense is the total denial of the offense to the authorities and sometimes to themselves . . . even in the presence of a long record of similar offenses documented by reliable witnesses.

If, after careful study, an offender is not considered to be a sex deviate, he is turned back to the court for sentencing under the regular Criminal Code. Out of 2158 offenders committed to the Department for observation and diagnosis in the first eleven and one half years of the program, 1119 (or a little over half) were found to be deviated, 95 were found to be actively psychotic—they were committed to Central State Hospital (for the Criminally Insane)—and 938 were found not to be deviated and were turned back to the court for handling by the usual criminal procedures. (Specific findings in the remaining 6 cases were not given.)

Naturally the definition of "sex deviate" becomes extremely important, and Dr. Pacht told me that the scientific staff is still trying to arrive at a satisfactory one. The law merely orders special treatment if an individual "demonstrates mental and physical aberrations for which treatment is recommended."

The Wisconsin scientists, however, consider that the sex deviate comes somewhere between the man who commits a sex crime, like any other type of crime, because of inadequate training or the environment in which he grew up, without being mentally ill; and the man whose sex crime is obviously the product of mental illness. It is not difficult to single out the men who offend entirely because of sociological or cultural forces, at one end of the scale, and the psychotics at the other end. The Wisconsin experience has indicated, though, that in most of the serious sex crime cases, the abnormal sex behavior has multiple causes and cannot easily be pigeonholed in one category or another.

"First, we look for an immaturity in the development of sexual functions," Drs. Pacht, Halleck and Ehrmann explained in their report to The American Psychiatric Association.

This is almost always a broad immaturity which also encompasses other areas of the individual's personality and social behavior. Second, we look for a deviation of the individual's normal sexual aim or object which he has little ability to control by conscious rational thought. [Such an individual commits a sexually deviated act with the knowledge that it is socially reprehensible and that he will probably be caught. He may even consciously disapprove of his own behavior.] Most psychiatrists agree that when an individual shows a combination of sexual immaturity and a compulsive need to act out his immature sexual cravings, he is likely to continue to be involved in sexual offenses until he receives treatment. For this type of individual, recommitment under the Sex Crimes Law appears to be most appropriate.

If the court re-commits the deviate to the Department, he is returned to Waupun. From now on he mingles with the general prison population and no longer wears any distinguishing marks. (He may, in fact, be working beside a general inmate who had committed the same type of crime but who was not diagnosed as a deviate.) He goes first into an orientation group and is introduced to prison routines, while the staff decides what type of therapy to give him. A few are placed under individual treatment, but most are assigned to one of a number of therapy groups, structured to serve different types of personality needs. There is a small one, for instance, composed entirely of forcible rapists. Most, however are mixed, so far as offenses are concerned, such as the first group I sat in on at Waupun.

Youth appeared to be the common denominator here, with the exception of the one thirtyish man, and intelligence may have been a factor too, since the men impressed me as being alert and fully aware of their problems.

The therapist's air of slight dissociation from the offenders was deliberate. The group members conduct the discussion and interrogate each other; the therapist is not supposed to intervene except to protect some individual from too-rigorous questioning or to keep the discussion from wandering too far afield. The green-cushioned chair was reserved for the group member on whom the rest were focusing for the time being. Each man had his turn in the cushioned chair, for a number of sessions. It was the function of the rest to question him mercilessly, in a way that staff personnel could hardly do.

Ernie, as I shall call the man in the cushioned chair at the time of my visit—convicted of having sex relations with girls barely in their teens—opened the proceedings by calling on another group member as witness that the girls in Ernie's home town were no angels. Other members demanded Ernie's reason for bringing this up.

"Are you claiming that all the girls in L—— are easy? Are you using that for an alibi?"

"Of course not," Ernie replied. "To do that, you would have to try out all the girls in L——; the very idea is ridiculous. I merely wanted to show that Bill knows these girls, too, and what their reputation is."

The thirtyish man squared away for a full-scale attack on Ernie.

"Aren't you afraid of sex, really? Isn't that why you took up with younger girls? Younger girls don't know much about sex, they'll believe what you say to them, they're more scared to tell. Wasn't that the real reason?"

Ernie denied that he was afraid of sex. His trouble, he contended, was that he had no job and too much time on his hands. Also he was in a wild gang and had merely gone along with the others. The group pounced on both these excuses.

"If the gang you were in was wild, why didn't you find some other gang?"

"Why didn't you take up some hobbies to occupy your time—some other hobby, that is?" There was a little laughter at this, for Ernie had admitted that the pursuit of young girls had been his principal occupation.

Ernie fielded all the questions coolly. He had tried to get in another, better crowd before joining the wild one, he said, but they wouldn't have him. He guessed his father wasn't prominent enough or wealthy enough to meet their standards. He had tried to get a job, but there weren't any. The only emotion he displayed was when he said his father had refused to take him into his business. "Dad wouldn't even take me with him on his business trips. I don't know why. It's no fun, sitting at home waiting for the telephone to ring. And it's no help to come home dead tired from dragging around, looking for a job, and have your mother say brightly, 'Why don't you go out and look for a job?' "

From time to time, the men would mention their own problems in connection with something brought out in the cross-examination of Ernie. A young man whose offenses against children occurred after his marriage had gone sour thought his original mistake had been in equating sex with love. His practice had been to have sex relations with his wife every noon hour when he went home for lunch, though it had made for a very busy schedule. "I thought that way I showed her I loved her. It never occurred to me to give her pretty clothes and good times. What I should have done was to do something nice for her on Monday and Tuesday and Wednesday, and sort of work up to the other for the week end. But when I tried that, I found she was using her sex against me. She was using her sex to get the things she wanted."

A young rapist chimed in, "My wife used her sex against me, too."

And the incestuous father said, "I know very well I did what I did out of resentment against my wife."

These remarks were made without heat, however, and the young men, nearly all of whom had been married, found excuses for their wives. "You've got these resentments, and you carry them into your marriage. It's why your wife gets these feelings. It's not her fault."

Another, "I didn't know actually what love was—there was none in my home, just quarreling and fighting." This young man added that, since his arrest and re-commitment to prison, his family had been doing lots of things he wished he might have done. "They're eating out of doors, for one. Maybe that don't mean anything to you fellows, but boy, it would have meant a lot to me! My father takes my sisters out to movies, things like that. I think they've started thinking about what they did to get me in here."

Several others remarked that their parents, too, had been shocked into realization of their own remissness by the son's conviction for a sex crime.

But they did not put all the blame on their parents. This phase of the discussion had started with an indignant outburst from Joe (all these names are, of course, fictitious) whose offenses had been against children. Several of the men mentioned that, like Ernie, they had had difficulty about being accepted socially. Leaning forward, Joe had demanded, "How could anybody expect you to make friends when you're locked away upstairs every time company came? What are people going to think when your brothers and sisters have birthday parties, but you're locked upstairs and never have your name on a birthday cake? Aren't they going to think there's something wrong with you?"

This was what had actually happened to Joe, who was the youngest in his large family, though there was nothing in Joe's appearance or manner to account for his having been hidden away. In equally inexplicable fashion, he and a sister had been locked up together at night, except for the times when the father took the girl out of the room to have sex relations with her. The mother had known of this. When Joe had had his turn in the cushioned chair, I was told, the other men had pounded hard at him, unable to believe that there had been no sex play between brother and sister under such circumstances, but Joe had denied this stoutly. His offenses had been against children of neighbors.

Joe was asked why he thought he had been hidden from visitors and excluded from parties.

"Believe me, I've put in a lot of time when I was locked up in my cell at night, trying to figure that out. I've decided it must have been one of two reasons. One, my mother already had all the boys she wanted, so when I came along she wanted to forget about me. Two, she already had all the children she wanted, so she kept me out of sight all she could."

To Joe, however, the big point was that his mother was finally admitting her responsibility for her son's sex deviation. "I've been trying to get her to face the issue for years. Now that I'm in here, she has to listen." But Joe voluntarily assumed part of the blame for his acts. "I didn't have to fool with those kids. Sure I hated my mother and father, my father especially for fooling with my sister. But I didn't have to take out my hate on little kids. I could have robbed a bank, or something like that!"

Others of the group said that their mothers, too, blamed themselves but should not do so because the erring sons had known right from wrong. As one put it, "I think we emphasize too much on our parents. It was still us that did the crime." In the end, Joe even found something good to say about his father who, in spite of drinking all the time, had supported his family. "He's done pretty darn well, raising all those kids on just a little bit of money."

Attention was focused once more on Ernie, the men still trying to elicit the reason why he had turned to girls so much younger than himself as sex objects. His home evidently had been on a higher economic level than those of most of the group, and there had not been the obvious reasons for his deviation—parental drunkenness, brutality or overt rejection—that had marked so many of the others. Nevertheless, Ernie's emotional turmoil had been so great that the staff had feared for a while he might break over into a psychosis. That he could submit calmly and coolly to the needling of his peers was a distinct advance for him, but he continued to put the blame for his transgressions on the feminine sex. His explanation for his deviation was that an older girl had twice got him into trouble with his parents by suggesting intimacies and then telling his parents he had made overtures to her. "I was the one that got punished. It scared me off from older girls." He admitted under the questioning that he had been obsessed by sex. "It was something I knew. It wasn't hard for me to do."

Ernie turned on his interrogators. "Let's face it. Is there anything you fellows do that you get more pleasure from than sex?"

There was a considerable stir and a shuffling of feet, the men cast sidelong glances at each other, but no one answered. So far as his offenses were concerned, however, Ernie insisted that he had been the victim of circumstance, in the form of female temptresses.

"I don't believe we've gotten to the bottom of this yet," the incestuous father on my left pronounced when the session ended.

Group therapy was first used at Waupun when men diagnosed as sex deviates began arriving under re-commitments, more to aid in maintaining discipline than for purposes of treatment. At that time the treatment was all individual. However, the sex offender groups soon proved to be an excellent treatment method for deviates, and, ever since 1951, the staff has been learning how to make it more effective.

Dr. Harold F. Uehling, who has been a therapist at the Facility from its inception, described the use of group therapy with sex deviates in a paper he delivered before the American Society of Group Psychotherapy and Psychodrama published in *Federal Probation* under the title, "Group Psychotherapy Turns Repression into Expression for Prison Inmates."

He mentions that the average person views the serious sex offender as a callous, socially aggressive person, fully responsible for his actions unless he is mentally ill or mentally limited. Nothing could be farther from the truth, Dr. Uehling says. Most are extremely unsure within themselves, cursed by serious inferiority feelings. Contrary to the popular belief that such a man has no conscience, no regard for the rights of others, he more often than not is overly aware of his delinquencies. "He has to act bad because it is the only way he knows of subduing a recurrent, guilty voice which keeps saying over and over 'you've been bad from the beginning, and you will have to suffer the consequences of being bad.' " Airing these feelings in a group of men who suffer from the same repressions, the individual may begin to see where his errors and true weaknesses lie.

No inmate at Waupun is forced to take treatment. A new group, consisting usually of eight members and representing a variety of offenses, is brought together as a result of requests for help from the members.

> On entering the group, each new individual is asked to explain what it is he is looking for. This he does in the light of his own experience and personal biases. Sensitive areas in his make-up are brought under focus through comments of other group members, all of whom are agreed that progress depends upon getting at these sore spots. Each is made very definitely aware that it is not a reasonable explanation so much as a resolution of feeling that we are driving toward.

Putting up each man in turn for intensive quizzing by the group is called the "hot seat" technique, though Dr. Uehling says that the group reaches a point where the members wait eagerly for their turn. The special, upholstered chair as the "hot seat" was a recent innovation. Dr. Uehling believes that it increases both the ability of the temporary occupier to take the needling and the depth of his penetration into his problem.

The technique of focusing attention on each group member in turn arose out of the small rapist group, previously mentioned. The four men in this group had been diagnosed as dangerously assaultive. Before the group was formed, all had had many hours of individual therapy, extending over a period of from five to ten years in different cases. Three had been deemed sufficiently improved to be paroled, then had been returned to the prison because of new sex crimes, following the same pattern as their original ones (in marked contrast to the repeater record of most of the deviates who have been released on parole). Their I.Q.'s ranged from good-average to superior, and they had used their intelligence to cover up their emotional problems.

They admitted later that they had held back from their therapists their fantasies and compulsive urges, some of which were definitely sadistic, and had deliberately given a false impression of insight, adjustment and conformity (the trait of serious sex offenders, as has been noted before, which often deludes lay officials and parole board members). They had learned to display a keen intellectual insight while at the same time solidifying their defenses against genuine emotional release.

When the four were formed into a group, they began to gain an awareness of each other's emotional difficulties, and the deep fear each one had of exposing the vulnerable core in his personality make-up. This led to emotional release, and at one point the emotions reached such a violent pitch that the group was on the point of breaking up. A member, in desperation, suggested that they work on one group member at a time. The others agreed. Under the merciless interrogation of the other three, each man at length disclosed the shameful and painful incidents he had hitherto concealed.

Two members of this group were among the men I interviewed privately and whose stories will be told in Part V. Eddie had been paroled and had committed another rape soon after he was released. He told me it was not until he had been returned to the prison and placed in the rapist group that he had realized there was anything the matter with him. "That was when I began to see where my thinking was wrong. That's when the change began."

Phil had been paroled twice and both times had committed further rapes which sent him back to prison. He did not feel that the therapy given him had had any effect until the other three group members had pinned him down by their questioning. "You see, you hide behind your defenses. But those guys are plenty smart. They keep after you until they've backed you into a corner and there's no place else for you to go. They never quit till all your defenses are torn down."

(Sex offenders at California's Atascadero State Hospital also help in the treatment of fellow patients but in a different way, as we shall see.)

The technique has been found helpful in other therapy groups, where men are less seriously disturbed, as I saw for myself in the larger, mixed group I have just been describing. Its members obviously were getting more insight into their own situations as they probed for one another's hidden motivations, and most were accepting responsibility for their acts. Dr. Pacht feels this is an important factor toward cure.

"It's true that the fault isn't entirely theirs, by any means. But they are grown men, and they know the difference between right and wrong. It is a decided step toward maturity when they accept the blame for their own wrong-doing."

But insight, alone, is not enough. The next step is to bring into the open the deep hostilities which characterize these men, so they can be dealt with, too. "When we get into that, the sessions can be very lively," I was told. "It takes a lot of skill for the therapist to keep control when from eight to ten men are mad enough to fight, maybe to kill each other."

(Eddie told me how furious the other members of his rapist group had made him. "One time I was about to shy an ash tray at a guy." He had had to be restrained forcibly.)

It is these hostilities, of which the men themselves are often unconscious, which impel them to make innocent persons the scapegoats for the wrong they have suffered in childhood. Until the hostilities are conquered, there can be no assurance that they will not commit the same crimes again, if released into the community.

Another therapy group that I sat in on, also made up of different types of offenders but most of them older men, did not attack as the young men had done and did not display a comparable flexibility. This may have been because these men had heavier matters on their minds. Most were heads of households, and they had failed their families. Children as well as wives were having to share the penalty for their misdeeds. Two fathers who had committed incest were up for parole in the near future. Nearly the whole discussion centered on the way they should conduct themselves when they returned home, and what the attitude toward them of family and friends was likely to be.

One of the two started things off by asking the advice of the rest about this. He was assured of a welcome from his wife, he said. He could show letters from her to prove it. But what about the daughter with whom he had been intimate? Would she hold his misdeed over him as a club?

The question the other man asked was what the father's attitude toward the violated daughter should be. "Can you treat her like a daughter?" He asked a third man who had been convicted of incest how *he* would act if he saw *his* daughter. "I feel awful sorry for her," was the emphatic, almost explosive, reply.

Another group member, who had debauched a neighbor's child, wondered if he would be viewed with suspicion if he were left alone in a room with a young girl. What ought he to do in such circumstances?

The big trouble in his own case, still another group member offered, was that a wall had existed between himself and his wife. "We couldn't talk to each other—she's been mad at me for eighteen years. And no wonder. I was drinking and running around with women." It evidently meant a great deal to several of the men that their wives had indicated they were anxious for them to return home.

The consensus of the group was that, when released, they should act in a way to give their families and communities confidence in them. "There couldn't nobody have any confidence in me, the way I was in the past," one said, but recognized that it would be up to him in the future.

Others expressed a fear that drink would be a problem again—it appeared to have been a factor with many in this group. "It's going to take years for things to get back to normal," one said, and another voiced his conviction that "They will never be normal again in my case."

But they all jumped on a group member who declared he would be at Waupun for the rest of his life and asked, "Anyway, what is there for me on the street?"

"It's up to you what you make on the street," one after another declared. The one who said his relationship with his wife would never be normal again was assured, "It will be if she loves you."

The advice the group offered for keeping out of further sex trouble was, "Get that part out of your mind. Don't think about those things and you won't do them."

While the topics discussed by the older therapy group did not offer the wide scope of the younger one, they did provide insight into the problems of the kind of father who helps develop sex hostilities in his children. In fact, the descriptions several members gave of themselves fitted the majority of the fathers of the sex deviates. These men are badly needed by their families as wage earners. If they can be returned to society more adequate as husbands and fathers, strong enough to resist drink and their aberrant impulses, they will much more than repay to society the cost of their special treatment.

Not all the therapy groups are of the same caliber as the ones I visited. Some are little more than teaching groups, for individuals who do not have the mentality to respond to a psychiatric approach. A few of the deviates are regarded mainly as custodial cases, probably never to be released.

Whatever the deviate's personality and capacity, however, he receives attention from the psychiatric staff. "We try some kind of treatment with everybody," said Dr. Pacht. "We are constantly revising our treatment methods, as we gain experience. Maybe someday we'll find a way to reach the cases that seem hopeless now."

How well has the professional staff of the program discharged the responsibility Dr. Benjamin Glover spoke of for guarding the "slowly won steps" toward medical control over scientific matters?

I found the heads of the Wisconsin State Department of Welfare and the scientists they employ to be deeply conscious of the great power over the lives of men placed in their hands by the Wisconsin Sex Crimes Law. The law itself protects the deviate by making mandatory a review of his case at the end of a year after his re-commitment and every year thereafter. This assures that no man will "get lost." A review may be had at any time within the yearly period on the request of a therapist and the concurrence of the staff. A deviate can be paroled at any time after his re-commitment that the scientific staff and the Special Review Board, set up to pass on deviates, are satisfied he is capable of making an acceptable adjustment to society.

The law protects society by allowing the Department to ask for a five-year extension of its custody if it believes a man is still dangerous when he has served the sentence that would have been imposed for his crime under the Criminal Code and would otherwise be discharged, and to repeat this request for extension of custody as long as the man is considered a bad risk, thus having the effect of an indeterminate sentence. The key word here is "dangerous." The Department sometimes discharges men before they are considered to be completely cured because it is unable to show that they would constitute a danger to the public, even though they might subsequently make nuisances of themselves (by nonassaultive and nonviolent behavior such as exhibitionism or Peeping Tom-ism). A considerable proportion of the new offenses committed by men who have been discharged from the Facility have been of the "nuisance" nature.

As has been proved repeatedly, however, the value to society of a law depends entirely on the way it is carried out, and I was impressed by the scrupulous attention the Department officials pay to both aspects of their "two-pronged" responsibility—the protection of society and the rehabilitation, insofar as this is possible, of the men placed in their keeping. Decisions about parole are especially delicate. "There is a point at which a particular man may be ready to take his place in society," Dr. Pacht said. "He may have received as much benefit as he can from an institution. To keep him longer damages society in the long run, but society can be damaged if he is released too soon. The timing is tremendously important."

When the program was started, men were paroled on the say-so of one psychiatrist. The average stay in the Facility was around ten months, and the repeater rate was spectacularly low. But the problem with the sex offender, motivated as he is by subconscious forces, is to determine the point when he will be able to maintain his equilibrium through unusual strains and stresses that may occur at some future time. Now an elaborate system of checks and counter-checks has been developed, to return rehabilitated men to society, on the one hand, and on the other to keep deviates under treatment until they are strong enough to stand up under the inevitable ills of life.

Before a man is paroled or discharged, another investigation is conducted in the field, similar to the one made before sentencing. The attitude toward the man of family members, neighbors, the community in general is ascertained; the job situation in his home town is explored. It is sometimes found that the deviate has been deceived about the willingness of his family, or his townspeople, to take him back. In these cases, it may be considered advisable for him to start out in another locality.

A report is obtained from the prison authorities with regard to his acceptance of prison routines and his work record; an evaluation is made of the progress he has shown under psychiatric treatment. The man then goes before the scientific staff, and is subjected to rigorous questioning about his crime and his present attitudes, and finally before the Special Review Board, which puts the man through another searching interrogation. This board, composed of a social worker, a psychiatrist and a lawyer, and entirely separate from the Parole Board which passes on general offenders, then makes a recommendation to the Department, which is acted upon except in highly unusual cases.

"The Review Board is composed of top-notch people," Dr. Pacht said. "We of the staff don't even make a recommendation to them any more, just a report on the progress we feel a candidate has made since the last review of his case. They don't always agree with us that a man is ready for release, and we are glad to have our findings checked by an independent judgment."

The session the deviate holds with the staff is called a "staffing," and staffings are held on every convicted serious sex offender before the pre-sentence diagnosis is made, before discharge, and at any time a therapist requests one for a man he is treating. In many, but not all, cases, staffings are also held before each yearly review of an offender's case and before parole. "To hold a staffing before every review and every parole is a goal toward which we are striving," Dr. Pacht said.

I attended a staffing that was held at the request of one of the therapists. The central problem of the individual to be interrogated, so acute as to approach paranoia, had been a tremendous hostility toward authority. He had six children, and his committal to prison had left his wife with no means of support. The therapist had learned that the man was nearly insane from worry about his family's security. Arrangement was made for welfare payments to his wife, whereupon the man had calmed down and his hostility had abated. The therapist thought he had improved enough to warrant a review of his case.

The staffing was held in the same large conference room—there are several in the Facility—in which the therapy group of younger men had met. This time the entire scientific staff of the prison was assembled about the table, and Dr. Seymour Halleck, the Department's chief psychiatric consultant, and Dr. Pacht, head of Clinical Services, were present. On occasion, as many as fifteen experts may attend a staffing. The questioning was conducted mainly by Dr. Halleck.

The candidate, a man in his late thirties whom I shall call Mark, greeted the group rather familiarly and appeared extremely composed. When asked about his crimes, he went back to the time when his relationship with his wife had first begun to deteriorate. "I was afraid of my family going into the same situation of quarreling and fighting that I had seen in my home in childhood." He felt sexually inadequate with his wife and would have consulted a psychiatrist, except for a fear that someone who knew him would see him coming out of the psychiatrist's office. The bickering at home increased; finally he began consorting with other women "to prove something to myself."

About this time he suffered a big financial loss, which did not help his home situation. "It began bothering me a lot when I heard the men I worked with talking about easy women. Sex had been a dirty subject all through my childhood. I hated women when they behaved toward me in a loose way." He stressed his resentment against women in general, and loose ones in particular.

When Dr. Halleck asked him for his opinion of the way women regard sex, Mark replied that he supposed they were not as aggressive as men and probably were more frigid. Nevertheless, in the crimes of which he had been convicted—attempted rape of women who were strangers to him—he accused the women of very blatant sexual overtures toward him, which, he said, had disgusted him and had ended the whole thing, so far as he was concerned. This in spite of the fact that the victims, in widely separated locations, had reported that he had used with all the same *modus operandi* for gaining entrance to their homes.

He diagnosed his trouble as hysteria. "My biggest failure was getting in a state of confusion. I would work too hard and burn the candle at both ends. I have learned a good lesson, to be more patient."

The staff, however, concluded that the man was dangerous. They considered that his demeanor had been too cool, under the circumstances, and that his transference of all blame to his victims was an unhealthy symptom. There were other, subtler signs which spoke to the experts of a badly disorganized personality.

"We assume that the men have committed the crimes of which they have been convicted," Dr. Pacht told me afterwards, "since all have been tried and found guilty. However, we don't pay as much attention to the crime as to the personality the man reveals. Even if Mark did not commit the crimes he was charged with, I believe every staff member would agree that he has a potentiality for violent, aggressive behavior, and that it is not safe for him to be at large."

Periodic psychiatric examinations of deviates out on parole or discharge are not mandatory under the Wisconsin law. "They aren't needed, because of our excellent parole system," Dr. Pacht said. "A parole officer can always request a psychiatric examination for a parolee, if he appears to be slipping, and a parolee can always have one by his own request. Men who have been discharged can always come back to us for further help."

This is the one point upon which the admirable Wisconsin system might be open to challenge. Would a parole officer, who lacks the intensive training of a psychiatrist, be able always to detect early signs of disturbance? I asked about this.

"Not *always*," Dr. Pacht replied, emphasizing the adverb, "but the same thing would be true of psychiatrists and psychologists. Our parole officers are trained and experienced clinical workers—the majority are trained social workers—who are skilled in their ability to respond to very slight clues. They see the man in his milieu over a period of time, which is probably far more meaningful than a brief office examination by a member of our staff."

Parole lasts as long as the time remaining from the sentence a man would have been given for his crime under the Criminal Code, and the men are under the supervision of Department field workers during this period. The latest figures obtainable at time of writing (for January 29, 1963) show that, since the program was started in 1951, 684 deviates have been paroled from the Facility. One hundred thirty-three of these have violated their paroles for a total of 152 times. Most of the men have been returned because they broke some provision of their parole, however, not for new sex offenses. Of those released to date from the institution on parole, less than 11 per cent (10.4 per cent to be exact) were returned because of further involvement in sex offenses, while the repeater rate of general offenders runs between 40 and 50 per cent. (You may recall, too, that 40 per cent of the sex offenders had served sentences before they were re-committed to the Facility.)

"When it comes to parole, we have to make an educated guess, and as the number of deviates under treatment increases we're bound to make more bad guesses," Dr. Pacht said. It seemed to me, however, that—short of keeping in prison, for the rest of his life, every man convicted of a serious sex offense, which would be both uneconomical and unjust—the Wisconsin system, when carried out with the thoroughness and dedication I witnessed, guards against error about as far as is humanly possible.

How have the courts reacted? They have cooperated marvelously, I learned.

By January of 1963, after the program had been in effect for eleven years and six months, 2158 individuals had been examined in the Facility in the 60-day observation period called for by the law before sentencing. Of the 1119 already mentioned who were found to be in need of specialized treatment, the courts re-committed 889 to the Department. (Compare this with the number of men given the indeterminate sentence by the courts of New York State since it was made available in 1950.) They placed 219 on probation, plus out-patient psychiatric treatment, and one individual was placed on probation with in-patient treatment (in an institution other than the Facility at Waupun). (The disposition of the remaining 12 was not specified.) The Department had gone before the committing courts 89 times to ask for an extension of sentence; it had been granted in 86 cases.

Members of the scientific staff make frequent appearances before groups of court officials and law enforcement officers. "They are eager to have a better understanding of the problems of the deviates. We give talks to civic groups as well. We consider this an important part of our job," said Dr. Pacht. Deputies and prison guards are invited to attend staff meetings. "Many judges have expressed regret that they can't commit 'permissive' cases to us in the same way as the serious sex offenders," Dr. Pacht continued.

By permissive cases, he referred to nonviolent sex crimes, such as exhibitionism and Peeping Tom-ism, and crimes such as arson, which are believed to be sex related. They are called permissive because, in this area, the court may use its discretion about their disposal. The Sex Crimes Law provides that courts *may* refer such cases to the Department, provided the Department will certify that it has the facilities to handle them and is willing to take them. In the early days of the program, about one half of the cases referred to the Department were of this nature.

"In recent years, however, our case load of serious sex offenders has grown so that we don't have the staff or room in the prison to provide adequate treatment for the others," Dr. Pacht said. "We wish we did. While it is generally considered that the exhibitionist does not commit violent crimes, a number of sadistic sex murderers have been exhibitionists too. Peeping Toms are not thought to be a menace. But when a man is caught looking through a window, how can one be sure whether he is interested only in peeping or is planning to enter and attack someone?"

The number of serious sex offenders at Waupun has grown from 11, when the program started in 1951, to 246, at the time of my visit, comprising one fourth of the entire prison population. The professional staff consists of a full-time psychiatrist, eight psychiatric consultants, one neurological consultant; two and one half full-time psychologists (one man divides his time with the probation and parole unit), two psychological consultants and two clinical social workers. In addition, the Facility has psychology and social work trainees. But there are vacancies in each of the disciplines which make up the Waupun staff.

"We are operating on a bare minimum in the Sex Deviate Facility. If we were to lose one clinical psychologist, our work would be seriously handicapped. It would not be fair to the patients or the Wisconsin public to take on more people than we can treat adequately," Dr. Pacht explained. "Our citizens assume that the men placed under our charge are getting the best therapy it is in our power to provide. We have to keep faith with them."

And how do the deviates themselves regard the system?

"You will probably hear some pretty vigorous criticism from the men," I was told, in connection with the individual interviews. However, the ones with whom I talked privately had little fault to find. One, who had occupied a position of some prominence in his community, spoke with feeling of his humiliation when the story of his arrest broke in the local papers. "I couldn't find weeds high enough to hide in. Such a disgrace—that's the thing that shatters you. Such a damnable trick to play on your family." This man said that his first few months in prison had been a nightmare. "Things were so different—my assignments, everything. I couldn't understand it. It was like a hell on earth. After that, though, I found I was treated the way I wanted to be treated." He believed he had benefited from the therapy.

In the therapy groups, the ignominy of being a "blue-bander" was mentioned in passing but shrugged off as though it had not been of great moment, as was also the name the deviates are given by the other inmates, which is "baby rapers." But none who talked with me seemed to feel they had been discriminated against in the prison.

"Some of the other inmates look down on you, sure, but there's always some people that like to look down on somebody. Most treat you just like you were anybody else."

One man whom I interviewed privately wanted to talk on and on. "There are so many things I'd like to talk about to somebody. That's the big trouble here. You think of things between the group therapy sessions, and you'd like to talk them over with someone, but you can't."

"Aren't there other men in your therapy group you could talk to?" I asked.

"Yes, but in prison there are ears everywhere. If the other inmates find out what you've done, they can make life pretty miserable for you." This man had committed offenses against children, considered in prison circles to be the most reprehensible crime, whether sexual or general. I learned that his statement was quite true.

In the therapy groups, however, there is no holding back with regard to what the members had done, and several of the men spoke enthusiastically about their groups. Mark was the only deviate I encountered at Waupun who denied his crimes and, aside from Ernie, the only one who tried to put the blame for his troubles on his victims. But to have their crimes broadcast throughout a prison is something about which the deviates are understandably sensitive.

One man complained because the deviates had not been given the new prison at Fox Lake, Wisconsin, a halfway house between the maximum security institutions and the outside world. Its general plan, in which gaily painted dormitories are scattered widely over a beautifully landscaped area, surrounded only by a wire fence, has already been followed in a federal prison in Illinois, down to the same round chapel with rich stained-glass windows and a reversible altar which can make it appropriate for a Roman Catholic, Protestant or Jewish service in a matter of minutes. The Fox Lake warden, John Gagnon, a dynamic man bursting with energy and ideas, is full of plans for preparing prisoners to become free men: one more first in Wisconsin's long record of pace-setting in social matters.

However, it was not so much the physical contrast with Waupun's high stone walls and cell blocks this deviate was thinking about as the fact that one cannot question any orders given in a regular prison. He felt that many deviates had suffered from an inability to express the resentments that boiled within them. Hence, these built up and exploded in aggressive acts against people who had done nothing to provoke them.

"We need to learn to stand up to people, tell them to their faces when we think they aren't doing the right thing by us. You can't do that with a prison guard. If we think an order isn't fair, we have to bottle up our resentment, the way we always have."

It is my understanding that the new institution for deviates will be medium security, like the one at Fox Lake, and the atmosphere will be more that of a hospital than a prison, like the institution for sex offenders in California, which will be described next.

All in all, it appeared to me that the disadvantages of having a special sex offender unit in a general prison were more from the standpoint of the prison than of the sex offenders, when the deviates are given the attention they need, as is done at Waupun. The therapy sessions cut into the prison work schedules. Comprising one fourth of the prison population, the deviates get 95 per cent of the psychiatric care. The Department would like to do much more for the general offenders, but cannot and still carry out its special obligation to the deviates.

It is undeniable, however, that rehabilitation might be speeded up considerably if the men were free to continue their discussions outside of their therapy groups. Also, types of treatment can be tried in a special institution which are not feasible in a prison environment. (We will see examples in the next two chapters.) In the long run, this would be a saving to the taxpayers and a benefit to society. The Wisconsin authorities look forward to much more rapid progress in therapy when they move into the special institution for sex offenders that the state is planning to build.

But Wisconsin has proved that it is not necessary to wait for the ideal situation before attacking the problem. Since 1951, many sex offenders have been rehabilitated in Waupun Prison, simply through the addition of an adequate staff of trained personnel, who have been learning as they went along. Any state in the union with a high-security institution could adopt this system tomorrow, with the advantage of Wisconsin's experience to draw on. The only added expense would be the salaries of the experts—a drop in the bucket when compared with the cost to society of turning violent, sexually dangerous men loose into the community after they have served their limited sentences.

# 16

# California's hospital for sex offenders— an adventure in therapy

While Wisconsin was the first state to begin intensive therapy of serious sex offenders, California was the first to set up a special and separate treatment institution for these men, after an investigation of the sex offender problem by San Francisco's famous Langley Porter Clinic. At time of writing, California's separate institution is still the only one that has been in operation long enough for its efficacy to be estimated. (The only other special institution for sex offenders, at Bridgewater, Massachusetts, was established fairly recently. As yet it has no conclusions to report.)

The California institution has to cope with the sex-crime problems of a big state, with big-city conditions and a considerable proportion of savage, brutal crimes, of a type not commonly encountered in Wisconsin. Moreover, the Wisconsin law, you may remember, bars murderers from the sex offender program, and insane offenders are sent to a state mental hospital. The California law bars no type of dangerous man from Atascadero State Hospital.

This institution has a certain long corridor which I traversed many times. Dr. G. Lee Sandritter, the present superintendent and medical director, told me that out of the 1000 or so patients whom I might meet in this corridor, 100 would have killed, another 100 would be there for violently assaultive crimes.

Nor is this all. California had never had a hospital for the criminally insane. When the law was passed which authorized the new sex offender treatment center, the criminally insane were included and also mental patients from other state hospitals who were considered to be major risks, either because of assaultive tendencies or because of a propensity to run away.

Whether or not the legislators were aware of the problem they were creating for the administrators of the new institution I do not know, but it was a formidable one. We have seen that the great majority of sex offenders are not insane or "mental" cases in either a legal or medical sense. As has also been mentioned, one of the blocks to treating sexually sick men and boys has been that the mental hospitals usually don't want them, deeming that entirely different methods are required for the insane and for the neurotic or immature. Few prisons offer psychiatric treatment intensive enough to be effective. At Atascadero, the only measuring stick would be whether or not the offenders presented a menace—a word later changed to danger—and whether or not they were amenable to treatment.

That is another difference between the California and Wisconsin systems. In Wisconsin, the Department of Public Welfare must take the responsibility for all the sex offenders who have been diagnosed as sexually deviated, whether or not they are considered to be capable of ever taking their place in society again. The California institution, under the law, need not accept sex offenders considered incapable of rehabilitation. But because of the assemblage under one roof of so many men who are dangerous for one reason or another, the staff must be responsible for security, taken care of automatically in Wisconsin at present by the high stone walls of Waupun Prison.

However, the California Department of Mental Hygiene, which was given jurisdiction over the new institution, accepted the challenge, and much time and thought went into planning. Six years before the institution opened its doors, the psychiatrist chosen to head it began visits to many institutions in the west and southwest, getting ideas for a design which would provide security while avoiding prisonlike features.

The site chosen is a tract of 1,162 acres astride the Salinas River, three miles from the town of Atascadero and about midway between San Francisco and Los Angeles. Named officially The Atascadero

State Hospital for the Mentally Ill Offender, but usually called just Atascadero State Hospital, the structure has no guard towers or cell blocks. At the present time the outer walls are painted in a variety of pleasing pastel shades. You walk past luxuriantly blooming flowers, to the big glass doors, and into a wide entrance hall which looks out on an inner patio, with a fountain and small pool. A reception desk is on your left, the administrative offices and executive conference room open off a hall to your right. When I was there, a patient was stationed beside the front door with a display of automobile seat belts in different colors. Selling the seat belts to visitors was a patient project, the man in charge reporting proudly that already they had sold twice as many as they had expected to.

The hospital proper, which you enter from the reception hall through a series of electrically controlled doors called the sally port (an officer in a barred cage must press a button before each door can be opened), is composed of separate though adjacent buildings. There are a number of courtyards, enclosed by the buildings, the whole giving the effect of a single very large edifice, with the buildings performing the function of outer protective walls. Easy access to the sections used most is provided by two long corridors, situated at right angles to each other.

The twenty-eight wards, containing anywhere from forty-five to seventy-five patients—the men here are never called inmates—are separate, self-contained units. Each one has a big lounge, usually looking out on a courtyard, with a small, barred-off office for personnel as you enter. The sleeping quarters consist of small individual bedrooms, each equipped with plumbing, ranged on either side of a long hall running off the lounge.

The lounges have various dispensing machines—for soft drinks, cigarettes and the like—and every ward has a television set and a coffee-making apparatus. I arrived on a holiday, when the usual hospital activities were largely suspended. Men were playing cards or watching television or stretched out on the cots at one end of the lounge of a ward I visited, evidence of the overcrowding at Atascadero, as at most other public institutions. Most, but not all, were wearing the khaki shirt and trousers provided by the state. A patient explained that they could wear their own clothing if they wished, and that most of the men liked to dress up for special occasions such as church, entertainments and visiting days.

At the time of my visit, a repainting job of the entire hospital, inside as well as out, was nearing completion. The drab "institution green" of the wards and halls had been replaced by gay, warm tints. The men had been allowed to choose the colors for their bedroom doors, and the halls running off the lounges presented a rainbow effect. Patients were being identified as "the guy with the green door" or the yellow or purple one, and they liked that.

The huge building was ready for patients in June of 1954, and at first all seemed to go well, in spite of the heterogeneous nature of the patient body and the complications incident to the different types of committal. Perhaps we should pause here and describe these matters in more detail.

First, the California courts are empowered to send to Atascadero, for observation and diagnosis, sex offenders, sexual psychopaths and other offenders whose mental condition makes them appear to be dangerous to themselves or to the community, though this is not a must, as in Wisconsin. In this system, a sexual psychopath is defined as a person who has been convicted of a sex offense or who has committed other offenses and is found to have tendencies to commit sex offenses. "It is established that there seems to be a pattern of deviant behavior which is a danger to the health and welfare of society." The term "sexual psychopath" in the law has been changed to "mentally disordered sex offender," but the patients continue to refer to themselves mainly as sexual psychopaths, and I shall use the original term for the sake of convenience. California has the indeterminate sentence, from one day to life, which permits retaining these men in custody as long as they are considered to be dangerous. The majority of the patients in Atascadero fall in this group, consisting, in July, 1963, of 859 men.

Second, there are the individuals designated in the law as "mentally abnormal sex offenders," called Masos in the hospital. These men are self-committed, under a special provision of the law. Any man may appeal to a superior court for hospital treatment. He must be found by the court to be a person "likely to be a danger to the health and safety of others," and must be released at the end of a two-year treatment period. In July of 1963 there were forty-two Masos at Atascadero.

Third, the courts send to Atascadero individuals found not guilty of crimes by reason of insanity at the time the crime was committed; and, fourth, those found too disturbed mentally to stand trial for crimes they had previously committed. In July of 1963, these two groups of the criminally insane together numbered 425.

After a 90-day period of observation, psychiatric examination and tests, the patients referred by the courts are returned to the committing court with a recommendation. Around one half of those sent for observation are found not amenable to treatment—the same proportion of untreatables found in the first study of sex offenders in Sing Sing—and the hospital recommends that they be placed in other California institutions. This would mean jail or prison for the untreatable sexual psychopaths.

Those considered amenable to treatment are reported to the court with a recommendation that they be re-committed to Atascadero State Hospital, there to stay until the doctors believe it is safe for them to be released into the community.

Usually the courts follow the hospital's recommendation, but not always. I sat in on a staffing of one man who, sent to Atascadero for observation under the sexual psychopath law, had been returned to the court with a statement that he was completely anti-social and untreatable and a recommendation that he be sent to another institution. Nevertheless, the court returned him to Atascadero.

The man had a long record of offenses, both general and against children. Twenty years previously he had been sent to prison for kidnapping and raping a 5-year-old girl. She had had to have eight stitches. That was before the indeterminate sentence was put on the California books, and after he was released he had served prison terms for burglary and drunk driving. His most recent offense had been procuring two little girls for another man—he was paid $20 for each child—and joining with the other man in rape attempts on both girls.

"He is a con artist of the first order," I was told. "He hasn't the slightest intention of changing his ways. What he does in therapy sounds good, but he is not talking about his real offenses. He describes something that is bad enough, but not nearly as bad as what he has done.

"We consider him a potential murderer. Certainly his pattern of continued savage offenses against children marks him as highly dangerous, because you never know how far those men will go."

After this build-up, I looked at the patient when he entered with special interest. He was a tall man of around 50, somewhat stooped and with what I took to be a prison pallor. The man admitted that he had molested his stepdaughter—he did not mention the procurement and attempted rape of the other little girls. "But I would like to say that before I did this I knew I needed some kind of help but didn't know where to get it. I knew I had to have a certain attitude toward society, but couldn't get hold of it."

The psychiatrist who conducted the examination said frankly what his recommendation would be—that the man was dangerous to little girls.

The patient looked at him wonderingly. "You think I'm *dangerous?*"

"Very dangerous."

The man nodded his head, as in acceptance of one more blow from an unkind fate, and said lugubriously, "I thought I had made a good deal of improvement. I can't see myself as you see me, that's for sure. And I try to see myself as others see me, too."

The two doctors who conducted the staffing—the assistant superintendent of the hospital and the man's own doctor—explained to me, "We won't get anywhere with this man as long as he retains these attitudes."

Suppose Emmett Hashfield had been required to run successfully a gantlet of this kind before he could be freed into the community, and *before* he had killed a child!

Speaking of offenders they consider untreatable, Dr. Sandritter told me, "Those fellows would be taking up the room here of a man we might be able to rehabilitate completely. If we have diagnosed them as sexual psychopaths, they have to stay in prison, under the indeterminate sentence. But eventually such a man might decide he wanted to be cured and be willing to cooperate. Then he would be returned here. If the time came when we felt he had gained sufficient control to be released, he could be released, the committing court consenting."

Contrasted with the foregoing patient was a youth of barely twenty, who had been recommended for recommitment to Atascadero as treatable, though he had escaped being a sex murderer only by the grace of God. He had preyed upon early teen-age boys and had conceived the theory that, while a boy walking along the street by himself would probably be hostile to homosexual solicitation, two boys walking together might have a homosexual bent and be more amenable. He carried his theory further. If he were to kill one of the two boys, he thought, the survivor would be more amenable still. He stocked his car with a variety of weapons, picked up two boys, drove to a lonely spot, stabbed one and tried, fortunately unsuccessfully, to finish him off by hitting him on the head with a hammer. Then he molested both boys.

Barbaric and irrational as this crime was, the hospital doctors believed there was hope for the perpetrator. "He has been here for two years. He will probably have to be here five years, maybe seven years, more. But he is trying."

A great virtue of the systems in both Wisconsin and California is that they enable intensive treatment to be applied when an offender with a potential for danger first comes to the attention of the law. After thirty years in and out of prisons, this young chap would probably be as impervious to treatment as the older rapist of little girls is now, and might well have succeeded in later murder attempts.

There is still another group, the mentally ill, mostly transferred from other California mental hospitals for security reasons. The California code defines a mentally ill person as one who is either (a) of such mental condition that he is in need of supervision, treatment, care or restraint, or (b) of such mental condition that he is dangerous to himself or the persons or property of others and is in need of supervision, treatment, care or restraint. This law permits other California mental hospitals to send their more difficult and dangerous patients to Atascadero, to stay as long as the staff deems necessary. In July, 1963, the mentally ill group comprised 264.

Let us go back now to the late 1950's and see what happened after the hospital's auspicious start. For the beginning could hardly have been more successful, to outward appearance.

The magazine *Federal Probation* for March, 1958, contains a report by Louise Viets Frisbie, a psychiatric social worker, on the results up to that time.

The first period covered was the thirty months from September 1, 1954 (the date the hospital opened) to March 31, 1957. During these two and one half years, of the 1414 sexual psychopaths held for treatment (almost exactly half the number admitted for observation), 902, or about 64 per cent, had been discharged from the hospital with a recommendation to the committing court that they would not benefit from further care and treatment and were not a menace to the health and safety of others.

Criminal proceedings were then reinstituted. However, superior court judges have for the most part granted probation upon a favorable recommendation from the hospital superintendent, unless limited by law. For instance, figures from a three-month-shorter period—shortened to permit a sufficient lapse of time for a significant showing of repeaters—to December 31, 1956, showed that, of the 782 sex offenders discharged to that date with a favorable recommendation, 686, or 87.7 per cent, had been released on probation. (Of the remaining 96, 67 went to state prison, 23 to the county jail, 2 to the State Hospital for the Mentally Ill, 2 were deported and 2 had died.)

Fifteen months later, by March, 1958, 52 of the 686 probationers had been arrested on new sex offense charges (in 50 per cent of these, no physical menace was involved), or a known repeater rate of 7.58 per cent, which is a very low rate indeed, in view of the fact that 43 of the 52 repeaters had had prior convictions.

The hospital had tried to keep track of the 902 discharged in the thirty-month period, and only 17 had been lost sight of when this report appeared. (A feature of the California law is that a discharged sex offender must register with the police chief of a California town or the sheriff of a county when he moves from one community to another.)

Marital status remained unchanged in all but 10 per cent of the cases, and the men seemed to have no trouble in finding work. The one remark appearing over and over in communications from former patients was a wish that they could have had the hospital treatment earlier. They felt that it would have prevented their crimes.

Significantly, no report on the work at Atascadero State Hospital appeared in a professional journal after Louise Frisbie's in 1958. For there was trouble in the hospital, and staff members have been too busy repairing it ever since to engage in outside writing. There had been difficulties, not unexpectedly, from the beginning. The surrounding communities were apprehensive. The new concept of therapy within a maximum security setting was confusing to many staff members, unable to decide whether they were working in a hospital or a prison. Was treatment the main thing, or security? Were the patients criminals who had preyed on society and should be punished, or victims of society who should be babied?

A progress report issued to California officials in 1962 says:

> There were local empires in the hospital. Many of the employees in one department felt that employees in another department were uncooperative and did not know the "right way" to go about treating the patients. Complicating this was the walk-aways of sexual psychopaths with ground privileges, and break-outs of patients from the security area. There was an average of fifteen absences-without-leave a year.
>
> Starting early in 1959, there was a series of unfortunate incidents—escapes, violent death of an employee, etc.—which resulted in an almost complete deterioration of morale and loss of confidence by the press, the public, the employees and the patients.

When the present superintendent, Dr. G. Lee Sandritter, took over in March of 1961, he found things in about as poor a shape as they could very well be. The first superintendent had left in 1960, and in the intervening year there had been two temporary superintendents. They had succeeded in holding things together, and some of the more dissident staff members had left. However, a number of the remaining employees were "disgruntled, unhappy and had axes to grind. The public, the employee and the patient morale was bad and all were at cross purposes."

Dr. Sandritter's first task was to win the support of the employees to a concept of treatment within a security framework, in which there would be no conflict between the two objectives. During a two weeks "get-acquainted" period, he familiarized himself with the hospital— the various departments, treatment methods and employees—and also made contacts with local citizens and citizen groups.

On April 1, 1961, he began the work of setting up aims for the hospital and a program for carrying them out, and, what was much more difficult, persuading the different departments and employees not only to accept them but to enter into them wholeheartedly. An Operations Manual was started, which set forth policies clearly, and lines of communication were set up between the different administrative groups.

May and June of 1961 were stormy months, as Dr. Sandritter endeavored to reorient the medical staff. A rump medical organization developed which attempted to seize power and control the hospital.

"Put yourself in my place," Dr. Sandritter said to me, "when, at a meeting of the doctors, I was asked what I would do if the whole medical staff were to resign in a body."

"What did you do?"

"I passed papers around the table, told them to write out their resignations then and there and sign them."

"And did they?"

"Not then. What happened was that most resigned later, one at a time." At present, only three of the original medical staff remain at the hospital.

But May and June also brought much progress in improving relations with the surrounding communities and the public at large. Their panic and indignation were understandable. At Atascadero had been gathered a large aggregation of all the types of offenders most feared by the average citizen—rapists and child molesters, not to speak of murderers, the criminally insane and the mentally disturbed who presented a danger—and they appeared to be out of control. Dr. Sandritter met with many local groups, explaining the hospital goals and assuring members of the community that they and their children would be protected.

In July a policy group was set up, which inside of two months was functioning smoothly and providing leadership to the administrators of the different departments. In this group were threshed out finally the problems of prison versus hospital and therapy versus security.

A year later Dr. Sandritter reported:

> It is slowly dawning on all our employees the fact that this is neither security nor therapy, neither hospital nor prison, but a unique organization and institution dedicated to using the best psychiatric treatment within a security setting in order to return patients as no longer dangerous to the community. With the awareness of the uniqueness of this institution, and as members have used their own creative efforts to accomplish the goals of the hospital, there has come slowly but surely an *esprit de corps* based on mutual appreciation of other members of the team because of the support each individual is getting from the team. [There is still too large an employee turnover, but it is decreasing all the time.]

While all this was going on, Dr. Sandritter was meeting frequently with the Emotional Security Program—referred to hereafter as ESP —the patients' own government, of which more will be said later, to reassure the patients and regain their confidence in the hospital's program. The sexual psychopaths, in particular, had become confused and disheartened by the breakdown in the hospital administration.

First a series of panel discussions was held, at which the patients aired their grievances and problems and Dr. Sandritter admitted administration errors frankly. When these sessions became repetitive and no longer productive, the ESP Council was given the responsibility for setting up a meaningful program for the sessions Dr. Sandritter was holding with all the patients mentally competent enough to attend.

The Council decided upon role playing, and, for the first one, a criminally insane patient was selected to play the part of a recalcitrant sexual psychopath, a child molester, who had resisted treatment to date and was being assigned to a new ward doctor. Dr. Sandritter played the part of the new doctor, with no previous briefing as to what was to occur. The format gave the patient an opportunity to reveal the desires of the patient body for changes in certain policies, and Dr. Sandritter to demonstrate the need for certain policies.

Both participants handled their roles so adroitly that the occasion was deemed highly successful, and two months later another psychodrama was presented for the patient body, with a Maso (self-committed mentally abnormal sex offender) taking the part of a criminally insane patient who had murdered his wife and child, had a history of hallucinations and had lost his memory. Dr. Sandritter played the part of a doctor who had treated the patient for a long time and was conducting a typical individual therapy interview with him.

These presentations were a great help in building better feeling among the different types of patients as well as better understanding of their individual problems. The ESP Council gained confidence from the trust shown in letting it set up the programs, and the patient body was given confidence in the new superintendent because of the competence he had shown in handling his end of the psychodramas. The patients also gained a realization that they could be helped, but only if they worked at it.

A patient with considerable administrative experience before he was committed to Atascadero in 1960 as criminally insane has described the process by which Dr. Sandritter raised the patient morale —after the darkness had lifted from his mind, this man continued to work in the hospital in a number of capacities—and has summed it up this way:

> The author has become convinced from his own experience and from working with many fellow patients that for successful treatment a patient must have two things. First he must have faith in himself so that he has the courage to work at changing his personality to become acceptable to society. Secondly, he must have faith in something more, be it a wife, a doctor, society, or God,

so that working at his personality has meaning. If one of these is obtained, the other can be developed, and the patient will be on the road to recovery.

I believe it is important for the public to know the situation which developed at Atascadero State Hospital through lack, on the part of the staff itself, of understanding of the special task imposed by a special institution of this kind. Similar difficulties may well beset other states which are moved to follow the examples that have been set by California, Wisconsin and Massachusetts, unless they are well warned. The noble California experiment might have failed before it got well started, and have been cited forever more as proof that you cannot treat sexual psychopaths in a hospital setting—the argument, so I am told, that to date has kept my own state, New York, from setting up a special institution for serious sex offenders—if a strong administrator had not entered the picture, to prove that you can.

In the two years after Dr. Sandritter assumed command there were only two walk-aways (in contrast to the fifteen a year which had prevailed before), no break-outs, and no serious "incidents" within the hospital. It is receiving inquiries from other states, interested in setting up similar institutions, and staff members have counseled with these outsiders. The home folks are pleased, as well. During my visit to Atascadero, the California Legislature commended Dr. Sandritter for what he has accomplished. A California editor who had been highly critical of the project admitted that his newspaper had received no letters from indignant readers condemning the hospital since 1961.

More concrete evidence that the special treatment now being accorded sex offenders and the dangerously insane is having an effect is provided by a story from the January 12, 1964, issue of the *San Francisco Examiner*. It reports that, while in San Francisco in 1963 there had been a 16 per cent increase in general crimes over 1962, there had been a decrease in the number of rapes and murders. Forcible rapes had fallen only by 2 per cent, from 221 cases in 1962 to 216 cases in 1963, but murders had dropped by 30 per cent, from 57 in 1962 to 40 in 1963.

The paper did not designate what proportion of the murders in either year had been sex murders. However, I myself saw enough men at Atascadero who were believed to have a potential for killing out of sex hostilities, and who can be held in custody as long as they are considered to be dangerous, to feel reasonably sure that the California system must be playing some part in that 30 per cent decrease.

But more than faith and self-confidence are needed to reconstruct habit and emotional patterns which have been built up over many years. From a numerical standpoint alone, the problem at Atascadero is staggering. With a supposed maximum capacity of 1500, the hospital now must house between 1600 and 1700 patients at any given time. There were around 1650 patients at the time of my visit. It had been expected that an average of 80 new patients would be received each month. The number of new arrivals averages 110 each month and some months goes as high as 150.

"We have to rehabilitate them as quickly as we can," Dr. Sandritter told me—he never uses the word "cure"—"in order to make room for the ones constantly coming in."

Dr. Sandritter reviews around 300 case histories every month. "I don't see all the patients myself, but I pass on every recommendation regarding accepting a patient for treatment or for discharge. The final decision is mine, and I take the responsibility for everything that goes wrong."

The hospital, at the time of my visit, had on its staff 19 doctors of various disciplines—psychiatrists, neurologists and general physicians—out of an authorized 22. There were 7 clinical psychologists, out of an authorized 8; 14 social service workers, all with Master's degrees and all experienced; there were 20 workers in the rehabilitation department, which includes occupational therapy, recreation, arts and crafts; and 43 nurses. Three hundred and seventy technicians complete the therapeutic roster. The remainder of the 685 employees, out of an authorized 705, are administrative personnel, security officers, and maintenance and other workers.

Dr. Sandritter told me, "I have been asked many times where I find replacements when staff members leave; that is to say, where I find men and women with the training needed to carry out so revolutionary a treatment concept. That problem runs through the entire professional personnel—doctors, psychiatrists, social workers, nurses, technicians. I reply that there is no place where I could find such people, for the places do not exist. In such a case, you take the personnel you have and train as you go along.

"As our patient load has increased, we have been meeting the lack of psychiatrists and other highly trained personnel by training more and more people to do things formerly performed by the professional staff."

The technicians, who play a very important part in therapy, are a case in point. In addition to the large group employed in the hospital, there are always from 30 to 50 in training. The only prerequisite is a high school education. Applicants spend a period on probation and, if they pass muster, must complete 300 hours of training within a year after the probationary period has ended. Then they must pass an examination given by a central board not connected with the hospital. When they have completed their course, they can do what a hospital nurse can do after two years of training, though they are not fitted to perform the medical techniques required of a graduate nurse. Their training continues, on the job.

The technicians, working in shifts like the "charges"—the employee in charge of each ward—and nurses, are in close touch with the patients at all hours of the day and night. They observe behavior, besides working with the patients to improve it, and keep the professional staff advised of each patient's progress or lack of it.

As in Wisconsin, everything at Atascadero was thrown open to me, and before I began my explorations Dr. Sandritter gave me a long briefing about the system.

He is a native midwesterner, born in Missouri, raised and educated in Nebraska. He had served in Nebraska institutions, in a variety of medical and administrative capacities, and also in the 147th General Hospital, in the Pacific, during World War II, before accepting an invitation to head Eastland State Hospital in the State of Washington, in 1954. Up to this time, Eastland had merely been a custodial place for the mentally ill. The Washington State Department of Institutions wished to institute treatment, and Dr. Sandritter was charged with setting up a therapy program.

When he arrived at Eastland, he found 170 patients handcuffed to their beds every night, and others locked in their rooms during the day or placed in strait jackets or in cuff or leg restraints and forced to sit all day in one place on the wards. When he left Eastland in early 1961 to become superintendent and medical director of Atascadero State Hospital in California, the only patients restrained to their beds were infirm ones who otherwise might fall and injure themselves. Some twenty thousand dollars' worth of handcuffs, leg irons and strait jackets were no longer needed, and the patient population, which had been 2500 when he went there, had dropped to 1700. It has continued to drop.

I found Dr. Sandritter to be a philosopher as well as a psychiatrist, interested in the whole range of human behavior and with a vast store of knowledge on every conceivable subject. He is a man not easily perturbed, and he heartily approves the gathering of the criminally insane, the mentally disturbed, and the sane but emotionally disturbed under one roof.

"In general hospitals, patients with many different kinds of diseases are treated successfully. That is because the doctors don't treat the disease, they treat the patient. Here, too, we treat the patient. It doesn't matter that our patients suffer from different kinds of disturbances."

There is no segregation according to types of illness. In the ward system set up by Dr. Sandritter, the criminally insane and mentally ill are scattered among the sexual psychopaths and Masos. When the sex offenders first come into the hospital, I was told, they are inclined to look down on the mental cases—a rather pleasant change for them from jails and prisons, where the sex offender is looked down on by everybody. But they soon become sympathetic, and the sane men in the wards are a great help in the treatment of the mentally unbalanced.

On one occasion I sat in the ESP office, talking to two young men, both of them "clean cut" in appearance, intelligent, well bred.

Neither would have seemed out of place in the office of a college publication, let us say. One was an officer of ESP; the other did in fact work on the two publications put out by the patients. One had been a child molester; the other had been transferred to Atascadero from a mental hospital.

"I was arrested for impersonating an officer," the latter told me. "I went into a police station, said I was a plain-clothes man, and asked them to pay for my taxi. I had nothing to gain by it; it was a crazy thing to do. I have thought I did it because I realized that I might do something worse, if I wasn't stopped." He always had warning, he said, of an approaching crisis.

This young man had completed high school by taking correspondence courses, while in a mental hospital, and hoped to be able to go to college after his discharge from Atascadero State Hospital. The child molester had had a year or two of college. Only an expert could have detected any difference between them, or that there was anything the matter with either one. In the wards, there would be a few men whom I took to be psychotics, because of their speech or actions, but everywhere the atmosphere was one of control and co-operation.

"There is no reason why the same thing cannot be done in any mental hospital," Dr. Sandritter said. "These men are all sick in one way or another. Why differentiate?" He hopes, in fact, that the day may come when general offenders, too, will be placed in treatment hospitals instead of prisons—Dr. Bernard C. Glueck, Jr., expressed the same wish to me—though he recognizes that we must have a much larger supply of psychiatrists, clinical psychologists and psychiatric social workers than we have now before it will be practicable.

The professional staff is not large enough to permit as much individual therapy as is given in the Facility at Waupun Prison in Wisconsin—Wisconsin, in fact, has very nearly as large a medical staff for its 240 sex offenders, when one takes the consultants into account, as California has for its nearly 1700 sex offenders and criminally insane and mentally disturbed. The same group therapy program is employed, and there is also a program of discussion groups, headed by technicians, to "loosen up" inhibited patients and help them to express themselves.

The team system, in vogue today in many branches of medicine, is employed to get optimum value from the professionals, consisting of a doctor, a psychologist, a social worker, a nurse, a rehabilitation expert and an occupational therapist. The ward technicians, though not professionals in the usual sense, are part of the therapy team. The entire administrative staff is broken down into teams in this same way.

But the heart of the therapy program is to have everything that happens to a patient throughout the day and night, every act he performs, everything in his environment, contribute in some way to his treatment. The repainting of the hospital, for instance, in attractive colors—it was done by patients—had been a part of therapy. A patient remarked, "It makes you feel better and act better, having pretty colors, that you like, all around you."

"The way we do this is by tight structuring," Dr. Sandritter told me. "We have a very tight structure now, and it is getting tighter all the time." By this he meant organizing so that closer attention can be given to every detail of each patient's life in the hospital, with ways found to make each one speed the patient's recovery. To this end, training programs are going on constantly in every department and at every level.

On one hand, there is a tightly structured chain of administrative command, with many groupings and frequent meetings together of department heads and teams of various kinds. It is Dr. Sandritter's thesis that good administration is therapy. It takes into account the human jealousies, resentments and biases of employees as well as of patients, gives opportunity for expression of hostilities between departments so that these can be resolved, and provides a framework within which employees and patients alike know exactly what is expected of them.

On the other hand is the patients' self-government organization, the Emotional Security Program, designed to allow as much independence, self-reliance and responsibility as individual patients can handle. The ESP is to me the most dramatic feature of the Atascadero system and an exceedingly important part of the therapy program.

Every ward has its own patient government, with officers elected by the ward members and standing committees which take care of the different ward activities. One of the ward officers is a "senator," the ward's representative to the council of the over-all patient government, whose officers are elected every four months in spirited campaigns.

The ward governments have a meeting once a week, which is attended by members of the ward's therapy team, the ward doctor meeting with them at least twice a month. Here matters of ward business are conducted and questions can be asked of members of the therapy team. The ESP over-all government also meets once a week. These meetings are open to all the patients holding hall cards, usually around 600, and 400 ordinarily attend. Once a month Dr. Sandritter comes and answers questions.

The ESP officers and council serve both to keep the administration advised of patient grievances and ideas for improvement and to interpret administration policies to the patients.

At a ward meeting to which the ESP president was one of my escorts, he was asked about a new ruling, forbidding patients to receive coffee and tea, in previously opened containers, from their families. He explained that employees had to empty out the contents of such containers, sift through them, and then return them to the containers, and they didn't have the time to do this.

"Why do they do it?" he was asked.

"Because some people send in narcotics in jars of coffee and tea," he replied bluntly. "As you know, drugs are a big problem in a place like this. We are here to get well as fast as we can, and it is against our own interest to have anything that interferes with recovery." He assured the group that the new ruling did not apply to coffee and tea sent in the manufacturer's original container, with the seal still intact.

(Another recent patient grievance had been a rule forbidding cakes from home to the patients, though cupcakes could be received. It had to be explained that you can't very well conceal a file or hacksaw in a cupcake.)

The ESP is responsible for the hospital's eighteen-page *Newsletter,* issued semi-monthly, and a small literary magazine, *Impressions.* The *Newsletter* is full of items about the doings in the hospital and various wards, and it was interesting to me that the concealing of patient identities, such an important factor in the Sex Offender Facility at Waupun Prison in Wisconsin, is not observed at all at Atascadero. The articles describe the activities of different patients by name and are signed. Patients welcome contacts with the outside world. The *Newsletter* for October 1, 1963, featured a story about a float which the patients had entered in the Golden Jubilee parade of nearby Atascadero, the town from which the hospital takes its name. Eighteen men, all named, were involved in the construction of the float, which was labeled "Stairway to Recovery." "It was done up in a blue and white floral design, with the steps of recovery listed as you climb the stairs. The steps were Commitment to Hospital, Recognition of Illness, Social Recovery, Return to Society, and Citizen. . . . The culmination came when the float won the Sweepstakes Trophy of the Golden Jubilee Parade, as well as the best float in its division, bringing much honor to the hospital."

There is no evidence of sensitiveness, either, about mental illness, the *Newsletter's* humorous column containing a number of cracks about "crazy" people or actions.

So that the public might have a better understanding of the hospital's work and goals, the ESP put on a Press Day, inviting California newspaper people and acting as their hosts. The *Newsletter* noted with pleasure that a group of school children, attended by their teachers, had visited the hospital on another occasion. This forthright facing of the public and their situation seemed healthy to me. It must greatly ease the strain of the return of the patients to their own communities, and appears to be a distinct advantage of a separate institution where there is no discrimination among different types of offenders.

Patients help patrol the halls and stand guard at the entrances to the different wards. The ward governments co-operate with the therapy teams in administering treatment. Here I should explain another important aspect of the philosophy underlying the treatment program. Dr. Sandritter refers to it as a kind of re-conditioning. Its aim is to replace destructive habit and emotional patterns with habit patterns calculated to enable the patient to control himself, so that he can become a good member of society. I would not describe it as a brain-washing process, however. The program is explained to the patients. In the therapy groups, and in ward life, they learn, as in Wisconsin, what has been wrong in their previous attitudes and habits. They must want to change, and they are taught that they must work earnestly to bring it about.

When a patient enters the hospital, he is assigned to a ward and a ward team, becoming the special responsibility of one of the professionals. He also is given a technician sponsor in the ward. Several days are spent in taking a complete history and in examinations and tests, "the beginning of our understanding of the pathology present in the patient," as Dr. Sandritter puts it. Most are placed in a therapy group, but some patients have to have individual therapy before they are ready for that.

The patient is at once pushed into assuming as much responsibility for his own and ward affairs as he can. His technician sponsor helps, but the ward government pitches in to make him feel welcome and to help him understand the benefits of co-operating. After he has learned to take his full responsibility in the ward, he is brought into matters affecting the hospital in general.

Those able to do so perform hospital jobs. Admittedly, this saves the taxpayers' money, but the jobs are also considered therapeutic. The majority of the patients are able-bodied and in the prime of life. It is felt that they are better off performing work that has a purpose. Much thought is given by the therapy team to placing each man in the type of job that will be best for him, in the range available—kitchen, bakeshop, laundry, painting, cleaning, landscaping and clerical work. The usual work stint is four hours a day, the rest of the time is spent in group therapy, or in the numerous activities provided by the hospital—occupational therapy, sports, music and the like. Care is taken to leave time in which the patient may follow interests of his own, and there are at least twenty different patient activities, such as Alcoholics Anonymous, a toastmaster group, a dramatics group, the *Newsletter,* participating in ESP, for the special interests of individuals.

"Every time we add a new activity to the list, tensions in the hospital go down," I was told.

In June of 1963 a chapter of the Junior Chamber of Commerce was introduced. It was the first Jaycee unit in any California institution and is believed to be the first in any psychiatric hospital in the world. It was suggested by the organization's chapter in the town of Atascadero. Governor Edmund Brown wrote to the sponsoring group, "By acting upon your concern with the rehabilitation of patients in the hospital, you have set an example of constructive cooperation which I hope will be widely followed." A State Senate resolution commended the town chapter for "its extension of service to humanity in this particularly challenging human cause."

The ceremony on June 29, 1963, when the hospital chapter was formally installed with thirty members was attended by legislators, state and local officials of the Jaycees, representatives of the California State Department of Mental Hygiene, and civic and community leaders.

When I looked into the big, fully equipped gymnasium on my get-acquainted tour of the hospital, it was well filled, though the usual activities had been suspended because of the holiday. A number of men, wearing regulation basketball costumes, were practising basket throws. Presently the group thinned down to what I took to be a team of young Negroes, taking turns at expert throws into the basket. Since there is no racial segregation, either, at Atascadero, I assumed that the five Negroes were teamed because of their excellence in the sport. A giant white man, also a patient, was coaching them. He appeared to know his business, and they listened intently to his instructions.

Hospital teams in the various sports play outside teams from nearby Army and Navy bases, as well as conducting inter-ward contests. In December of 1963, the hospital held an invitational basketball tournament with eight teams taking part, including teams of commercial organizations as well as several from U.S. service bases.

At the other end of the gym, men were lifting bar bells and punching dummies. The dummies offer an excellent outlet for aggressions, and two wards have "Swinger" groups. The aim is to learn to go to the gym and punch the dummies, when hostilities arise, instead of people. A visiting scientist had suggested a "Hate Without Hitting" group as the next step. The administration had the idea under advisement.

The *Newsletter* is full of items about entertainments and inter-ward contests, for all of which the patients themselves are responsible.

One sees a great many women inside the hospital proper, in marked contrast to the Waupun practice. Many of the nurses are women, including those in the wards. This, too, is a part of therapy. "The men behave better, they take more interest in their appearance and manners and watch their language, when women are present," Dr. Sandritter told me. He said the same thing was true in women's wards in mental hospitals, when there are male attendants.

There are women employees even in Ward 14, the locked ward, where the most violent and intractable patients are placed. It is called a locked ward because the men assigned there never leave it; everything is brought to them, including occupational therapy. The therapist, a woman, came in while I was there and showed me the excellent weaving and other handwork of the ward patients, which was done in a heavy wire cage, with padlocked door, provided for the protection of the materials when no classes were being held. The therapist, however, needed no protection. When we emerged from the cage, the patients crowded close around her, but no offense was meant and none was taken. It was like the crowding of small children around a favorite teacher.

It might be contended, in fact, that the safest place for a woman in the whole United States is inside the electrically controlled doors of Atascadero State Hospital. I was struck by the number of women I saw, walking alone through the busy main corridor, sometimes past a whole ward of men walking in a body to the dining room. I knew by this time that hall privileges had to be earned and that undependable patients were escorted. But I thought of the psychotics who would inevitably be found in any ward group and asked what the possibility was that one might go berserk and attack a passing woman. On this occasion I was accompanied by a male attendant and a nurse supervisor.

"The possibility is very slight," the male attendant replied. "And there are plenty of men employees within call if a patient should decide suddenly to clobber a woman. But the chances are that other patients would get there first."

"The patients *would* get there first," the nurse supervisor said, "and they'd have the man down on the floor in no time. He would be lucky if he could get up and walk away. The patients wouldn't even have to like the woman," she added.

When a patient comes up for a staffing, either the routine ones commanded by the law for every patient every six months or a staffing looking toward release from the hospital, he is interviewed by a panel consisting of the assistant superintendent, who is a psychiatrist, his own doctor, who presents him, his own psychologist, social worker, his technician sponsor and the charge from his ward. The psychiatrist has the benefit of the evaluations of all those who have worked with the patient, down to hourly observations of his behavior. Recommendations regarding parole or discharge are passed on to the team of department heads, who make a recommendation, and thence to Dr. Sandritter, who makes the final decision.

Like the authorities in Wisconsin, Dr. Sandritter does not consider that the system is perfect—facing facts squarely is part of his creed. He took out a pencil and did some figuring for me.

"Out of every one hundred men sent to us for observation, we return around one half with an adverse recommendation—that they are untreatable and should be placed in a prison or another mental hospital. That leaves fifty whom we accept for treatment. Out of the fifty, we fail to improve ten. That leaves forty who are finally discharged as no longer constituting a danger to the community. Our records show that, out of the forty, ten will be completely rehabilitated. Ten will have problems but will be able to maintain their equilibrium. They will not commit any more crimes. Another ten will have more difficulty, but will manage to stay out of trouble—at least, they won't be caught. Ten will repeat their offenses. Out of the hundred original cases, only thirty will cease to be problems and burdens to society.

"But that does not mean that the work isn't worth doing. Under the

California law, the fifty we diagnose as untreatable and the ten we fail with can be held in custody as long as they continue to be dangerous. That removes sixty dangerous men from the community. Of the forty eventually released, we will have been able to keep one half from performing antisocial acts again. One-fourth will not commit serious crimes. The other fourth, because of the time spent in custody, will commit fewer crimes than they would have otherwise."

Also, Dr. Sandritter has a strong faith in the human race and in the increasing effectiveness of treatment as therapists gain more experience in the problems they are dealing with. The average stay in Atascadero of men eventually released as rehabilitated is eighteen months. Dr. Sandritter believes this could be cut to ten months by doubling the number of professionals on the staff.

"Because of California's steady population growth, there is already talk of building another hospital like this one. That wouldn't be necessary if we could rehabilitate most of our patients in half the time it takes now. We could do it with twice our present professional staff, or even by adding seven people to it, if they were the right people. I know who the people are, and I could get them."

This is the pattern Dr. Sandritter would like to see adopted in treatment centers—larger therapy staffs provided in existing facilities, rather than setting up more and more large hospitals, at great cost to the taxpayers.

Dr. Sandritter has been considered something of a controversial figure because of his constant insistence upon larger staffs and more intensive treatment, but this does not disturb him. He recognizes the need for security institutions where dangerous men can be confined, but adds, "The more therapeutic the program, the less the need for physical and mechanical confinement, and the sooner many can be returned to their homes and communities as good citizens."

# 17

# The California system in operation

My second day at Atascadero State Hospital, the holiday makers were back and hospital activities were in full swing. It is a great place for meetings, and these hold the secret of the smoothness with which the intricate system operates.

In addition to the regularly meeting therapy and discussion groups of the patients, the weekly meetings of the ward governments and the over-all patient government, there are many meetings on the administrative side. There is a weekly meeting of the medical staff and a weekly meeting of all the department heads, both of which Dr. Sandritter attends. At this latter meeting, new methods of therapy are discussed, procedural matters are threshed out, guidelines are set up. Changes are made from time to time in the rules and procedures, but only after long consideration and debate. For once a rule has been agreed upon and signed by Dr. Sandritter, it becomes law throughout the hospital, so that the effect must be carefully estimated in advance. Responsibility for carrying out the rules and for their departments in general rests with the department heads, and channeling to the different departments and teams is strictly observed.

For more direct connection with each other and with patients, the hospital administrative staff is split into six divisions, whose members hold weekly meetings of their own, which Dr. Sandritter does not attend. The first meeting that morning, at 8:30, was of the top team of one of the divisions, comprising the heads of the psychiatric, nursing, rehabilitation and social service departments of this division. The discussion concerned a patient's family who, on the Sunday before, had asked to see the man's social service worker. Because of a newly established command channel, they had been made to wait for more than half an hour. It was pointed out that some families had to drive several hundred miles to get to the hospital and had to return the same day. If the new procedure could cause unnecessary waiting around by a patient's loved ones, should it not be reconsidered?

At 9:00, the medical staff had its weekly meeting in the conference room of the reception area of the hospital. I found eighteen doctors, including Dr. Sandritter, sitting about a long table. The question before this assemblage when I came in was whether or not to continue touch football and other contact sports rather recently instituted. The impression had been that bruises incurred by attendants who took part in these sports with the patients had been offset by a drop in assaults on attendants in the wards, but the matter was up for reconsideration. After some discussion, it was decided that the benefits of the contact sports still outweighed the disadvantages and that they should be retained.

My guide and I left the meeting at this point, because a ward government meeting was scheduled in Ward 14, the closed ward where the "hard cases," the most violent and dangerous of the psychotics, are kept and where sexual psychopaths are sent when all other devices to get them to co-operate have failed. I had pictured this ward as a kind of bedlam and was curious to see what a meeting here would be like.

The entrance to this ward is always kept locked, in contrast to the others where patients with hall cards are free to come and go. As we walked down the long hall which led to the lounge, about midway my guide and I passed a patient who was sitting huddled over a record player, which was tuned low, as though this was the only way the patient could have uninterrupted enjoyment of his records.

No sooner had we entered the ward lounge than a young man came up to me. In one hand he was holding a cup in which were a safety razor and shaving brush. He extended the other hand to me, told me his name, and asked me for mine. He held his head stiffly high and back, his face was expressionless, he spoke in a slow, uninflected drawl. I think I suppressed a little gulp before taking the proffered hand and telling him my name. He asked me more questions about myself, which I answered; then other patients came up and were introduced to me. Soon I was passing out cigarettes and lighting them, at the request of different patients, after getting permission from my escort. In other wards, dependable patients are allowed to have lighters with nonexplosive fluid, but, as one of the patients here explained to me, in the closed ward no one may have a lighter or matches. The men can have cigarettes, and many had their own, but they had to depend upon the attendants for lights.

The meeting was called to order, and I was invited to sit with the ward officers, my guide whispering as he sat down beside me that this was an honor. In this ward, as in the others, the patients elect their officers, and two of the five were Negroes, though there were few Negroes in the ward as compared with whites.

We sat in a row of chairs against the wall, facing the ward members, all of whom were assembled, with the possible exception of the music lover in the hall. (Attendance at the ward government meetings is not compulsory.) At the end of the front row, doubled over the arm of his chair, his back to the rest of us, was a very tall, emaciated man, who from time to time uttered moans and bleating sounds.

The chairman of the ward government, a tall, slender young man of fair complexion, rose and called for reports from the officers and committee chairmen. All were addressed by their last names, prefaced by "Mister," and there were no interruptions. One committee chairman reported that Ward 14 had lost a volleyball game to another ward, but that their team had tried hard. Others reported on the fund for buying coffee—coffee appears to be of prime importance throughout the hospital—and similar ward affairs. Suddenly two technicians rushed to the moaning man in the end chair, pulled him upright and to one side, and began to undress him! They stopped, however, with the removal of his shirt and undershirt. The patient had dropped a lighted cigarette into his clothing. The fire extinguished and the garments replaced, he was seated again in his chair by the technicians, but his moans and bleatings grew louder until, finally, the technicians led him from the room. Throughout this incident, the other patients paid no attention to the disturbance but kept their eyes fixed on the row of officers and their minds on the matters at hand.

The minute the meeting was thrown open to the group, my friend of the shaving materials was on his feet, demanding to know what had happened to $2 he had contributed toward an entertainment which apparently had not been held. He was frequently on his feet thereafter, as were several others whose questions and comments, though always possessing a queer kind of logic, did not contribute much to the proceedings. The ward chairman would hesitate sometimes before recognizing one of these compulsive talkers for the fourth or fifth time, then would let him speak. Nor did the clear-minded among the group exhibit any impatience with these men.

"I believe we are more truly democratic in the hospital than the people are outside," the ESP president said to me, a little later (while a staff member remarked to me that, in some of its decisions, the ESP council was more conservative than the United States Supreme Court).

One man rose to suggest that more ward members should go out for volleyball, to insure a full team of able-bodied players when they had a contest with another ward. "Some of our best players are under heavy sedation when the time comes for a game. We should have plenty of substitutes to take their places when this happens."

All the usual medical measures are employed with the psychotics when needed, including shock therapy, tranquilizers and sedatives, though they do not take the place of therapy designed to alter a patient's habit and emotional patterns. This ward would have an unusually high percentage of patients requiring such measures.

There were some acid comments about the hospital personnel. One patient wanted to know where the ward psychologist was. "He hasn't been around for some time."

"What psychologist?" inquired another, with fine sarcasm. "Do we have a psychologist? I've been in this ward for six weeks and I haven't seen one yet."

I found that, throughout the hospital, the patients are very jealous of the prerogatives they are allowed and expect the staff members to be punctual and meticulous in carrying out their duties. This is quite natural in a community shut off from the outside world, where small details of daily living assume a disproportionate importance.

By hurrying, I was able to get in on the latter part of the staffing, mentioned in the preceding chapter, being held in another section of the hospital. (I shuttled so many times from one section to another, and went down so many long hallways, in addition to the main corridors, that I have only the foggiest idea where in the big hospital I was much of the time.) This was a routine staffing, held for every patient at six-month intervals, and none of the patients was being considered for discharge.

The assistant superintendent, a psychiatrist, presides at a staffing and questions the patient. As at all formal staffings, present were the members of each patient's therapy team—his own doctor, psychologist, nurse, social worker, and technician sponsor, and the charge of his ward. The patient's case file was at hand, and team members filled in the psychiatrist on recent developments before the patient entered.

The first patient to come before the panel after I arrived was a highly educated man of superior intelligence, oriented in all spheres but given to violent actions. On one occasion he had thrown gasoline on a house, ignited the gasoline by shooting tracer bullets into it, then had shot tracer bullets into the fire truck when it arrived. I gathered it was on another occasion that he had shot up a police car, in a fit of rage. He admitted wryly of the latter episode, "That was not one of my better days."

He told the panel that he thought he had been trying to get himself killed. He had a large family and was under a great deal of pressure from his family and other sources. "I was carrying too heavy a load. I was in a spot and I couldn't get out of it."

A big, genial-appearing man with a perpetual smile, he was given to taking punches at people in the ward, it appeared. He said he realized he had to find a way to get the hate out of himself. "Maybe I can get it out verbally. I'll try." He had joined a "Swinger" group, he added.

The next patient was the raper of little girls already mentioned. I was told that in the ward he, in contrast to the previous patient, did fairly well until pressured too hard.

Next was a psychopathic delinquent, turned over to the hospital by the California Youth Authority. Sex was his problem, and I assumed he had been transferred from the Youth Authority for the protection of other youngsters in their care. He got into trouble first at the age of 15, for molesting a 5-year-old girl, and two years later had been committed to the Youth Authority by a court because of aggressive and incorrigible behavior.

"How do you feel about trying to rape this little girl?" the psychiatrist asked him.

"I felt real bad about it, but recently I don't feel so bad."

"But you realize it was a bad thing to do?"

"Yes, I do."

However, he answered all questions frankly and admitted having propositioned several female employees and having suggested a homosexual relationship to some other patients. He said he knew the hospital disapproved of this. But it had been some time since he had solicited anyone, and he appeared to be making some progress, though it was slow. Whether or not this youth is ever enabled to control his strong and indiscriminate sex impulses, at least keeping him in custody will save children from nasty, damaging experiences.

The high point of my visit to Atascadero, however, so far as meetings were concerned, was a ward government meeting in an open ward, much more representative of the system than the one in Ward 14, interesting as that had been. (I had to depart before the next meeting of the over-all patient government, to my great regret.)

It was considerably more structured than the one in Ward 14. The officers sat at a long table, facing a much larger assembly of ward members. In front of each officer was a neatly lettered placard, giving his office. From left to right the placards read: Ward Co-ordinator; Senator (the ward's representative in the ESP council); Ward Chairman; Secretary-Treasurer; Activities Co-ordinator.

The chairman, a short stocky man who might have been in the middle or late fifties, his dark hair gray at the temples, presided with quiet authority. The treasurer reported a balance of $7.50 in the ward treasury after coffee had been bought that morning for the week. The Activities Co-ordinator announced plans for celebrating Christmas and a volleyball game with another ward. The chairman of the canteen committee reported that there had been complaints about "the lousy taste of the fish served last Friday." The complaints would be passed along. Another committee chairman told the group, "The line has been looking pretty good going to chow, but it's still a little ragged. We can tighten it up."

A ward technician was then called on to give his opinion of the results of the neatness campaign the ward had been conducting. He said the ward had been looking pretty good but could be better. "It's a hassle to keep things neat in a place like this."

Meanwhile the ward charge, seated at the front of the room next to the official table, had been looking toward the back of the room and making florid gestures. He explained to me that all the deaf men and deaf mutes in the hospital were in this ward. Through sign language, he was keeping them posted as to what was going on.

Now two new patients were introduced. Each stood up and gave his name and the town he was from, to hearty applause. The ward group is a patient's family while he is in the hospital; the *Newsletter* items reveal a great sense of loyalty to the ward on the part of its members, a pride in its achievements, and a keen interest in the events, good or bad, which befall the other members.

The ward doctor was to attend this meeting, and he was fifteen minutes late. The group members began to ask where he was, what had happened to him. As soon as the doctor came in, with apologies and the explanation that he had been held in another meeting, he was peppered with questions by a patient just out of seclusion. This young man had been commenting rather freely throughout the ward government meeting, and it was explained to me later that he was an epileptic with an organic brain disease and a mind on about the 8-year level. He was not assaultive or violent but, never having been taught how to live with people, created a constant disturbance in the ward. "The men endure it as long as they can, then in open meeting ask if he can't be put in seclusion for a week, to give them a chance to catch their breath."

Gene, as I shall call him, had just returned from seclusion, looking forward to taking his place again in the ward, and flew into a rage when the doctor told him he was to be transferred to another ward, where a neurologist was trying out a new type of therapy involving a great deal of sleep.

Gene cried out that he wouldn't go to the new ward, they couldn't make him. If they dragged him there, he wouldn't co-operate. He had said he would co-operate in this ward, he had been promised another chance. He left his chair in the second row and took a stand before the doctor, who was seated at the front of the room. The ward charge hurried to interpose himself between Gene and the doctor; two technicians moved in behind the angry young man.

Gene, ignoring them, asked permission to tell the doctor what he, Gene, thought of him. The doctor, after a momentary hesitation, said, "Go ahead."

Gene then poured out an impassioned indictment. It was the grievance of a small boy but delivered with a mature marshaling of thought and of expression. "You are supposed to observe, but you don't see anything. You are supposed to know all about me, but you don't know anything about me. You are supposed to be a doctor, but you are no doctor—" On it went in this vein for minutes, the doctor listening composedly, a very slight reddening of his face his only betrayal of emotion. Gene ended his diatribe with an explosive, "You—are—a—*fool!*" I believe everyone present sighed with relief at the final invective, it could have been so much worse. The doctor commented, in fact, that the usual epithet applied to him in such situations was "four-eyed bald-headed bastard," at which the other patients, who had been sitting quietly, watching the incident, laughed appreciatively. (I should like to say here that at Atascadero, as in Wisconsin, no off-color word or expression was uttered by a patient in my presence.)

The next development was a fascinating thing to witness. The patients took over the task of trying to reconcile Gene to his new assignment. The ward co-ordinator, a man with a sensitive face, started it off by asking the doctor if he might talk to Gene. Up to this point, the men had addressed each other as "Mister," as in Ward 14, in token of the solemnity of the proceedings, but from now on they called Gene by his first name.

"You must remember, Gene," the ward co-ordinator said in a

kindly tone, "that the men here in the ward have been trying for two years to help you. Maybe the move will be a good thing for you."

Gene, who had sat down in the front row across from the doctor, wailed, almost tearfully, "But I promised I would co-operate!"

Other patients then spoke up to remind Gene that he had promised to co-operate many times, in the two years he had been in the ward, but hadn't been able to keep his promise. They urged him to give the new ward a try. One said he knew some of the fellows on Gene's new ward, that it was a good ward, he thought Gene would like it.

A man just across the aisle from me, also with an intelligent and sensitive face, who had taken no part in the proceedings heretofore and had looked as though his thoughts might be far away, leaned forward now.

"I believe Gene's feelings are hurt. He thinks we want to get rid of him. That isn't so, Gene. We like you. You're not going to lose us. We will still be your friends."

Another patient, picking up the cue, asked the doctor if Gene could not be permitted to visit his old ward from time to time, and if they could not visit him.

Next they tried kidding. One man offered to take Gene's place in the new ward. "That new treatment sounds like a good deal. You like to sleep, and all you'll be doing there is sleep." Tossing a cigarette to Gene, he added, "The doctor has promised to bring you a package of cigarettes there every day," a big laugh, in which the doctor joined, greeting this ploy, for the doctor had made no such promise. The big, smiling man with a propensity for shooting up things, who was an officer in this ward, suggested genially, "If you don't want to change wards, Gene, why don't you fake it for an hour and act sane?"

The ward charge ended the episode by giving Gene a friendly slap on the knee, telling him briskly to get his things together—"I bet you're going to be real happy in the new ward"—and hustling him out before Gene quite knew what was happening.

It was difficult to tell, in this ward, which men were sexual psychopaths or mentally ill or criminally insane, because they all, with the exception of Gene, had appeared so normal and had behaved so normally. But mentally disturbed men were present, and I would have imagined that the defiant and abusive patient would have touched off a general upheaval. The Atascadero system proved itself to me when the only reaction of the ward body was to come to the support of the therapist.

I had a further illustration of its workings at the meeting of the ward therapy team, held just after the ward government meeting. Crowded into the tiny inner room of the ward office were the ward's doctor, social worker, psychologist, rehabilitation worker, the ward charge and a technician or two, the chairman of the ward government, the ESP president, and myself. (Let me remind you that the chairman of the ward government and the ESP president were both patients. I had frequently to remind myself that a gentlemanly, intelligent, well-spoken man with whom I was talking was a patient, and not a member of the administrative staff.) Having the ward government chairman present at these meetings was a recent innovation. The ESP president had come to the ward to escort me to my next appointment and had been invited to attend the therapy team meeting. The ESP president expressed his appreciation at being taken behind the scenes, and said he thought it would be good for ESP officials to do more of this, since the council acted as liaison between the patients and the staff. The doctor, smiling, said he would see what could be done.

The ward government chairman presented a number of cases for the consideration of the professionals. These were ward members with whom a committee formed of patients in the ward had been working. They had recommendations to offer regarding these men, subject to the ruling of the professional team.

With regard to Case No. 1, the ward committee asked simply if there was any reason why the man should not be given a hall card which would permit him to go about within the hospital proper. The therapy team took that one under advisement.

Case No. 2, the chairman said, had been doing well on his painting job. The committee of patients thought the man merited canteen and courtyard privileges—he already had a hall card. The therapy team decided to mete out these new privileges one at a time. They granted canteen privileges. If the patient continued to do well after a week or two, he could have courtyard privileges also.

Case No. 3 had puzzled the therapy team. He had a strong artistic bent and the professionals had thought it would be good for him to be put into the creative art group, but he had resisted. The ward government chairman said his committee had been talking to this man. They had learned his resistance had stemmed from the fact that when he got involved in an art project he would slip into a dream world, and he wanted to stay in the real world. (He had previously been addicted to glue-sniffing.) The ward committee thought this was a good explanation for what had appeared to be an unco-operative attitude and asked if the patient might not be given full privileges. The professional team agreed, suggesting starting the man off with some limitations, granting him canteen privileges first, and gradually extending them.

One patient had refused to do his work in the ward. The committee suggested that he be denied spending money. (The rebellious patient, a college graduate, also refused to bathe and had gained fifty pounds in the hospital.) The therapists agreed to the recommendation.

But hall card and canteen privileges were requested by the ward patient committee for another man. He was doing well in the laundry, the ward chairman said, and the patients on the ward had worked hard with him. A technician spoke up, saying that if the ward recommended those privileges, he thought they should be granted. The therapy team granted the patient a hall card to go to and from his laundry job (he had been escorted up to this time) and canteen privileges.

Still another was a tough case; the committee of patients was not recommending anything for him now, but the ward government was working on a program for this man. It would be laid before the therapy team when the patient group was satisfied with it.

So it went through a considerable list; then the ward chairman withdrew, and the therapy team continued with a consideration of cases brought forward by the technicians.

These are some of the ways in which the staff works with patients, patients work with each other, and staff and patients work together at Atascadero State Hospital.

In Wisconsin and California, we have today two systems for rehabilitating sex offenders, different in many ways, both admirable. California demonstrates the advantages of a special, separate institution, where the entire program can be directed to therapy. Wisconsin demonstrates that sexually sick men can be treated effectively in a maximum security prison in smaller states, whose sex offender population may not warrant a special institution. With adequate therapy, the indeterminate sentence, now practically a dead letter on the books of many states, would have meaning. Judges would be less hesitant to invoke it if they could be sure that the man sentenced under it would have the best chance for recovery that science can provide and that his rights would be protected as they are in Wisconsin and California.

I am not as sure as Dr. Sandritter is that all the different types of particularly dangerous men—the mentally ill, the criminally insane and those with a propensity for sex violence—could be mingled together in any and every mental hospital. It seems to me that his peculiar genius for organizing and administering, for engaging the loyalty of the staff and the faith of the patients, has a very great deal to do with the present smooth working of the California system. I would personally advise any state body considering such a plan to study the procedures at Atascadero State Hospital long and carefully before venturing to follow this particular example.

However, a hospital atmosphere and treatment plan for sexual psychopaths is proving its advantages triumphantly in California.

But these things cost money, someone is sure to object, and our taxes are high enough as it is. We tend to overlook the fact that police forces and man hunts and jails and reformatories and prisons cost money too. Studying the annual budget for my own little county, of around 18,000 population, I have figured that the cost each year of the criminal division comes to at least $140,000. This figure covers only the cost of the sheriff's office and jail, the criminal court, its officials and employees, and building maintenance. It is borne entirely by the county residents. The figure does not include the expense of the state troopers, who help local authorities, and does not include the expense of the state prisons, mental institutions and hospitals for the criminally insane, which we help to pay for, as individuals, through our state taxes.

I have never heard anyone complain about the cost of our county criminal apparatus or question it in any way. We take it for granted that we must have it for our protection, and have it we must. But it was a struggle to get a county mental health clinic set up, designed to prevent the development of criminals and mentally ill persons, who will become a burden on the community if their problems do not receive early attention. The last annual budget allowed for the mental health clinic at time of writing was around $36,000, of which the county pays half, the other half being contributed by the state. Actually, the direct cost to us local taxpayers is less than $16,000, since clinic patients pay something when they are able to pay, and it was estimated that the county's share would not exceed $14,500 and probably would be less than that.

One board member had objected to the budget, because it carried an increase of $300 over the budget of the preceding year, to provide services for the increasing number of residents who were making use of the clinic. How could he, as a board member, explain this increase to the taxpayers? he asked.

I don't know just what fraction of a cent the $300 increase represented for each county taxpayer, but I paid my share gladly. (I am happy to say that the board member withdrew his objection.)

In California, too, the patients at Atascadero pay what they can, in keeping with the practice in any general hospital when a person is hospitalized for illness or injury. Although the patients have been committed as the result of court action, all who are under commitment through provisions of the Welfare and Institutions Code pay for their room and board, which averages $275 a month, if they are financially able to do so. The mentally ill patients committed under various sections of the Penal Code also contribute what they can toward their keep while in the hospital.

Where sex offenders are committed to prison, the taxpayers carry the full burden.

The Wisconsin authorities once figured out that if a clinical psychologist is able to keep just one and one half sex offenders from being an expense to the community for one year—through keeping him from committing another crime, being apprehended, tried, convicted and supported by the state while in prison—the psychologist will have saved the taxpayers his own year's salary. The ratio is probably closer now, since this comparison was made some years back, and the cost of crime has risen more steeply than have psychologists' salaries. Also, the ratio does not take into account the fact that, many times, the offender's family must be supported from welfare funds while he is in prison.

The Emmett Hashfield case shows what can happen to a county's budget when the ghastly, unspeakable sex murder has been committed. The money that has been spent by Warrick County, Indiana, alone, for Hashfield's defense, and the legal proceedings the county residents have had to underwrite would pay for a good deal of psychiatric attention to Indiana sex offenders, which might be able to save a number of sexually sick men from proceeding to sadistic murder or, at the very least, keep them from being released into the community while they are still dangerous.

The most adequate therapy program that one can conceive, built up regardless of expense, would still represent only a small proportion of the over-all expense of our criminal courts and protective systems. In the end, it would save the taxpayers far more money than it would cost, in addition to the anguish and horror it would spare individuals and the community.

# 18

# Prevention, in California and Massachusetts

Just as it appears inescapable that the place to start an attack on the problem of serious sex crime is with more enlightened and effective handling of offenders who come into the hands of the law, so the first efforts at prevention should be toward improved handling of children and teen-agers who come into society's hands, either because they have committed crimes or because of defective home situations.

We have seen that many serious sex offenders had their personalities further distorted, and got their initiation into aberrant sex, in institutions set up supposedly to correct, or in institutions for children whose only crime has been that they had no parents or the ones they had, for some reason, were unable to look after them. The same conditions have prevailed in many detention homes, where children are placed temporarily while awaiting disposition of their cases by the courts.

A few years ago I was driving through a charming New England village—the kind whose soaring steeples, elm trees and beautiful old houses, grouped about a green, drew visitors from many miles away —with a woman judge who was investigating the facilities where children were held. She asked me to stop at the village jail. "I am a great dropper-in at jails." Very often, she explained, she found children locked in cells or placed in bullpens with adult offenders, quite contrary to the law. The idyllic village where we stopped was no exception. Talking with youthful offenders, she had learned that many had been convicted and sentenced to correctional institutions with no lawyer to defend them, though the law in that state set forth plainly that no person should be tried on a charge involving commitment unless represented by a lawyer, to be supplied by the court if the defendant has no funds.

It would seem that in many localities the constitutional rights of youngsters who have no one to fend for them do not carry much weight.

It is a truism in enlightened penological circles that to detain little boys with big boys, or adolescents with older men, is to "throw them to the wolves." I don't know that anyone has tried to calculate how many of the young victims who might otherwise have attained a normal sexual adjustment grow up to be sex offenders, but the number must be impressive. There can certainly be no doubt that a youngster coming from an inadequate home, where he has been deprived in his emotional needs and possibly brutalized as well, will not be helped by further brutalization and sexual exploitation in an institution to which society has consigned him.

As far back as 1940, the American Law Institute approved a statute which it called "A Model Youth Authority Act." It proposed that youths committed for offenses—of any type—should be turned over, mandatorily, to a state-wide panel to be known as the Youth Correction Agency. Commitment would be for an indefinite period, though the youths could not be held beyond a specified time without judicial review. The agency would have continuous control of the offender from commitment to discharge, would be made responsible for a genuine study and treatment program, and would be given power to utilize as it saw fit the various facilities existing throughout a state and to construct its own facilities as funds were appropriated.

This law was offered as a model to the various states, and by 1951 five states—California, Massachusetts, Minnesota, Texas and Wisconsin—had adopted the general program, each with some modifications. Bertram M. Beck, who studied the program as it was operated in the aforementioned states and reported his conclusions in a book entitled *Five States,* found that, in all five, diagnostic and parole services had been improved. Delinquency prevention programs had been established which had stimulated community interest in improving services to children and youths in local communities.

Persons trained in the sciences of human behavior have been added to the correctional staff. . . . The programs . . . have conclusively demonstrated that the new agency is capable of attracting superior personnel to leadership positions . . . the key to the improvement of correctional facilities.

Some compromises had to be made in passing the law through the various state legislatures. But the youth agency, by whatever name it is called, is free in the five states named to develop treatment methods and institutions, and out of the Model Law have come some new, imaginative and, to me, intensely thrilling ways of dealing with unfortunate, unhappy youngsters.

California was the first state to adopt the program; its central agency, called the Youth Authority, was set up in 1941. One of the most felicitous treatment systems for delinquent youth so far devised grew out of the very necessity of the Authority to find some place to put the youthful offenders when the courts began turning them over, after the law was passed by the California Legislature, since the three institutions already existing were not adequate to hold them. Forestry camps were set up as the quickest and least expensive way of housing the youngsters. The plan has proven so effective that it has become a permanent part of the California system and has been adopted by Michigan, Illinois, Washington, Massachusetts and New York State. (In 1963, a law was passed in California calling for the setting up of a forestry camp for nondelinquent but out-of-school, unemployed youths, too.) Meanwhile, new institutions were built for girls and for boys for whom the forestry camps were not considered suitable.

It was my privilege, some years ago, to visit several of the institutions that have been provided by the California Youth Authority to meet the special needs of boys and girls entrusted to them. One for girls was a handsome building, in whose many-windowed and sun-flooded rooms girls were being taught to sew, to type, to cook, and to acquire other skills and arts which would give them a means of earning a living or enable them to function more efficiently as wives and mothers. The atmosphere was that of a place of opportunity, rather than of punishment or correction.

But it was the forestry camp I visited which most captured my imagination. These camps can be used only for selected youths, who can be trusted not to "walk away," for they are built and conducted on the order of any mountain summer camp for youngsters whose parents can afford the price. The difference is that the boys in the Youth Authority camps perform a valuable service by clearing and replanting the forests, clearing streams, and fighting fires. A group from one of the forestry camps re-built a dam. The evenings are spent in sports, or games, or reading, or listening to records. A well-known athlete, I am told, learned the rudiments of the sport which has brought him fame and honor in a forestry camp conducted by the California Youth Authority.

Some of the youths whom I saw playing baseball after supper, or having friendly boxing or wrestling bouts, or off in a corner, reading, had committed very serious crimes, but the counselors explained to me that these were not inherently bad kids; most had just never had the breaks. A number had merely reacted according to the patterns of the particular culture into which they had been born and had lived until they came into conflict with the law. With many Mexicans, for instance, who constitute a sizable element in California, it is a sign of manhood to carry a knife and to use it if one is insulted. In other cultures, if a boy doesn't respond to a challenge to fight, he will get a licking from his father when he goes home. As for the truly tough cases, when one knew the life stories of the boys, it was not hard to figure out how they had gotten that way.

I was told about the "toughest kid in camp," who had proved impervious to all the approaches used with him. It was observed, however, that at night, after he was in his bunk, he would stealthily draw a piece of paper from some hiding place, read it, and cry. One of the counselors succeeded in finding the mysterious piece of paper. The writing on it by now was nearly obliterated, it had been unfolded and re-folded and re-read and cried over so many times. But it was a letter from the boy's mother, the only one he had had from her and the only sign of interest in him she had displayed after his arrest.

All the different institutions conducted by the California Youth Authority—at time of writing there are thirteen, including four forestry camps—emphasize both academic and vocational education and improved health. All have chaplains, who work with youngsters individually as well as conducting religious services. A constant effort is made to fit the education, treatment and facilities to the individual needs of the youngsters.

In 1957, the Authority was given the responsibility for providing psychiatric treatment to youngsters with severe emotional problems, short of actual psychosis. (Psychotics are referred to mental institutions.) This includes boys with a propensity for sex crime, for whom special psychiatric treatment units have been set up. Each boy usually sees his therapist twice a week, and therapy groups are used also. The case load per therapist ranges from eight to twelve patients, so that each child needing it is able to receive intensive psychiatric treatment. Special living units have been provided in the boys' training school at Preston and the girls' training school at Los Guilucos for emotionally disturbed youngsters, which include an academic classroom, a group therapy room and an occupational therapy room. The special units make possible closer relationships with the therapy staff and more flexibility in treatment methods.

In addition to the four big forestry camps—called "Conservation Camps" now in recognition of the service they render—each with a capacity for 80 boys, there are two smaller ones, and California boasts forty-one county camps which are state subsidized. There are camps for girls as well as for boys.

For boys from 8 to 14, the Authority has a ranch school permitting such outdoor activities as hiking, fishing and camping. During the summer, all the boys in the ranch school spend ten days at a camp set up on the order of a Boy Scout camp, where they participate in all the scouting activities.

When one reviews the list of camps and schools of various types that have been built up by the California Youth Authority since it took over the responsibility for the state's unfortunate youngsters in 1941, one must agree with Governor Brown that "In California, under the guidance of the Department of the Youth Authority, we have provided the best institutions in the nation for the rehabilitation of juvenile delinquents."

The distance problem in California, with its great sprawl down the Pacific Coast, has been met by having two reception centers, one in northern and one in southern California, and parole offices scattered in fifteen major cities throughout the state.

California deserves the greatest credit for the use it has made of its famous climate and unsurpassed natural resources, in behalf of its troubled youngsters, and for the valiant attack that has been made on the problems created by the tremendous population influx. The number of boys and girls turned over to the Youth Authority has been increasing by close to 1,000 per year. In August, 1963, the Youth Authority had 6,568 charges in institutions and 12,453 on parole. The Authority expects these figures to be doubled by 1970.

Instead of throwing up their hands in dismay, Authority officials are devising new treatment methods. One is to rehabilitate youngsters in their own communities by professional teams in place of institutionalizing them. Prevention is being stressed, through improvement of juvenile court, probation, law enforcement, welfare, education and other community services. Although additions have had to be made to present facilities, the plan is to avoid swallowing up youngsters in huge institutions by building two constellations of small institutions, one at Stockton in northern California, the other in southern California out from Ontario.

But not all of our states have mountains, great forests and a mild climate, and none, with the exception of New York, has a population problem comparable with California's. I shall therefore cross the continent to Massachusetts, whose system vies with California's in its enlightened and devoted attack on the handling of youngsters in trouble and has the added advantage, for our purposes, that its situation is typical of that in most other states. Its system could be put into effect by any state wishing to join those already operating under the Model Law.

In Massachusetts, the central authority is a three-member Youth

Service Board, composed of professionals who give their full time, appointed for staggered six-year terms by the governor with the advice and consent of the Executive Council. (In California, the State Senate has to approve the governor's choices.) The Board has the legal custody of all delinquent children committed to its care by the juvenile courts of the Commonwealth, as Massachusetts is officially styled, and makes all decisions, on an individualized and flexible basis, about the type of handling and treatment each child shall receive.

The decisions of the Board are carried out by a Division of Youth Service, headed ex-officio by the chairman of the Youth Service Board. The Division operates the reception and detention services, training schools and juvenile parole services of the Commonwealth. In both California and Massachusetts, a citizens' advisory committee, made up of representatives of various organizations and disciplines, keeps in close touch with the work of the central agency. The crux of both systems is that youngsters who come before the courts are not committed to specific institutions, as is done under the traditional plan, but to the central authority, which is given full discretion to place and to care for them wherever and in whatever way it feels will be to their best interests.

In Massachusetts, boys and girls committed by the courts remain under the jurisdiction of the Youth Service Board until the age of 21, and in some cases after that. As in California, the Board has charge of the institutions for youths and is empowered to provide such other ones as it feels are needed, and funds permit. It is also empowered, out of its experience, to make suggestions to the Legislature for changes in the law, which will enable it to do a still better job of protecting and rehabilitating.

While the Model Act was originally intended to apply to the "youthful offender," the designation used for those between 17 and 21, both Massachusetts and California have adopted it for delinquents, offenders under 17. Under the Massachusetts law, children between 7 and 17 who commit offenses, and those labeled "stubborn children" (youngsters who are too much for their parents, and are taken into court by their parents) may be adjudged delinquents by the juvenile courts and, if not placed on probation, may be committed to the Youth Service Board. Truants and school offenders may likewise be committed to the Board, but only until age 16.

The "stubborn children," I was told, frequently are more severely damaged than out and out delinquents. A complete restructuring of their attitudes is called for in many cases. The "stubborn child" provision makes this possible at an early age, before there has been overt delinquency.

Since the establishment of the Massachusetts Youth Service Board in 1948, the annual rate of commitments has gradually increased from 500 to 1000 boys and girls. At any given time, the Board has approximately 1000 children in institutions and 1500 more on parole. Approximately 1000 more children each year are committed to the Board by the courts for brief periods of detention (that is to say, custody, with or without clinical study) prior to final disposition of their cases by the courts.

When the law was put into operation in 1948, the Massachusetts officials, like those in California in 1941, were faced with the problem of putting into effect a new program involving diagnosis, better treatment methods and higher parole standards, without proper facilities for doing these things. The Massachusetts climate is not favorable to outdoor living the year round, and the three-member Youth Service Board, which was given the task of operating the new program, had to get along with the three institutions—a training school for boys, one for girls, and a security institution for boys—already provided for juvenile offenders.

Existing staff had to be re-trained and re-oriented for the new approach; a staff of professionals had to be built up. The makeshift reception centers were overcrowded and did not permit separation of young boys from older ones. There was a serious lack of proper detention facilities. The original law, moreover, had left a weakness in the chain of command. The first three years of operation showed that a three-member board, with no official head, did not make for efficient administration.

The advisory committee of citizens pointed out these defects, and in 1952 the Legislature set up the present Division of Youth Services as a separate entity, under the control of a director. Mr. John D. Coughlan, the man the advisory committee had wanted as director, received his appointment from the governor on December 24, 1952, and has continued in the post to time of writing.

On the outskirts of Boston, now, there is a big reception center for boys and another one for girls. Both also offer detention services (temporary custody and diagnostic study of children awaiting final court disposition) for eastern Massachusetts. Small detention centers serve central and western Massachusetts. The Lyman School, for boys up to 16 (the first training school established in the United States), has been added to, its program revamped, to make it truly a place for rehabilitation.

The existing security school was expanded to serve boys in their later teens. It combines academic work, leading to a high school diploma, with training in various trades. It has a full sports program, a forestry day-work program, and a cottage plan. The last named serves both as a reward for achievement and as preparation for re-entering the outside world, on parole or discharge.

The original industrial school for girls also gives academic and vocational training and a complete program in sports and music. A fully equipped beauty parlor not only provides a vocational outlet but emphasizes the value of a neat appearance and adds to the girls' self-respect.

All the foregoing are "open" institutions. There is a further "closed" one for boys, called the Institute for Juvenile Guidance, which provides security for the public while offering more intensive treatment. University extension courses are given here in all high school subjects, as well as training in upholstering, carpentry and bookbinding. A special music program, in which more than half the boys participate, has been found to be a good treatment tool. An honor section for those being prepared for parole stresses initiative, responsibility and merit. In all the Youth Service institutions there are remedial classes for those with special gaps in learning.

Massachusetts has one forestry camp for boys, on Cape Cod, to which youngsters may be referred directly from the reception center or from any of the institutions. As in California, the forestry camp has a great appeal for many youngsters, and the chance of referral there is a spur to achievement.

Finally, there is a special school for little boys, from 7 to 12, whose problems are not too serious as yet.

In addition to its own facilities, moreover, the Massachusetts Youth Service Board uses foster homes, private schools and many schools of a variety of religious faiths, depending upon the type of setting deemed best for the individual youngster. The law even empowers it to place its charges in schools or institutions outside Massachusetts, if the type of help it is felt some youngster needs is not available in the Commonwealth.

At the time of my visit to the Board headquarters in Boston, the Commonwealth was paying a yearly tuition of $5000 to a special school for a boy whom officials considered to be a special case. "We can't do that for very many, it's obvious." But to me an outstanding feature of the Massachusetts system is the consideration each youngster receives.

As I sat in the office of Mr. Ernest W. Mitchell, the assistant to the director of the Service, conferring with him and with Mr. Joseph M. Ambrose, the supervisor of special services, phone calls came in from workers in different parts of the Commonwealth. Each concerned a problem of an individual youngster, and both Mr. Mitchell and Mr. Ambrose knew about the youngsters. One concerned a request from an overwrought, neurotic mother to be allowed to visit her son, who was having a difficult time adjusting. The officials were trying to decide whether it would upset the boy more to see her at this particular time or to have her visit put off. This kind of protection and guidance, from trained persons concerned for the youngster's welfare, continues until a boy or girl is old enough to stand alone.

Much thought is given to the return of individual youngsters to their own homes and communities. It is not unusual for a boy who has had a good record up to that time suddenly to explode just before his parole or discharge, perhaps to run away. Experienced workers recognize this reaction as a symptom of fear, lest he fail to make good or that fantasies of his homecoming that he has built up will fall short of reality.

Pains are taken to prepare those going out for the situation they are likely to find; the parole officers work with them closely after their return to their community. This is a crucial point, where better understanding on the part of the family and the community can be a decisive factor toward permanent rehabilitation.

All the children and adolescents committed, from whatever source, go first to one of the reception centers. Here complete social histories are compiled, psychological tests are given, and usually each newcomer is seen by a psychiatrist as well, as a preliminary to placement. Not many juveniles are committed for sex offenses, but when there is a sex problem the offender is always seen by a psychiatrist, both at the reception center and again if release on parole is contemplated.

The diagnostic facilities of the centers are also at the service of the smaller courts of the Commonwealth, which do not have their own facilities for evaluations. The Youth Service co-operates in this way with seventy-two courts, providing the state-wide court-connected clinic service mentioned in Chapter 4.

I visited three of the Massachusetts Youth Service institutions for boys and think that these three might well serve as models, or at least inspirations, for other states which must start an improved program with existing facilities and add to them, or alter them, without drawing too heavily on public funds.

The combined reception and detention home for boys, on the outskirts of Boston, was built especially for the function it performs. A big block of masonry, with no pretension to architectural distinction, it allows effective separation of youngsters committed by the courts because of delinquency—those who have stolen cars or raped or even murdered—from those being held on detention, perhaps runaways picked up by police or youngsters removed from their homes through no fault of theirs. It also separates little boys from bigger ones.

The locked doors to the various sections give a jail-like atmosphere upon entering, but within their sections the boys are free to come and go as they please, and many ways are provided for passing the time. There are two recreation rooms on each floor, each one with a television set, and there is a big gymnasium where the little fellows can run, or tumble and wrestle on big mats, and the bigger ones can play volleyball or basketball. Boxing matches with outsize boxing gloves help to relieve aggressions, but there cannot be such articles as dumbbells or Indian clubs, with which boys might do real damage to one another.

"The boys are frightened and filled with hostility when they come in," I was told. "Most are in need of external control. Many are mentally retarded."

A big enclosed yard for outdoor exercise and a big indoor swimming pool complete the recreational facilities. "We think we can say our boys are the cleanest ones in the Commonwealth," my guide remarked. "Every one gets two showers a day, and at least one swim!"

Short as is the stay of each boy—under the law, they cannot be held longer than two weeks on detention, and those committed to the Youth Service are passed along as soon as their diagnosis is completed—academic classes are carried on in a charmingly decorated schoolroom. There is a big industrial arts shop, and the staff lounge was decorated with samples of the boys' handiwork. Religious education is compulsory; there are chaplains of the principal faiths.

In addition to the psychological tests and psychiatric examinations —the same professional staff serves the girls' reception and detention center—made of those committed to the Youth Service by the courts, each youngster is given a physical examination. Many have medical problems, such as rheumatic heart or epilepsy. The nurses' office is a favorite spot for the boys. Many seek it just to see a woman. "They miss their mothers and long for them, even when the mothers don't seem to take much interest in them," the nurses told me.

Mr. Francis H. Maloney, the superintendent, is a big, solid, quiet man who might have been a varsity football lineman at some time in his career, a man well able, I should think, to maintain a firm but kindly hand over an ever-shifting population containing some youths as tough and dangerous as they come.

The Lyman School, for boys 12 to 16, occupies a large tract of ground at Westboro, Massachusetts, about twenty miles from Boston.

It forms a small community, its buildings ranging from an old frame edifice, used as headquarters, to a brand-new brick cafeteria and gymnasium. The head of the Lyman School, Mr. John M. Borys, is a Dartmouth graduate of not too many years back, whom one can envisage as shooting rapidly upward in any commercial organization, because of his energy and flow of ideas, but who prepared himself to help youngsters in trouble. And the boys at Lyman have been in trouble. All have been sent here after a trial on probation has not worked out. Their offenses range from those of the stubborn child and school offender to murder, though the most common ones are motor vehicle thefts and breaking and entering. The intelligence quotients range from 40 to 145.

"A considerable number of the boys have been deprived of ordinary human experiences for many years," Mr. Borys told me. "Many have tremendous physical problems, too, such as rheumatic hearts, epilepsy and club feet. They are full of hostility. One of our basic functions is to give them normal and wholesome attitudes."

Those needing special medical care receive it; all manner of dental problems are taken care of. The school furnishes a complete academic program, designed not just to give as good an education as in public school but to make the boys want to continue their education after they have left Lyman. There are Boy Scout and Sea Scout groups, and groups are provided for boys interested in airplanes, electronics, radio and similar matters. One of these groups has completed a color organ, another has constructed a miniature railroad, with the help of citizen advisers from surrounding communities.

The resources of the nearby communities, in fact, have been drawn upon in numerous ways to round out the lives of the Lyman boys with normal experiences of which they have hitherto been deprived. Harvard students come to Westboro on a volunteer basis to head discussion groups and work with the youngsters in swimming, wrestling and boxing. An ex-Marine from Westboro teaches skin diving; members of the Veteran Boxers' Association instruct in boxing and stage boxing exhibits. The Jewish-American Veterans in nearby Worcester put on entertainments at the school. The Framingham Kiwanis Club gives a very fancy dinner each year as a reward for excellent performance by the Boy Scout and Sea Scout groups. Other townspeople work with individual youngsters in the cottages, in the evening.

Each month a birthday party is held at the school for the boys whose birthdays fall in that month, different community organizations taking turns in providing games, refreshments and presents. There are special parties for youngsters who have no one to take an interest in them, and children from the school are invited to parties in homes in the different communities. The community friends provide cook-outs, picnics and hundreds of trips to football and basketball games.

In the big, new dining hall, where the staff and their charges select their food, cafeteria style, the kitchens have the latest equipment for large quantity cooking, and I was assured that the baked delicacies are unsurpassed anywhere. The chef has a wide variety of menus and a repertory of at least twenty desserts, to prevent monotony.

My visit was at the Christmas season, and, as at the reception-detention center, there were Christmas decorations everywhere. In the Lyman reception office, where newcomers to the school check in, a table was covered with plates of cookies and other goodies as a welcoming gesture.

Their greatest difficulty, Mr. Borys told me, is in getting the home communities to accept the youngsters again when they leave Lyman, though the surrounding communities help with this too. Representatives of a citizen organization, the Friends of Lyman School, visit the school authorities and other community sources beforehand and try to convince them that these youngsters do not constitute a risk, but the problem remains. I was told by a friend outside the Youth Service of a sad episode. A boy who had committed an unpremeditated murder— the one crime, so penologists say, that any of us might commit under force of circumstance—had been rehabilitated and accepted at a private school where the Service wished to place him. The Board of Trustees of the school discharged the principal who had accepted him.

Another difficulty is overcrowding. Two hundred and fifty is the ideal population for the facilities, with a maximum of 300, but the usual population is 350. (The same thing is true of nearly all our public facilities set up for juveniles, including the public schools.)

My last call was at John Augustus Hall, at West Boylston, Massachusetts, for the little fellows from 7 to 12 whose main need is for a better environment than the one they have had. For this purpose a big old brick mansion was purchased, standing on a hilltop and surrounded by wide lawns and shade trees. Additions have been made to provide a capacity for 80 youngsters.

The attempt here is to create as homelike an atmosphere as possible. There is no regimentation, there are no locked doors, the boys run about freely. Women on the staff provide the mother figure needed particularly by little boys. "We are tolerant of things we wouldn't stand for in older boys," Mr. Patrick F. Creeden, the softspoken superintendent, told me.

Here are sent "stubborn children," school problems, and arsonists, whose own homes have proved incapable of giving the kind of direction and guidance youngsters need. They stay until they are considered ready to return to their homes, the average stay being one year. However, parents may get their youngsters back at any time they wish without having to go to court.

Whenever possible, a boy is released at the end of the school year, so that he may start in his home school the next fall with his class. At the Hall, school runs from a special Grade 1 through Grade 6. The morning I was there there had been a fresh snowfall, and the pupils were out skiing down the hill or sliding down on big metal trays. "They are only kids once," Mr. Creeden said. "We want them to enjoy it while they can."

Unlike the practice in most institutions, at mealtimes the food is placed on the tables before the children come in and they serve themselves. Staff members do not sit at the tables but are at hand to give help where it is needed. Some of the smaller boys have to have their meat cut.

"Many are like little savages when they come to us," Mr. Creeden said. "They have lived mainly on jam and peanut butter and won't eat turkey until they see others doing it. Boys have gained fifteen pounds in the first month after they entered the Hall. All are craving attention and love, someone they can believe in."

In summer they are taken swimming and on picnics, and on weekly expeditions. John Augustus Hall, like the Lyman School, has its Friends organization, who give a birthday party each month and, on the weekly game night, come to the Hall and play with the youngsters. Here, too, medical and dental problems are taken care of, even to the extent of operations to repair cleft palates.

But the Massachusetts Youth Service has not stopped with a program for children in trouble, as enlightened and efficacious as devoted personnel can make it. It has built up a system for ferreting out and bringing help to youngsters headed for trouble, *before* they have done something to bring them into court. Community representatives assigned to certain areas of the state, and workers attached to selected agencies, advise on the establishment of local programs for helping pre-delinquents.

A very important branch of the prevention service is the School Adjustment Counselor Program, started in 1955. The Youth Service Board at the time of my visit in late 1962 was co-operating with 90 counselors in 75 school systems. The local school boards select the counselors, but the Youth Service supervises the program and sets standards in personality factors and professional training. The Commonwealth paid $4500 toward the salary of the first counselor in each system and $2250 toward the salary of each additional counselor. I was told that if a counselor succeeds in keeping just two youngsters out of institutions each year he saves his own salary.

The counselors' function is to work with children who are neglected, maladjusted, emotionally disturbed, or showing other signs of potential delinquency, and with their parents. They work with the school authorities and community leaders, too, to improve general conditions for youth in the town or city.

This excellent system for preventing delinquency through the schools is also in effect in Connecticut and Illinois, in both cases under the State Department of Education. From the standpoint of preventing serious sex crime, it gives the community an opportunity to bring help to youngsters seriously deprived emotionally before they have reached the stage in their illness where only the most intensive psychiatric treatment can cure them.

The Massachusetts Youth Service officials nevertheless are far from satisfied with the job they are doing. There is not nearly enough psychiatric help; the mental health clinics are understaffed and many more are needed. "We don't have sufficient facilities to help all the parents who call us asking, 'What should I do with my youngster?' "

They would like to have more forestry camps, and the budget does not permit a large-enough staff to make the best and fullest use of the one they have. While the heads of the Service feel that steady improvement has been made in treatment and diagnostic methods since 1952, they suffer from the occupational disease of government agencies—inability to pay high-enough salaries to attract and hold persons with the training and experience needed for the difficult task of remaking human beings. Though the Service maintains an in-service training program, taking young people from college and sending personnel to college, it is constantly losing personnel to better-paying positions. I observed, however, that a number of the officials I met, holding responsible positions, had been with the Service since its inception, indicating that in many instances the gratification of being part of an inspiring program can transcend the lure of higher pay.

As was noted in Chapter 4, there is a problem in the disposition of truly dangerous cases—the delinquents who are mentally ill, with a bent for violence. The mentally ill fall within the province of the Department of Mental Health, which is not equipped to handle delinquents, and the Youth Service facilities are not equipped to handle the mentally ill. "We don't get a great many of these youngsters, but what to do with the ones we get is a big headache. We haven't been able to solve it satisfactorily yet," one of the officials told me; very few states have solved this problem. Yet it is from this group that future perpetrators of violence are most likely to come.

Another lack felt by the Massachusetts authorities was in the field of research. "We now have around 10,000 case histories stored up, containing background information about 10,000 boys and girls, but we have been unable as yet to take advantage of this information. The

Commonwealth of Massachusetts spends many millions of dollars on its youth program every year. Another hundred thousand spent for collating and analyzing the material in our files and the records made by the youngsters after leaving us could enable us to improve our treatment and parole procedures immeasurably."

I was told of these same difficulties wherever I went. It is good economics to keep as many people out of public institutions as possible and to speed as safely as possible the rehabilitation of those committed to institutions.

But when one sees the job that is being done, and the way it spreads understanding of troubled youths throughout the community, it appears very well worth doing, even though it may not yet be done perfectly.

We cannot calculate how many lives of women and children are being saved by youth agency programs or how many more will be spared a horrifying and damaging experience, for one can never know what crimes would have occurred that did not occur because preventive measures had been instituted in time. But we can be certain that a considerable number of boys are being turned from sexually antisocial behavior by the humane and understanding treatment they receive. We can also be certain that many boys and girls, as Mr. Ernest Mitchell remarked, are being rescued from hostilities and neuroses which might make them the kind of parents who rear children with criminal or violent tendencies.

# 19

# Further possibilities for prevention, and some early symptoms of the sickness

Scientific methods are being developed for singling out youngsters in need of special help, even before any symptoms have appeared. A ten-year study made by the New York City Youth Board and completed in 1962 found predictions as to whether a young child will in time become delinquent to be amazingly accurate. The study tested tables for the prediction of delinquency drawn by Drs. Sheldon and Eleanor Glueck of the Harvard Law School.

In 1952, 301 6-year-old boys entering first grade in two New York City schools in a district with a high delinquency rate were checked by the Glueck tables as to their likelihood of becoming delinquent within the next ten years. The three major factors on which the predictions were made were (1) supervision of the boy by the mother, (2) discipline of the boy by the mother and (3) family cohesiveness—the extent to which the family enjoyed doing things together, inside and outside the home. As originally planned, the study was to have gone into the father's relationship with the boy, but this aspect was dropped when it was found that many of the homes lacked a male parent.

It was predicted in 1952 that 33 of the boys, or more than 10 per cent, would become delinquent by age 16 and that 243 boys would not become delinquent. Twenty-five were rated as having an even chance to become delinquent.

Ten years later, only 5 of the 33 considered potential delinquents had stayed out of trouble, giving this prediction an accuracy rating of

85 per cent. The prediction for nondelinquents proved to be 95 per cent accurate.

On the basis of this check of the Glueck tables, a manual has been prepared which gives full details for setting up a predictive test among first-graders, including the way to approach the families, questions to ask and method of scoring the answers. "A Manual of Procedures for Application of the Glueck Prediction Table" may be obtained from the Youth Board Research Institute of New York, 79 Madison Avenue, New York, N.Y., for $1.00.

A number of authorities have pointed out the difficulty, however, of predicting which youngsters headed for delinquency will have a propensity for committing serious sex crimes. Dr. Ralph Brancale, director of the New Jersey State Diagnostic Center, told me that it is hard to define the dangerous adolescent, the one who is likely to explode. It is necessary to distinguish between adolescent mischief, or temporary turmoil, and deep-seated disturbance.

He suggests, "We have to start with those who express their problems in a violent way. The group to be worried about is one with a sustained pattern of repetition, no matter what you do in treatment."

Society's practice for the most part has been to confine the repeaters in training schools which do not have the facilities to treat those with destructive, antisocial tendencies.

"Eliminating a potentiality for violence is a deep-seated, insidious problem," Dr. Brancale said. "It is not going to be easy with tough kids, whose emotions have been battered out of shape by their early experiences." But through the work of clinics similar to the New Jersey one, Dr. Brancale hopes insights will be gained which eventually can be applied in prevention.

Dr. Manfred S. Guttmacher has called for more investigations like the Kinsey studies and for more and better biochemical researches. He mentions "the superb clinical material passing through our courts" and calls for "more intensive and better scientifically controlled studies of those patients along psychoanalytical lines. The Rorschach and new specially created psychological tests should be intensively explored to test their usefulness as diagnostic and predictive techniques. Sociological methods of assay, like those used by the Gluecks in their study of juvenile offenders, should be applied to sex offenders."

Another authority, Lewis J. Doshay, has maintained that it is juvenile general offenses, rather than juvenile sex offenses, which are related to later criminal behavior. "The prediction prospects for any juvenile sex offender should not be based on the sex offense but on the criteria of background personality configuration, nature of response to school and play, and general behavior."

However, reviewing a serious sex offender's history with the benefit of hindsight, it is usually not too hard to see the signs which pointed the way to future trouble, as in other types of mental illness. The Michigan Report previously referred to said, in 1951, "The childhood of nearly every deviated sex offender contained signs of a gathering storm and by the same token presented a series of opportunities which were too often misunderstood or ignored."

Quite often the "first offense" of a person charged with a serious sex crime was not a first offense at all. Whenever a sex murder is committed and a plea of not guilty by reason of insanity has been entered, the defense dredges up many incidents from the client's earlier life which betoken abnormality. But it is not until a deadly crime has been committed that anyone has paid attention.

People are inclined not to report sex incidents in which no great harm has been done. I would not have reported Jack Smith if he had not reverted to a manic condition. I did not realize, then, that my forbearance might have had grave consequences for someone else. Alarming behavior should be reported. Little Edith Kiecarius might be alive today if one of the women or children to whom Fred Thompson exposed himself had reported him. But we should also be assured that the person we report will be given the help he needs, by the law and medicine.

There are some attitudes in youngsters which are considered to be indicative of a possibility of later criminal sexual behavior. These include a lack of guilt feelings about sex misconduct; unusually aggressive, hostile relations to others; an abnormal lack of affection for family and intimates; a tendency to seek immediate gratification regardless of the rights of others or the individual's own best interests.

(The last came out many times in my interviews with serious sex offenders.)

It has been suggested that acts of sexual delinquency inconsistent with a youngster's chronological age call for investigation and treatment or segregation, before more serious offenses are committed. High on the list of warning signals is deliberate sadism in torturing animals or younger playmates. Sadism is partially a sexual trait and a definite sign of something wrong.

A psychiatrist at a clinic I visited showed me a baby doll, about half of life size, made from some composition material. The doll's arms had been bound closely to its sides with tape. A knitting needle was thrust into one eye, and another knitting needle had been plunged clear through the head from the back; a scissor blade protruded from the doll's chest.

"What would you think if your ten-year-old son were to do something like this to a doll?" the psychiatrist asked me.

"I would be very disturbed!" I replied emphatically.

The boy's parents were disturbed and, being highly intelligent, well educated people, had at once brought the boy to the clinic. He had not harmed any flesh and blood creature, and there may have been an innocent explanation for his treatment of the doll. However, if the action was an expression of deep hostilities, future heartache could be avoided by starting treatment at age 10.

We are justified in believing that a great deal of sexual sickness could be nipped at tender ages if every community or group of communities had a child guidance or mental health clinic, to which every parent in the area could have access, when a child's behavior is troubling or merely puzzling.

Much childish behavior that baffles or bothers parents is simply childish behavior, and I would not have parents anxiously looking for sinister signs or hauling a youngster to a psychiatrist or clinic every time a problem comes up. But they should be able to get expert help when a problem has defeated their own best efforts. In many cases, their own attitudes are at fault, and learning this and being helped toward better ones can prevent much future antagonism between parents and children, at the least, and may prevent the development of an unhappy youngster into an "unknown sex fiend."

Dr. Manfred S. Guttmacher believes that the key to prevention of sex crimes lies in establishing better attitudes within the home. He quotes Spurgeon English for the kind of home background that will foster children with healthy minds and emotions.

1. The child should have warmth from the mother. With the warmth, the mother should combine affection so that the male in particular has memories of pleasant experiences with women and will want to re-establish ties of intimacy with women in later life.

2. He should have a sexual enlightenment free of taboos or disgust in relation to heterosexual union.

3. He should have the interest of a man during his growth, so that he identifies himself with masculine attitudes, particularly those pertaining to responsibility and home formation, including a satisfaction in parenthood. The first and second rules apply also for the woman. Third, she should have from early life the warm interest of a man so that she feels a kinship with the life of a man. When we consider how many fathers ignore their daughters rather completely during their whole development, it is not surprising that there is so little ability for women to like men and get along with them. In certain instances where warmth and understanding of men and pleasure in physical intimacy with them is lacking, a leaning toward emotional and physical satisfaction with women is the result.

Lesbianism may not be the only consequence. Women who marry though subconsciously hating men tend to be the ones whose sons turn out to be woman-haters, sometimes working out their hatred in violent sexual ways.

The Michigan Report said wisely, "The next generation can have fewer sex offenders than the present one if the misinformed and anxiety-ridden attitudes of many adults can be corrected."

In fact, anything that can be done to help parents achieve the right attitudes toward their children can help to cut down the sex-crime problem. The trouble here is that the parents who most need this help are the hardest to reach. They are the ones least likely to read books and articles on child rearing, to attend lectures. Many fight expert help with all their might when it is offered to them. Visiting children's courts, I have heard parents deny with vehemence that there was anything wrong with a child who showed many signs of deep disturbance. I have seen an attractive, well-dressed woman pace up and down like a tigress in a judge's chambers, furiously countering the charges of hair-raising neglect of her children brought against her by saying they were *her* children, it was her right to do with them as she pleased.

It is very easy to become indignant at parents who are selfish and smothering or callous and brutal. Yet if we go into their backgrounds, in the way a good clinic goes into the backgrounds of troubled youngsters, we find that they treat their children as they themselves were treated, not knowing any other way.

The very fine Westchester County, New York, Children's Court for many years has worked as sedulously with the parents of juvenile offenders as with the youngsters themselves. The improvement brought about in many homes that appeared to be hopeless has made me feel that in any parent who keeps a child—does not abandon it but provides some kind of home, any kind of home—there is something that can be reached if someone cares enough to try. This is a stupendous task, and one outside the capabilities of many communities at the present time. But it is a goal to work toward.

Stressing, in the Mayo Clinic study referred to in Chapter 10, the difficulties of effecting a cure in a "full-blown" sex deviant, Drs. Johnson and Robinson strongly urged that pediatricians and family physicians make it their business to educate parents who have damaging attitudes. These doctors are in a position to gain insight into bad family situations while children are small. Preventive measures could be carried out then by relatively simple efforts on the part of the attending physician.

A number of authorities who have suggested better education in sex matters add that this education should not be limited to youngsters and problem parents. The general public, too, should be given a better understanding of what is normal sexuality and what abnormal.

One might think that no one in our present culture who can read, if he possesses ordinary intelligence, could escape knowing all there is to know about sex. Nowadays it is not even necessary to avail one-self of the "how to" books advertised freely in family journals or of so-called pornography. In many popular novels, love is portrayed as the immediate bedding down of a man and woman the moment attraction is felt, often with full details supplied. It has become com-monplace in "whodunits," once distinguished by their lack of sex and sentiment, for lovely women to be represented in avid pursuit, for undisguisedly sexual reasons, of newly met males. Women as individuals possessing dignity and entitled to respect from men are becoming, in a literary sense, a vanishing species.

Abnormal sex is openly propagandized. At the Institute for Sex Research (founded by Dr. Kinsey) in Bloomington, Indiana, I was shown a sadistic picture magazine and told that the greater propor-tion of under-the-counter publications are devoted to sadism. This particular magazine showed a pretty, scantily clad young woman engaged in tying up another pretty, scantily clad young woman in a variety of ways and postures—that was the theme of every picture in the magazine. The authorities could do nothing about it because no whips or other pain-inflicting instruments were involved, and both tier-up and tiee were beaming in evident enjoyment of their rather odd form of divertissement. One must imagine the kind of thing that is barred from the mails but finds ways to circulate to a large audience.

A number of persons who work with sex offenders have assured me that their charges have not been influenced by the pornographic or near-pornographic literature that abounds today, because they don't read it. Sex offenders, as a group, have on the contrary been found to be poorly informed about sex and to have many miscon-ceptions about it. But if they were born after 1940, they could hardly fail to have read or seen comic books of a type prepared for children beginning with the early 1940's. Dr. Frederic Wertham exposed these children's comics as a vast hotbed of violence, sex and sadism in his book, *Seduction of the Innocent*. It was the result of a long study made by Dr. Wertham and his associates at the Lafargue Psychiatric Clinic in New York City's Harlem, both of the comic books themselves and their effect on the children who were referred to the clinic. The connection between children's crimes and the comic books prepared especially for them had escaped attention previously because few adults had any idea of the contents of the books.

Dr. Wertham describes many in *Seduction of the Innocent* and reproduces sequences from a number. One of the pictured sequences exceeds in horror the crimes of Albert Fish and the murder of Avril Terry. I would not have believed this possible had I not seen the actual comic reproduced, with its gory text, in Dr. Wertham's book. Sadistic and abnormal sex are frequently mingled with gangster-type shootings and brutality. In the crime comics, the criminals are the heroic figures, the police are shown as inept bunglers.

Youngsters who came to the Lafargue Clinic would report that they spent hours every day poring over these primers in crime, sex and horror. Those who could not read the text, whether because they were too young or by age 12 had not yet learned to read, nevertheless could follow the story from the pictures. Dr. Wertham gave the figures for the many millions of these children's comics, produced every year, and re-sold and traded back and forth so that their readership is multiplied as is no other type of publication. Parents alerted to the problem found themselves unable to keep these atrocities from their children, because they could be obtained sub rosa from other children.

It is easy to see where the disturbed 15-year-old described to me could have gained his impression that what you did with girls was to grab them and hurt them. Dr. Wertham mentions a number of cases where children were found hanging, a children's comic, open to a hanging sequence, on a chair or on the floor nearby. The 10-year-old boy who had tied up a doll and skewered it with knitting needles and a scissor blade could easily have derived his inspiration from a comic book designed for children.

The children's comic books, thanks to the efforts of Dr. Wertham and others, are not as bad as they used to be, but at time of writing the postal authorities are trying to prevent unsolicited mailings, to children, of out and out pornography.

With literature, as with money, bad currency drives out good. A well-known woman writer, whose books on idealistic themes have always sold well, decided some antidote was called for and wrote a novel of wholesome family life—there is still quite a lot of it in the U.S.A.—but her publishers turned down her manuscript, the first one of hers they had ever rejected. Her editor remarked that they had in the office at the time a manuscript so filthy he could not read it, inured as he was to such material.

"You're not going to publish it, are you?"

"Of course we're going to publish it! It's what the public wants!"

I am told that there are now organizations of homosexuals, and that magazines are published glorifying their particular idiosyncrasy. In one of our big cities, I blundered into a bookstore which evidently specialized in this type of thing. I didn't stay long. As I scanned the rows of books on exhibition and saw that every one dealt with some form of sex aberration, a weird male creature swam out of the dimly lighted rear portion of the store, a welcoming leer on his face, and I got out of there.

Where may boys and girls from unfortunate backgrounds learn about normal sex, normal love, normal family life? Whether or not it is true that the average sex offender is uninfluenced by the current stress on sadism, violence, immorality, amorality and aberrant sex, many authorities believe that frank and forthright sex instruction in the schools could clear up conflicts in the minds of many troubled youngsters. It could hardly make them worse.

Such a program should educate not merely in biological facts but in normal sex behavior: the impulses and desires normal at different stages of growth, the personal and social reasons why society has demanded that we control certain impulses, the bases of a happy and successful love relationship, the factors of maturity. Classes should be conducted in such a way that pupils can ask searching and intimate questions without embarrassment—one way is through written questions, unsigned—and receive honest answers. Perhaps a seminar of parents would be a good way to start this off, so the parents too may become informed and have an idea of the way the school class will be conducted. We had better find *some* way to counteract the spate of sadism, promiscuity, homosexualism and other abnormal forms of sex which today's youngsters can hardly avoid encountering in one guise or another.

In a broad sense, we must recognize that the troubles of the serious sex offender began far back in his ancestry, one generation of persons ill equipped for parenthood producing another, and so to the present day. The pace may even accelerate as the age for marrying becomes lower, with a larger proportion of immature parents, and modern life makes increasingly heavy demands on the stability of our citizenry.

One authority has suggested, perhaps with tongue in cheek, that the way to wipe out sex crime is to make all parents perfect. Dr. Asher Pacht of Wisconsin and I agreed, in our final talk together, that if we wait for this to happen we will wait a very long time indeed.

"But we *can* break the cycle, in many instances," Dr. Pacht said, "by providing proper treatment for those who display serious effects of misguided parental attitudes. Their children and grandchildren can have the chance at normal, wholesome development that they never had."

This is not only the humane and enlightened way to deal with the sex offender. It is the only way women and children can be safe from the "unknown sex fiend."

# FIVE

# The sex offenders speak

# Ten ways to make a
# sex offender

In the course of my investigations I had read many case histories and general conclusions about sex offenders; I had talked with many experts who have dealt with them. I had learned a great deal about sexual psychopaths, sociopaths or deviates, as one may choose to call them, but it was all at second hand.

I wanted to see for myself what these men were like, hear from their lips what they thought about their crimes. The generous co-operation of the Wisconsin authorities and of Dr. G. Lee Sandritter at California's Atascadero Hospital gave me an opportunity, unexampled for a layman so far as I know, to do this. The California system, which must deal with large cities, mixed races and nationalities, and sex offenders of all types and degrees of menace to the community, was a valuable supplement to Wisconsin's more homogeneous and rural situation.

In Wisconsin, the selections for private interviews were made by the professional staff. I asked to be permitted to see men who were articulate and would be able to express with some accuracy their thoughts and feelings. All those chosen had been under therapy for a considerable time, in some cases for a number of years, and most had an excellent comprehension of their difficulties and the underlying causes.

In California, members of the Emotional Security Program (the ESP referred to in Chapters 16 and 17) helped in singling out offenders who would present a good sampling of the different types of sex cases. Several of the men I talked with there had responsible posts in the patient government, and one ESP official offered his own story, saying he would not even mind being identified if undisguised facts would help toward better understanding of the sex offender and his problems.

A woman nurse was present at my private interviews in California but took no part in the proceedings. At Waupun Prison in Wisconsin, no one else was present, and the door of the office loaned me for the interviews was kept closed, after I learned that it embarrassed my interviewees to be in full sight of persons passing by. For the benefit of the curious, I was not in the least apprehensive, nor was there any reason for me to be.

When you sit across a desk from a succession of men found guilty of crimes considered loathsome and inexcusable by our society, you are struck by the lack of any signs marking them off from the rest of the human race.

One young man who had preyed on boys in the pre-pubertal age range had the same mental age as his victims. In actuality, he was not so much debauching young boys as engaging in sex play with his mental peers. Small and delicately constructed, he looked much younger than his chronological age, which was 21, and in an institution where he had been confined previously he had to have a guard to protect him from the advances of other inmates. Alec was a gentle and amenable chap, who meant no harm and represented the sex offenders whose crimes stem from a mental lack and who will always require either careful supervision or lifelong detention.

The rest with whom I talked ranged from men with advanced college degrees to those who had not completed high school, which made for a difference in vocabulary and grammar, but, with only one or two exceptions, all the men revealed good minds. Several were more than ordinarily attractive in appearance. I can only think of two whom I would have distrusted if I had met them in ordinary situations.

I began every interview by explaining that I was writing a book on sex offenders and would like to have their viewpoint on the problem. I promised that I would write nothing which might serve to identify them to friends or townspeople. They seemed to accept this unquestioningly. Their manner during the interviews was serious. I felt that, like the ESP official, they welcomed an opportunity to help the public to a better understanding of the sex offender.

The layman, of course, must beware of being taken in by glib parroting of psychiatric terms and concepts which people under therapy pick up, but I was able to confirm, from their case records and from their therapists, that again, with only one or two exceptions, the men were frank and truthful—though several did withhold particularly heart-rending childhood episodes, perhaps considering them too indelicate for my ears or possibly considering it unmanly to appear to be making an appeal to my sympathies.

Dr. Asher Pacht, head of the Clinical Services in Wisconsin, had spoken of the myriad elements which bring about sexual deviation and which make impossible a "magical" solution—effecting a cure by uncovering a long-forgotten childhood experience—a concept gained by many intelligent and well-educated people from reading popular psychoanalytical literature. The interviews confirmed the varied and complex nature of the underlying factors in sex crimes.

In some cases, the childhood backgrounds fell into the classical patterns that have been found by many investigators. A middle-aged man who had been a molester of children for many years had had a rough, indifferent father, whose work took him away from home a great deal, and an overly affectionate mother, to whom he had been bound too closely. "I was very sick, as a child. That forced her to be with me lots." But the mother had also made him afraid of females by her severe condemnation of his attempts, in childhood, to find out how little girls were made. All of his victims had been little boys.

"When I grew up I was too timid to approach women. I felt inferior to other adults. I was always very shy, though I pretended to be rough, like my father. I got along well with children, I could be myself when I was with them." He said that, as a result of therapy, he now enjoyed grown-ups and felt at ease with them.

This man has a benevolent face and a warm smile. I asked, "Did you ever hurt the children you tampered with?"

"Oh, no, I love children, I would never hurt them. There was one funny thing. I was living with a family once when the wife had to go to the hospital. While she was away I took care of the children, cooked their meals, washed their clothes, bathed them, did everything for them. You know, I never did a thing wrong with those children. Somehow, that was different."

Even in this typical example of a background which predisposes a man to have a sexual relationship with children, the fact that my interviewee had been given the responsibility for these particular children had barred them as sexual objects.

Allen was a 17-year-old exhibitionist, very withdrawn and repressed, who had committed himself to the Atascadero State Hospital under the Mentally Abnormal Offenders statute. "There were no real charges against me," he told me. "I just want to keep out of society for a while, until I can learn to control myself. I never could talk things over with my parents. I think that now, maybe, I can."

Allen's exhibitionist episodes would follow a frustrating experience, when he felt let down and lonely. "I would get mad at everybody. I would want to call attention to myself." He had gone through an exhibitionist period at the age of 15, when his girl friend had broken with him, and again two years later when his own parents, and the parents of a girl he had been dating at this time, broke up the relationship. "My parents objected to the girl because they said she had a bad reputation."

"Did she?"

"Yes, but it wasn't her fault. Some fellows had told things about her that weren't so. Her parents didn't want her to go with me, either, and wouldn't let me see her. I got mad and despondent. I would get in my car, and when I passed a woman driving alone I would exhibit myself. I knew it wasn't right and didn't do me any good, but I couldn't help myself."

Allen also admitted a tendency to argue and fight when he was crossed, instead of working out a problem in a reasonable way, another result of over-frustration in childhood. Allen's task is to learn to react to problems in a mature fashion.

Marvin, a chronic Peeping Tom, in his middle twenties, good-looking, married and a father, lacked the outward signs of repression Allen showed, though his story was much more bizarre. His parents appear to have been wildly irresponsible—Marvin said his father had won his mother in a card game—and had led a wandering life, leaving their children behind them in orphanages or with relatives. Marvin was the youngest of a large family and the only child they kept. "I think the only reason they kept me was because I was expected to be the heir of a rich uncle."

There had never been any affection in Marvin's home, he said, and he had tried to commit suicide when he was 12. When he was 13, his parents were divorced, Marvin remaining with his father. Marvin grew up knowing nothing of love. "I thought of love in terms of sex. Everything relating to women was sex to me—sex on a Hollywood basis."

Going into the Service when he was 18, Marvin was given a dishonorable discharge for stealing a car and, ashamed to face his father after that, did not return home but worked as a door-to-door salesman. It was after he married and had two children that his peeping began.

"I wasn't ready for the responsibilities of a family. I felt that I was a failure. I didn't like having to go from door to door, selling, but didn't know what else I could do. I felt trapped. I started going out at night, peeping, and masturbating while I peeped, to get rid of tensions."

Marvin now recognized that he had always been thinking defensively. "I argued excessively and bore grudges. I was ashamed to admit that I loved my wife. Even now my voice trembles when I speak the word 'love.' I was afraid to love for fear of getting hurt in the end."

What triggered his peeping, he finally realized, was arguing and feeling unhappy. "I would get into an argument at the plant, that night I would go out and peep, and afterwards I would feel worse."

But the peeping itself became obsessive. He started doing it in the daytime as well as at night, sometimes several times in a single day. Being arrested and sent to jail did no good; he would resume the peeping and masturbating as soon as he was released, though he knew it was harming him and he didn't want to do it. Marvin several times had asked to be committed to Atascadero State Hospital under the

California Mentally Abnormal Offender program but was refused, because he was endangering no one else. Finally his wife interrupted a trial to beg the judge, in open court, to let her husband have the help he needed. The judge granted her request.

Marvin told me he had been brought up on a philosophy that what is to be will be. "In the hospital, I am beginning to see the opportunities I have for change and improvement. I have returned to the religion I had abandoned. Now, instead of arguing, getting all wrought up, and then going off to myself and masturbating, I go off, get hold of myself, and go back and apologize. I'm beginning to be more aware of consequences, learning to stop and think before I say something I shouldn't."

Marvin said, his voice not trembling, that he loves his wife, he believes he will be able to conquer his defensiveness. When that time comes, he will be able to control his tendency to revert to infantile behavior.

Incest ranks high among the crimes of sex offenders in both Wisconsin and California, and varied indeed are the routes by which a man may arrive at such a relationship with a daughter or stepdaughter.

Van had been selected for me as an example of a pattern interrupted fairly early which, if continued, could have become much more serious. The only man I talked with privately who had displayed sadistic tendencies, he was the only one who in talking to me suppressed the most alarming feature of his crime—the overt hostility, violence and sadistic overtones in the sex relationship he had had with an 11-year-old stepdaughter. He also placed the blame on his victim, a characteristic often found in sex offenders, in contrast to general ones.

Van was in perhaps his middle thirties, tall, dark and handsome in a rather sullen, lowering way. He told me that his mother had been very religious and had dreamed of his becoming a preacher. He had been held down very strictly until he was entering adolescence, when his mother had a nervous breakdown and the severe restraints were removed, though not the resentments they had engendered. He believed, however, that his hostile attitudes had dated from his first marriage. His in-laws had been against it. When the marriage broke up and his wife took their children and went to live with her parents, he felt his family had been taken away from him unjustly.

An added injustice, he said, was that, though he was a union man, the union in the state where he and his wife had been living wouldn't accept him. "Having to live on charity burned me up. I went with a gun to get my children out of the state. I was so emotionally sick that I was ready to sacrifice my own life to accomplish this."

When threats of violence failed to move his in-laws, Van married again, a widow with a little girl, and his disturbance was exacerbated when he found he couldn't handle the emotional problems created by his new marriage. "I felt so guilty about raising another man's child, and another man raising my children."

Van said he got along well enough with his stepdaughter for two years. "Then I began clamping down on her, like a parent." By this he meant punishing her, but he did not confess to the brutal whippings, and keeping the girl tied in a chair for many hours, that I had been told about. He also insisted that the sex relations, begun when the girl was 11, had been at the child's suggestion and had followed a beating or whipping.

"You were a grown man," I pointed out. "If she solicited you, why did you consent?"

He looked up at me from under heavy, dark brows.

"I resisted the first time," he replied. "But the next time—well, I guess I weakened."

He told me there had been only three sexual episodes when he was arrested for whipping the girl—he said it was because she had stolen some money—and the district attorney had extracted the incest story from the child. It was—and is—an interesting aspect of the incest cases that very often the authorities were not notified, even when the mother knew what was happening. In many instances, the truth either came out by accident or was revealed when the wife wished to get back at her husband for some wrong she felt he had done to her.

Van made no mention of the strong hostilities which must have been engendered by the restrictions and frustrations of his own childhood, and which had inspired the cruel and extreme punishments he had meted out to a child whom he used as a sex object. He ascribed his troubles to selfishness, greed and lack of consideration for others, but that was by no means the whole story in his case. It is well that the laws in both Wisconsin and California make it possible for the authorities to hold such a man in custody as long as his hostility and sadistic impulses are unresolved.

Another incestuous father—he had had sex relations with a stepdaughter, his own daughter and the daughter of a mistress—had a childhood background the direct opposite of Van's, one of license and debauchery as opposed to Van's strict religious upbringing. This man, whom I shall call Fred, did in fact become a preacher in his adult years, the dream Van's mother had had for her son. A principal difference between the two men, however, is that Fred's crimes had no tinge either of the violence or the sadism that had characterized Van's antisocial reactions. Fred had been under treatment for several years and was reaching the point of discharge. A man of excellent intelligence, with nearly six years of college and graduate work, he had a clear understanding of the background factors which had shaped an immature and irresponsible personality.

"My parents were transient workers, never paid very well. We kids were allowed to do whatever we pleased. We lived in the South when I was little, in houses built up on stilts. It was during prohibition. The big folks would hold home-brew parties on the first floor, we children would be on the ground underneath them, drinking too, and having intercourse.

"We moved north when I was 13, and for five years I lived a normal teen-age life. That is to say, I went to school, I didn't drink or carouse around. Though I would slip out at night and look in at windows, hoping to see women undressing.

"When I was 18 I went into the Service, and there I had a wild life, low morals and everything else. But I was looking for something better. When I got out of the Service, I went to college and then married a woman with a 3-year-old daughter. She had been a school teacher and was as good as I had been bad, very religious and with high moral standards. I think maybe her standards were too high, she was too good and proper for me.

"I had been raised by a mother and sisters and spoiled rotten; I wasn't ready yet for true manhood and marriage. I had an emotional age of about 8. My trouble was that at a point of terrific disappointment I would become a child again and would go to a child for sex. When my stepdaughter was 8, I molested her. Her grandparents found out, though they didn't report me. I wish now they had. My wife forgave me but held my offense like a hammer over my head.

"I had always basically wanted to be good. I loved God, I wanted to make up for what I had done. I went to a seminary, became a minister, and preached for several years. But I had done this against my wife's wishes. She kept telling me I wasn't fit to be a minister." By this time, Fred had two daughters of his own. When the older one was 10, he molested her.

"My wife learned about the relationship with my daughter. I quit the ministry, we moved in with her parents, I was under the hammer worse than ever there. I built up a sales route, and we were able to have our own home again, but whenever we would visit my wife's parents, her father would keep taking digs at me.

"I knew I needed help. I went to a psychologist. He turned out to be a homosexual—the last thing I needed! One day during a treatment session, he came over to me and kissed me on the forehead. That was the end of that. I went to a Veterans' Hospital clinic, and the doctor I was assigned to said to me, 'They ought to shoot an s.o.b. like you.' I applied to another clinic by letter but never got an answer.

"Things kept building up and building up. I was under heavy pressure to make a go of my sales business. I was in bad trouble with my wife. I moved in with a woman I had become acquainted with on my route. She had a little girl. After I had a big quarrel with my wife, and another with my mistress, I had sex relations with the little girl."

Fred has a full realization of the immaturity which had led him to react to unhappiness and pressure by turning to children for sex. "I felt no shame until I came here. I did have guilt feelings, but they were not true guilt. I had to learn the meaning of not gaining my pleasures at the expense of others. It was the shame I had brought on my family that made me realize I had been infringing on the rights of others. Then I was so ashamed that I never wanted to leave the hospital. I have learned that the sexual life is not a necessity, that a life of activity and productivity is the answer."

Fred's wife has improved in her attitudes too. Through discussions with Fred's therapist at the hospital, she now sees how she had added to the strain under which her husband was laboring. Fred has talked to his children about his crimes and the shame he has brought on his family. "They understand. I think they have matured better because of it."

He stressed the difference between the men who are trying to re-make their personalities, and sex offenders who don't want to change. "We are sick men, just as much as if we had tuberculosis. We have to be shut up while we are sick, but we want to be cured. All we ask is that the public will give us a chance to show we mean it."

Still another incestuous father traced his difficulties to his mother's desertion of the family when he was 6 years old. (His therapist con-curred in this.) Ron and his brothers and sisters had been placed in institutions and foster homes; his father had paid them small atten-tion. Ron's life from then on had been characterized by a search for the maternal love and tenderness of which he had been deprived.

"Did you ever see your mother after she left home?"

"I make it a point to see her every twelve years, whether she wants to see me or not!" he said with considerable force.

He had never made many friends and formed a strong attachment to the first girl he ever went out with. He had expected to marry her; it was a severe blow when she refused, after several years of close association. The second girl he went out with was the one he married, and the first five years had not gone badly. After that she began to tire of the excessive demands he made on her for sympathy and un-derstanding. Finally she left him, and he was forced to put his chil-dren in institutions and foster homes, as his father had done.

"I soon saw that was no good. The same thing was happening to them that happened to my brothers and sisters and me. So I set up a home and took care of them myself."

The incestuous relationship with the oldest girl had grown out of his attempts to provide the children with the love and warmth he had missed in his childhood, though he admitted that male passion had entered in as well. He did not think the relationship had harmed the girl particularly, though he realized it hadn't helped her either. But he knew it had been wrong and a sign of weakness and emotional immaturity on his part. His worst punishment was that, since his imprisonment, his children were again scattered in institutions and foster homes. "They're traveling the same road I traveled."

This man was not looking forward to adjusting his difficulties with his wife or to a happier marriage with someone else. "I know I could never live with any woman." He recognized that he must become strong enough to go the rest of his lifetime without a close human relationship, before he will be ready for release.

Varied also are the factors which breed the kind of hostility leading to violent sex attacks on innocent persons, often strangers to the attacker.

I had been told by Atascadero authorities that in every sadistic-masochistic case studied in the hospital—and there many such cases had been studied—the offender had been subjected to brutality himself in childhood. I knew, from the case histories of the men I talked with, that a thread of emotional deprivation ran through their stories, and in a number of cases investigators had described the mothers as being rejecting or dominating or seductive, or as combining seductiveness with domination or rejection. However, none of the rapists I talked with spoke of their mothers in these terms, and the only references made to sex matters in connection with the mothers was that several had disciplined severely for manifestations of normal childish curiosity, and in a number of the homes sex had been regarded as dirty.

Whatever the men may have known in their hearts or revealed to a therapist or in their therapy groups, they were not exposing their mothers' more serious inadequacies to the outside world. I admired them for this. On the other hand, they freely admitted their own derelictions, but without coarseness and without going into the details of their crimes. I felt the same innate gentlemanliness in these men that I had sensed in Jack Smith.

With two rapists I talked with at Atascadero, racial prejudice had triggered the offenses. One of the men was white, the other a Negro. In both cases, hatred, rather than sex desire, had inspired the attacks.

Paul, the white patient, was a slight, shy young man of Spanish descent who had been convicted of a sex assault on a 14-year-old Negro boy. To look at Paul, gentle-appearing, soft-spoken, introverted, you would not connect him with violence at all. Paul thought there was significance in the fact that when he exploded a Negro had been the victim.

Paul's own father had died; his mother had married a Negro when he was 9 or 10. Paul had not resented his stepfather particularly, nor had he been abused by him. "He didn't pay me much attention. As a man, he never figured much." But the mixed marriage had badly confused the youngster. "I always felt pulled between the two races, I never felt that I belonged anywhere. I guess I developed a lot of resentment against Negroes, only I never let it out."

It was perhaps as a result of his confusion and over-sensitiveness that Paul became a drug addict and served a sentence on a narcotics charge. After his release, he was ashamed to go back to his former employer. He returned to his mother's home and lived there for a year, a recluse, hiding from people he knew. He was alone in the house when the Negro boy called to collect money owing him. Paul's resentment against Negroes and against life in general flared up, and the sex attack on the boy was the result.

Since he came to Atascadero State Hospital, Paul has begun to accept the fact that his mother had married a Negro. But Paul was an example of the shy, inhibited youngster, mentioned by Dr. Ralph Brancale in Chapter 10, who occasionally explodes into sex violence. It is perhaps more significant of Paul's improvement that through working in the ESP he has been developing self-confidence.

The Negro offender had raped four women unknown to him, three of them white women, before he was arrested. Though Negroes are not pre-eminently sex offenders, as has been shown by Dr. Gutt-macher's and other studies, I suppose that to whites the Negro rapist is the most feared of all criminals. Yet the Negro who entered the office where my interviews were being held was far from being fear-inspiring.

He held his tall and lithe but broad-shouldered and muscular frame erect, his features were finely cut, his face and bearing gave one an impression of intelligence, competence and manliness which was borne out by his manner of speech and the frankness with which he confessed his wrongdoing. John was in his very early thirties, was married and the father of four children. He had attained the highest noncommissioned rank in one of our Armed Services, he had fought for his country in Korea and had been wounded, and he had never been in trouble in his life until he was arrested for his third rape of a white woman.

John's parents, though poorly educated and limited to the harder, more grueling ways of making a living, evidently had had aspirations for their children. John's two older sisters had graduated from a teachers' college. When John, having graduated from high school, joined the Service at the age of 18, it was with the idea of going to college later on himself, under the G.I. Bill. While he was in boot camp, getting $85 a month, he had sent $25 a month to each of his sisters, who were in college at the time, and $20 a month to his mother.

John liked the Service so much and had done so well in it that, by the time he had been wounded and invalided home from Korea, he decided he would make it a career. The girl he fell in love with and married liked it too.

I had been told that John had had much suppressed feeling against racial discrimination, but I gathered that it had not bothered him in the Service, up to the time when discrimination had precipitated him into a situation he saw no way out of. Apparently he had always had access to his commanding officers, and they had listened sympathetically. He mentioned that he had passed the test for radio school, then had been assigned to cook school. He went to his C.O., and his assignment was changed to radio school. There were several incidents of this kind. His record of promotions and salary—at the time of his debacle he was getting the top pay for a noncommissioned officer, with an extra $30 a month for proficiency—indicated that he had been judged on his merits.

He did say that he felt frustrated when he was in an all-Negro group, but he also said that he never felt entirely at ease in any non-Service group. The Service appeared to be the determining factor. "I felt uncomfortable whenever I was off the base. There was no real reason, I thought it was something I could cope with." He stressed his happiness in the Service, his complete dedication to it. It was his home, his life, the only thing that counted, so far as the world outside his own family was concerned.

The bad time began when he decided to apply for service in Germany. He would be able to take his wife and children with him. They would have to spend some time in a post on the East Coast, but their parental families were on the East Coast; they would get to see their relatives as well as having the experience abroad. John's application was accepted, the move was made to the East Coast. John had the facts of discrimination brought home to him when he tried to find housing for his family.

It took him a while to catch on. There were no vacancies close to the base, but that was not unusual. He heard of an apartment house twenty-five miles away, phoned, and was told that they had a number of vacancies. But when he showed up in person to see the apartments, the superintendent said a mistake had been made, there were no vacancies. Several white buddies, arriving after he had, were immediately accepted there. Then John knew.

Eventually he had to settle his family in a city eighty-five miles from the base—it was the nearest housing he could get. He had planned to stay on the base during the week, driving home only for week ends. But his wife, pregnant with their fourth child, developed complications; two of the children came down with asthma. John was needed at home, and he had to make the long drive every week night and morning.

His wife's condition grew worse; the doctor said she would have to stay off her feet or they would lose the baby. John went to his C.O., who arranged to have a Red Cross worker help out during John's working hours. "That was fine, but the Red Cross looked at my salary and said I was able to pay for the helper. They didn't take into account the hundred dollars or so it was costing me every month for transportation—gas and oil, and repairs and upkeep on my car."

The bills piled up, and John's salary would not cover them. The crowning irony was that, when the new baby was two weeks old, John was ordered back to his former post in California and assigned to electronics school. Arriving back July 1, he had just a week to find housing and get moved in before starting electronics school on July 7. The electronics school meant hard study; at night John had to help his wife, not yet recovered from childbirth, with the household tasks and the children.

John said, "Everything happened in just two months' time, after we got back on July 1. My debts in the East began to catch up with me around the middle of July. I couldn't pay them, so the collectors went to my C.O. He called me in, I said I could pay them off in time, but couldn't then. He understood. But the collectors kept pestering him, and in early August, he called me in again and said they couldn't have that. I would have to pay the bills or get a dishonorable discharge."

It was the threat of a dishonorable discharge that broke John. "That was when I became hostile. I thought, 'Society has done this to me. I will let society pay.' They had spoiled the image I had of myself. They were making me seem a bad person. I would be the person they wanted me to be.

"I began going out at night and entering houses, stealing any money I could find. At first I felt guilty, and I never got enough money to be any help, just five dollars, or ten or twenty. I would look in the paper the next morning, but there was never any write-up of my burglaries. I decided I wasn't hurting people. That was what I wanted —to hurt them the way I had been hurt.

"I kept on with the burglaries, every night. My wife couldn't understand why I was going out every night, and I couldn't explain. She moved into another bedroom, I became hostile toward her. I wanted to be punished, but at the same time I didn't want to, because I hadn't yet accomplished my mission."

John's humiliation as a man and a provider became complete when his wife got a job in a laundry, just six weeks after the baby's birth.

"I hit the ceiling when I found it out," John said. "My mother had worked in a laundry when I was a child. I remembered how she would come home exhausted, her hair plastered to her head because of the heat and steam. I would have died before I would have had my wife doing that kind of work. But she told me she had a light, easy job on the third floor, where it was air-conditioned, so I calmed down. She worked on the afternoon and evening shift. I would go home and get supper, so we could let the babysitter go. One night I cooked a supper I was rather proud of and I said to the kids, 'Let's surprise your mother. Let's take the supper to the laundry, and eat it with her,' so we packed up the supper and got into the car. But I didn't find my wife on the air-conditioned third floor. She was on the hot, steamy second floor, doing heavy work, just the way it had been with my mother. We didn't eat supper with her. I turned around and took the kids and the supper home."

When John described his shock at finding his wife reduplicating his mother's hard lot, a tear formed in a corner of his eye. As he talked on, it made a long, silvery streak down his dark cheek.

"After my wife got home, we had a terrible quarrel. I tore out of the house, got in my car and looked for a place to burgle. I entered a house. A white woman was there alone, asleep in her bedroom. In the next room I found her purse, with two hundred eighty-five dollars in it. I took the money, and left.

"Two hundred eighty-five dollars—now that would have been a real help on my debts. But I kept driving around. I still wasn't satisfied. I wanted a reaction from the white people. I wanted them to suffer. I thought of the way they valued their women, while debasing ours. That was the way to make them suffer! I went back to the house I had burglarized. The woman was still asleep, on her bed. I went in the kitchen and got a knife. I held the knife on the woman and—I raped her.

"The next morning I looked through the paper, but there was nothing about the rape. I still hadn't hurt them. That night I went out again, found another house where a woman was alone, took a knife from her kitchen, held it on her and raped her. I wasn't fearful the first time, but this time I was. I got up and ran and ran and ran."

But there was nothing in the paper the next morning. John went out again that night but learned, too late, that his third victim was a Negress.

"I felt horrible when I found it out. I went home and vomited. I wanted to die." But he still felt unavenged, so far as the whites were concerned, and raped a third white woman. A neighbor of the victim had noticed John's car, where he had parked it late at night, and had taken the license number. Two hours after John got home, the police were at his door. That was on September 1.

"The minute I was in jail, I felt as if all my troubles had rolled off me. It was one way of making restitution, and I thought I could get help. I believe now that my burglaries and rapes were my way of saying, 'Please help me.' I felt so comfortable and relieved, in that jail cell!"

I asked John whether he thought he might eventually have murdered.

"I don't know," he answered. "When I would pick up the knife in the woman's kitchen, I certainly had no intention of using it. But I can't say for sure but that some time I might have."

But discrimination alone does not produce sex violence, otherwise there would be many more Negro rapists than there are. (It is worth repeating that the majority of rapists, in ratio to their proportion of the population, are native-born white men.) John realizes that there had been a certain rigidity in his personality, though he did not call it that. His inability to feel comfortable except on the base, among Service people, might have been one indication, and the almost obsessive commitment to his Service, his need to excel in it, another. He told me that he had been the only Negro in radio school, and he had been the only Negro in many other Service situations. "I felt I had a duty to be a credit to my race, that I should be a Crusader. I prided myself on my ability to get things done." I was told, in fact, that in the hospital John had a reputation for getting things done, expeditiously and well.

The way John expressed it was that he had found, after coming to Atascadero, that the men in the ward didn't like him. "Wanting to get things done had given me a personality that offends people. I guess I was too driving. When you've got fifteen people in a therapy group and they all say the same thing, it's something you've got to think about."

At the end of ten months in the hospital, John was recommended for a white card, a reward for outstanding improvement and performance, but the recommendation was turned down. "That hurt," John said. "I think it hurt because it was a disappointment for my friends, as well as for me. Maybe the therapists did it for that reason. I want to change, to become more humble. I have to learn to give my services without expecting a reward for them."

John now regrets his crimes wholeheartedly and is working to change the personality structure that had caused him to break when the pressure had been applied too heavily. His wife has stood by him. "She is as sorry as I am about what I did, but she knew I was sick. When she took the laundry job, she was trying to help in the only way she knew."

There was no racial, social or economic factor in the cases of Eddie and Phil, the two members of the small rapist therapy group at Waupun Prison, Wisconsin, mentioned briefly in Chapter 15. Both were white and native-born, their families were comfortably situated. Their problems appeared to rise entirely from family relationships. Eddie was not yet 20 when he was first committed to Waupun after criminally attacking a woman his mother's age; he had been paroled and then returned to the prison after attacking another middle-aged woman. It had been noted in his file at that time that he was essentially immature, appearing older and more confident than he really was. He had done poorly in school. The good adjustment he had made in prison previously had been superficial, to cover feelings of inadequacy. (The reader may remember that before the special rapist group was formed, the four rapists who composed it had been using their intelligence to counterfeit improved attitudes, while their emotional disturbance had not been touched.)

Both his parents were efficient workers, both were employed. The only home trouble Eddie reported was with his father, over his own drinking, which he said had been heavy. His mother was described in Eddie's case history as capable but rather cold. Eddie had never been able to stay away from home very long, but the investigators felt his attachment had not been due to love for his home but to a continued hope that he would get something there he had never had to date. His rape attempts seemed to be closely related to his failure to find the warmth and acceptance he longed for in his own family. He combined dependence on his parents with severely hostile, destructive feelings toward men and women. The relationships he had had with girls prior to his first crime had been in the interest of sexual experimentation, rather than in the girls themselves. He had never had a warm and lasting friendship with a girl.

When I talked with Eddie, he was about to be given another trial on parole, he had improved so much since joining the special rapist therapy group. He was relaxed, but his manner toward me had no tinge of familiarity. He said his great trouble had been that he had felt shut off from his parents. "I just didn't seem to be with it. I thought they didn't love me, but I know now that they did."

I asked Eddie whether he thought the lack of communication with his parents was due to the fact that his parents weren't interested, or whether he might have been closed up within himself, so that they were unable to get through to him. He believed the latter was the explanation. He said that school had been sheer nightmare to him, and when I asked if this might have been because he was shut into himself, he answered, "I never thought of it that way, but maybe it was." He went on to say that he had made a valuable discovery, working at his prison job, which had been preparing him for a trade in the outside world. "This is something I've got to tell my sister. She could do things well, and I used to think I couldn't do anything. I've learned, though, that if I work at something, I can do it. I could have gotten my school lessons, too, if I had worked at them. Maybe not as fast as she did, but I could have done them." Since Eddie has a good average intelligence, he is probably right about this.

Eddie has decided that, much as he would like to return to his home, it will be better for him to start out somewhere else, stand on his own feet. When I asked if there would be anyone he could go to if he felt the need of advice or encouragement, he said, "Oh yes, I'll have my parole officer. I can call on him any time."

And then there was Phil, the second member of the special rapist group. His intelligence quotient is high enough to have assured successful completion of a course in a good college, if the circumstances of Phil's life had ever brought him within shouting distance of college. But at the age when a more fortunate youth would be entering his sophomore or junior year, Phil was matriculating in the Sex Offender Facility at Waupun. He was now in his late twenties, two attempts at parole, at considerable intervals, having ended disastrously. Phil recognizes that he has some years more to go in the Facility. His crimes of forcible rape had been committed against girls with whom he was acquainted and, in at least one case, in a situation which might have given Phil some reason to think his attentions would not be entirely unwelcome. But he did not advance these facts as an excuse for his actions, or even refer to them. He volunteered that his crimes had been motivated by an impulse to belittle and degrade his victims, rather than by sex desire. He also was aware of a strong homosexual element in his resentment against the female sex.

Phil felt that his trouble primarily had been conflict between his father and himself. He had had a deadly fear of his father ever since he could remember. "It cut so deep that for a long time, when the fellows in my therapy group would ask me questions about my father, my mind would go blank. Just lately though, there's been an improvement. I get a little flash of something before I blank out. I still don't understand what made me so afraid of him. My therapist says maybe I was more sensitive as a child than I think I was."

His father was an irascible man, given to violent rages. Phil could never please him, no matter how he tried. "I kept on trying, because I wanted to make him love me. I knew I never could, but I couldn't stop trying. It's like we are about death. We all know we are going to die, but we keep hoping we won't. That's the way I was about getting my father to love me. I was always afraid to do anything or say anything that would make my father mad at me."

"Were you a model boy, then?"

Phil grinned wryly. "I was anything but! I was in trouble all the time." But that was when he was away from home. He didn't dare misbehave at home.

He had learned early not to reveal his feelings. "My mother told the folks here at the prison that I was always happy as a boy. When I look back, I can't remember a single day when I was happy."

He passed very lightly over the part his mother had played in the development of his strong and aggressive resentments against the female sex, which had led to his sex crimes. The investigators had considered her to be an emotionally depriving mother, and Phil told me that sex had been treated in the home as something repulsive and dirty.

But the only complaint he expressed was that his mother was "pushy" and loud in carrying on the business she and her husband conducted, though not that way with her children. "I hated noise and pushiness, I hated violence and quarreling. She and my father used to fight a good deal. I would think a lot of times there wouldn't have been any quarrel if she had just kept still, but she would goad him. I resented it, and I guess that's why I resented women."

One aspect of the parental relationship that Phil considered especially damaging to him—and his therapist agreed—was that his father became violent over small derelictions but never punished his children for big ones. "When I did something really bad, he never said a word. When I got into trouble with the law, my parents were right there, they did everything they could. But as long as I was good, they didn't pay any attention to me."

Phil felt his basic trouble now was an inability to release his emotions, so long suppressed. "I've got to learn to feel things, and to be able to express what I feel. And to do that, I've got to get to the bottom of the reason I was so afraid of my father. I'm not going to be here the rest of my life," he added with quiet assurance. "But I know it is going to take a long time."

I asked Phil what he would say if he could speak to all parents, everywhere. He hesitated. I thought I saw moisture in his eyes, then dismissed the possibility.

Phil had been composed throughout his recital of his attempts to win his father's love; he had stressed his lack of feeling as his principal problem. After a second or so he replied, speaking slowly, "I would say to them, talk to your children, help them to understand you."

He paused. There could be no doubt now about the tears in his eyes. Suddenly he bowed his head into his hands and began to sob. It was several minutes before he could control himself sufficiently to go on.

"I guess what I mean is," he said, head still bowed in his hands, tears trickling through his fingers, "I'd say to them, 'Love your children.' "

# Appendix

## Laws of the separate states regarding serious sex offenders and sexual psychopaths

In order to have the latest possible information as to the laws and procedure for handling and treating serious sex offenders in the fifty states, the following questionnaire was sent to the attorney general of each state:

> Will you please indicate, by checking the appropriate boxes below, what your state statutes call for with regard to the handling of men and boys charged with sex offenses involving violence—forcible rape, attempted forcible rape, molestation of children—and who are a potential physical threat to the community.

1. Do the statutes of your state call for psychiatric examination in the above cases: (1) Upon arrest ☐; (2) Before trial ☐; (3) Before sentencing ☐?
2. If psychiatric examination at one of the above points is mandatory, is it conducted in: (1) The jail ☐; (2) A psychiatric clinic connected with the court ☐; (3) A mental hospital or residential clinic to which the accused has been sent for observation ☐; or (4) Is place of examination left to the discretion of the court or local authorities ☐?
3. In such cases are the examining psychiatrists bound by: (1) The M'Naghten rule ☐; (2) The Briggs rule ☐; (3) The Durham rule ☐; or (4) other— please fill in if none of the first three.
4. Are men charged with one of the aforementioned serious sex crimes permitted to plead guilty to a lesser offense: (1) Never ☐; (2) Occasionally ☐; (3) Frequently, unless the crime is one of special brutality ☐?
5. Does your state have an indeterminate sentence for sexual offenders or sexual psychopaths? Yes ☐ No ☐
6. Does your state have a special institution to which men convicted of sexual violence, or shown by psychiatric or psychological examination to have propensity for sexual violence, may be sent and receive special therapy? Yes ☐ No ☐
7. If there is no special institution for the handling and treatment of offenders, do your prisons or reformatories provide any special measures for treating them, such as: (1) Special wards, with psychiatric treatment ☐; (2) Psy-

chiatric treatment while they mingle with the rest of the inmates ☐? (3) No special measures ☐.

8. Do your statutes require psychiatric examination of a man or boy convicted of sex violence: (1) Before he is released on probation ☐; (2) Before he is released on parole ☐; (3) After his release when he has served his full sentence in a penitentiary or has been discharged from a mental hospital ☐?

9. If a man or boy has been found not guilty by reason of insanity when charged with a serious sex crime, does your law require that: (1) He be released forthwith into the community ☐; (2) He be sent to a mental hospital for treatment before being released ☐?

The following tables, plus summaries that were too detailed or different to be readily tabulated, are based upon the answers received from this questionnaire, either from the attorney general or an aide, though in a few instances I found that the attorney general's office was forbidden by law to perform such a service, and the information had to be obtained from another state department.

A number of officials who filled out the questionnaire wished to have it made plain that they were acting in a personal rather than an official capacity, and that their answers should be taken as their own impressions of the matters inquired about. It is of course understood that the attorney general's office of a state does not make the laws, and that criminal prosecution is the province of local authorities. The many state officials who gave their generous co-operation did so as a courtesy, which was greatly appreciated by the author.

The answers revealed, as mentioned in the text of this book, that a few states have a special facility for the treatment of sex offenders in a mental hospital, similar to the one in Wisconsin's Waupun Prison, and distinct from the routine practice of committing a mentally deranged offender of any type to a hospital for the criminally insane. (I hope the reader will understand by now that the majority of sex offenders are not insane by legal or medical standards.) My Question No. 7 therefore should have read: "If there is no special institution for the handling and treatment of [serious sex] offenders, do your prisons, reformatories *or mental hospitals* provide any special measures for treating them . . ."?

In some states, the laws and procedures may already have been changed since this book went to the binders. The following must be taken as representing the situation in each state as of 1963, in the opinion of my various informants. Readers might check to see if improvements have been made since then.

| | I | 2 | 3 | 4 |
|---|---|---|---|---|
| | *Psychiatric examination mandatory?* | *Place of examination?* | *Rule for determining sanity?* | *Permitted to plead guilty to lesser offense?* |
| ALABAMA | No | | | Occasionally |
| ALASKA | At court's discretion | At discretion of court or local authorities | M'Naghten Rule, but not as limitation on evidence[1] | Frequently |
| ARIZONA | At court's discretion[2] | At court's discretion or by agreement of counsel | M'Naghten Rule | If judge and county attorney consent; or to lesser degree of offense charged |
| ARKANSAS | Not mandatory but customary before trial | Mental hospital or clinic | M'Naghten Rule | Occasionally |
| CALIFORNIA (see Chapters 16 and 17) | Mandatory before sentencing | In mental hospital after preliminary hearing by court-appointed board of 3 psychiatrists | M'Naghten Rule | Never[4] |
| COLORADO | Mandatory before sentencing | At court's discretion: jail, mental hospital or clinic | None[5] | At discretion of court or prosecutor |
| CONNECTICUT | Only at request of defense on being | None specified | M'Naghten Rule | Occasionally |

[1] M'Naghten Rule applicable in charge to jury, but not as a limitation on evidence or on testimony or on report of examining psychiatrist.

[2] Psychiatric examination upon conviction is not required; however, "a person shall not be tried, convicted, or punished for a public offense while he is insane." If the convicted person is found to be insane at any time prior to carrying out the sentence, the sentence is suspended and the defendant is committed to the state hospital until such time as he is declared sane. The request for a sanity hearing may come from the superintendent of prisons or from the defendant himself.

[3] Arizona law provides severe sentences for serious sex crimes. For instance, a convicted rapist may be imprisoned for any term of from five years to life. A person guilty of kidnaping a child for the purpose of lewd acts is punishable

| 5 | 6 | 7 | 8 | 9 |
|---|---|---|---|---|
| | | | Psychiatric examination (before or after release)? | Disposition of those found not guilty by reason of insanity? |
| Indeterminate sentence? | Special institution? | Treatment elsewhere? | | |
| No | No | No | No | Release forthwith |
| No | No | State contracts with outside institutions | No | At court's discretion |
| No[3] | No | State mental hospital if insane | No[2] | Committed to mental hospital if still insane; released if found now sane |
| No | No | No | At intervals while in mental hospital; none after serving sentence in prison | Law permits release forthwith but usually committed to mental hospital |
| Yes | Yes | | During confinement and before release | Committed to mental hospital |
| Yes | No | In state hospital or in prison while mingling | Mandatory before release on probation; usually before release on parole | Committed to mental hospital |
| Not answered) | No | No special measures | Sometimes ordered by state | Committed to mental hospital |

by death or life imprisonment without possibility of parole if the child suffers serious bodily harm. If the child is not so harmed, the culprit is punishable by imprisonment of from twenty to fifty years without possibility of parole. If a lesser offense is repeated, the penalty is doubled.

4 Civil proceedings may be invoked at the court's discretion upon any criminal conviction, whether for a sex offense or not, if there is cause to believe the subject is a sexual psychopath. Hence the acceptance of a guilty plea to lesser crime does not come up, the issue being whether or not the accused is a sexual psychopath. See Chapters 16 and 17 on the California system.

5 The examination is not to determine if the offender is insane but, I assume, whether or not he is a sex deviate.

| | 1 | 2 | 3 | 4 |
|---|---|---|---|---|
| | *Psychiatric examination mandatory?* | *Place of examination?* | *Rule for determining sanity?* | *Permitted to plead guilty to lesser offense?* |
| | charged; though sometimes by state before sentencing or probation | | | |
| DELAWARE | Not mandatory but customary before sentencing | Mental hospital or clinic | M'Naghten Rule | Occasionally |
| FLORIDA | Not mandatory but permissible before sentencing | At discretion of court or local authorities | M'Naghten Rule | Occasionally, at discretion of court and prosecutor |
| GEORGIA | Before trial, if insanity is a defense | At discretion of court or local authorities | No specific rule; test is insanity at time of crime | Never |
| HAWAII | Before sentencing at court's discretion; before trial only at request of attorneys, court-approved | At discretion of court or local authorities | M'Naghten Rule | Occasionally, depending on circumstances |
| IDAHO | Before trial, if insanity is a defense | Mental hospital or clinic | M'Naghten Rule | May plead guilty to one charge, not guilty to another |
| ILLINOIS | At court's discretion | None specified | M'Naghten Rule | Occasionally |
| INDIANA | During trial, if a criminal sexual psychopath; by court-appointed doctors if insanity is a defense | Initial, jail or hospital [6] | M'Naghten Rule, with slight variations | Infrequently |

[6] Sixty days of observation in a mental hospital before commitment at state mental hospital.

[7] Sexual psychopaths may be committed until they recover. Sentence for rape: anywhere between two and twenty-one years.

| 5 | 6 | 7 | 8 | 9 |
|---|---|---|---|---|
| | | | Psychiatric examination (before or after release)? | Disposition of those found not guilty by reason of insanity? |
| Indeterminate sentence? | Special institution? | Treatment elsewhere? | | |
| No | No, aside from hospital for criminally insane | (None noted) | Not mandatory but customary at various times depending on case | Committed to mental hospital |
| Yes | No | No | Not required by law | Would depend on circumstances |
| No | Yes (Nature of institution not stated; may mean hospital for criminally insane) | | Before release on parole, if insanity was a defense | Committed to mental hospital |
| Not as such, but sentences are indefinite | No | Available in prison while mingling | Not mandatory but given in some cases | Release forthwith |
| No | No, though may be referred to state mental hospitals | None noted | No | Committed to mental hospital |
| Yes | No, but special wards and psychiatric treatment provided in various institutions | | Before release on parole and after discharge from prison or mental hospital | Committed to mental hospital |
| Yes[7] | No; sexual psychopaths to mental hospital | In prison while mingling (some cases to special unit) | Not mandatory but customary, before release or parole | At court's discretion[8] |

[8] There is usually a determination as to the probability that the patient would commit a similar act again. If a high probability is found, the patient is sent to a state hospital for at least two years.

| | I | 2 | 3 | 4 |
|---|---|---|---|---|
| | *Psychiatric exam-ination manda-tory?* | *Place of examination?* | *Rule for deter-mining sanity?* | *Permitted to plead guilty to lesser offense?* |
| **IOWA** | Sexual Psycho-path Law (not defined) | At discretion of court or local authorities | M'Naghten Rule where in-sanity plea entered | |
| **KANSAS** | Mandatory be-fore sentencing | State hospital after conviction and before sen-tencing | No specific rule[9] | Occasionally |
| **KENTUCKY** | Reports that the laws make no distinction as to sex offenders, except with regard to those who are insane. | | | |
| **LOUISIANA** | Not mandatory; at request of de-fense counsel in insanity plea | Discretion of court or local authorities | M'Naghten Rule | At discretion of prosecution |
| **MAINE** | At request of de-fense if plea is insanity | State mental hospitals ordinarily | Durham Rule for insanity but does not apply to sexual psy-chopaths | Occasionally, depending on strength of case |
| **MARYLAND** | No | | M'Naghten Rule | Never as far as known |
| **MASSACHUSETTS** | Mandatory be-fore sentencing | Mental hospital or clinic | Mass. General Laws C.123A, "sexually dan-gerous persons" | Occasionally |
| **MICHIGAN** | See page 348 for special procedures regarding sexual psychopaths | | | |

[9] The psychiatrists decide whether the subject is so mentally ill or deficient that it is advisable for the welfare of the defendant or the protection of the community to commit him.

| 5 | 6 | 7 | 8 | 9 |
|---|---|---|---|---|
| *ndeterminate sentence?* | *Special institution?* | *Treatment elsewhere?* | *Psychiatric examination (before or after release)?* | *Disposition of those found not guilty by reason of insanity?* |
| s | No | Therapy at State mental hospital for those considered criminal sexual psychopaths. Also see page 346 | Before release on probation | Committed to mental hospital |
| s | No | Yes[10] | Mandatory before release for any reason | Committed to mental hospital |
| ; may be cuted for e | No | None noted in prisons | While in prison | Depends on whether insanity claimed at present or at time of crime |
| rape only | No | In prison at warden's discretion | No from prison; yes from mental hospital | Committed to mental hospital |
| , for ective nquents | Yes, at Patuxent, for all defective delinquents including sex offenders | See No. 6 | No mandatory statute | Committed to mental hospital |
|  | Yes, at Bridgewater | See No. 6 | (Unanswered) | Committed to mental hospital |

[10] Nearly all sexually sick men are sent to the Larned State Hospital in Larned, Kansas.

| | 1 | 2 | 3 | 4 |
|---|---|---|---|---|
| | *Psychiatric examination mandatory?* | *Place of examination?* | *Rule for determining sanity?* | *Permitted to plead guilty to lesser offense?* |
| MINNESOTA | At court's discretion (presentence for all criminals; for minors at any step after arrest) | At discretion of court or local authorities | No specific rule | At county attorney's discretion; occasionally or frequently, depending on county |
| MISSISSIPPI | No | | | Occasionally; depends on district attorney's recommendation and court |
| MISSOURI | See page 347 for special sexual psychopath procedure | | | Frequently |
| MONTANA | No | | No specific rule | Never |
| NEBRASKA | Not mandatory but permitted before sentencing | No provision in statutes | M'Naghten Rule | Occasionally |
| NEVADA | Not mandatory, but at request of attorneys | Discretion of court or local authorities | M'Naghten Rule | At county attorney's discretion |
| NEW HAMPSHIRE[12] | Mandatory upon arrest when violence used; otherwise discretionary | Mental hospital | Its own standard, close to Durham Rule: "ability to control one's impulses" | Never[12] |
| NEW JERSEY | Mandatory before sentencing | Clinic (see Chapter 4) | M'Naghten Rule | Never |

[11] Sex offenders are held under the sexual psychopath law in a special security building at Lincoln State Hospital and can be released only on the order of the court which committed them. Such action may be recommended by the hospital superintendent.

[12] This state was one of the first to pay serious attention to the problem presented by the sexually sick man who is not insane, and the first state to

| 5 | 6 | 7 | 8 | 9 |
|---|---|---|---|---|
| *Indeterminate sentence?* | *Special institution?* | *Treatment elsewhere?* | *Psychiatric examination* (*before or after release*)? | *Disposition of those found not guilty by reason of insanity?* |
| No | No | May receive treatment in criminal ward of state hospital | Before parole, at discretion of Adult Corrections Commission | Committed to mental hospital |
| No | No | None required by law | Unanswered | Depends on mental condition at time of trial |
| Confined until considered cured | No | No special measures in prisons | No mandatory examination | Sent to mental hospital if still insane |
| No | No | None except state mental hospital | No | Committed to mental hospital |
| Yes | No | Special ward at State mental hospital [11] | No | Committed to mental hospital |
| Yes | No | No special measures | Mandatory before release on probation or parole | Committed to mental hospital |
| "Commitment" as distinguished from "sentence" | No, but sent to special ward at state hospital | | Periodic examinations and reports mandatory during commitment | Committed to mental hospital |
| Yes | No | No[13] | Mandatory before release on probation or parole | Committed to mental hospital |

excuse the criminal offense if the accused is found to be a sexual psychopath. Hence the question of pleading guilty to a lesser charge does not arise.

[13] No special institution or provision at time of writing, but my informant said that Governor Hughes was planning something along these lines "and if money becomes available, we will move into this area."

## Laws of separate states regarding serious sex offenders and sexual

| | 1 Psychiatric examination mandatory? | 2 Place of examination? | 3 Rule for determining sanity? | 4 Permitted to plead guilty to lesser offense? |
|---|---|---|---|---|
| NEW MEXICO | At any time upon showing of reasonable doubt | None specified | See below[14] | At final judge's discretion |
| NEW YORK | Mandatory before sentencing[15] | Jail, state hospital or place recommended by hospital director | No specific rule[15] but examination bears some relationship to Briggs Rule in purpose | At discretion of district attorney and judge |
| NORTH CAROLINA | Mandatory before trial | Mental hospital, clinic or at court's discretion | M'Naghten Rule | Occasionally |
| NORTH DAKOTA | At judge's discretion, at any stage, where defendant's mental condition is in doubt | At discretion of court or local authorities | Not stated in statutes but M'Naghten Rule usually followed | Occasionally |
| OHIO | Mandatory before sentencing | Discretion of court or local authorities | M'Naghten Rule | (Unanswered) |
| OKLAHOMA | Not mandatory but may be ordered by court | Mental hospital or clinic | (Unanswered) | Occasionally |

[14] As a result of disease of mind: (a) did not know the nature and quality of the act or (b) did not know that it was wrong or (c) was incapable of preventing himself from committing it.

[15] A report must be made by examining psychiatrists to the sentencing judge which should state all the relevant circumstances that will aid the judge in imposing sentence.

[16] Defendant is committed to the Commissioner to be placed in an institution

| 5 | 6 | 7 | 8 | 9 |
|---|---|---|---|---|
| | | | *Psychiatric examination (before or after release)?* | *Disposition of those found not guilty by reason of insanity?* |
| *Indeterminate sentence?* | *Special institution?* | *Treatment elsewhere?* | | |
| Yes | No | Rarely | No | Insanity proceeding frequently instituted after acquittal |
| Yes, for certain sex offenders | No | Psychiatric clinics in all correctional institutions and Board of Parole | Examinations and reports to Board of Parole before parole | At discretion of Commissioner of Mental Hygiene[16] |
| Yes, in some cases | No | Special wards in state mental hospital | Examination before release | Committed to mental hospital |
| Yes | No | Men found to have a propensity for violence sent to state hospital; conviction for serious sex crime usually means prison with treatment if needed at the State Psychiatric Clinic | At discretion of Pardon and Parole Boards | At court's discretion |
| Yes | No | Usually at Lima State Hospital for Criminally Insane | (Unanswered) | Committed to mental hospital |
| Yes | No | No special measures | No | Released forthwith |

for observation and examination for sixty days. The Commissioner then decides whether the individual shall be released as not dangerous or shall be committed for treatment as long as deemed necessary. He may at certain times be conditionally released, and if, after five years, his record is clean, his release becomes absolute. If he is for some reason returned to the institution during a period of release, the process starts over again.

| | 1 | 2 | 3 | 4 |
|---|---|---|---|---|
| | *Psychiatric examination mandatory?* | *Place of examination?* | *Rule for determining sanity?* | *Permitted to plead guilty to lesser offense?* |
| OREGON | Mandatory either before trial or before sentencing | Jail, mental hospital or clinic | M'Naghten Rule where insanity is at issue[17] | Frequently |
| PENNSYLVANIA | Not mandatory but at court's discretion | Discretion of court or local authorities | No specific rule (ordinary psychiatric standards) | Probably occasionally |
| RHODE ISLAND | Not mandatory but upon court order at request of prosecution or defense, before sentencing | (Unanswered) | M'Naghten Rule where applicable | Occasionally |
| SOUTH CAROLINA | No | | | Determined by the facts |
| SOUTH DAKOTA | No | | Bound by no rule | (Unanswered) |
| TENNESSEE | After conviction | In the jail | M'Naghten Rule | Frequently |
| TEXAS | Not mandatory but permitted before trial | At discretion of court or local authorities | M'Naghten Rule | Occasionally |
| UTAH | Mandatory before sentencing | At discretion of court or local authorities | No specific rule[18] | Occasionally |

[17] However, Oregon has a statute very similar to the Iowa one (page 346) in which "sexually dangerous persons" may be brought before the court upon a written complaint, setting forth facts tending to show that the accused is a sexually dangerous person or a person who has voluntarily filed an application for commitment as a sexually dangerous person. This person is defined by law as one, not insane, who by a course of repeated misconduct in sexual matters has evidenced such lack of power to control his sexual impulses as to be dan-

| 5 | 6 | 7 | 8 Psychiatric examination (*before or after release*)? | 9 Disposition of those found not guilty by reason of insanity? |
|---|---|---|---|---|
| *Indeterminate sentence?* | *Special institution?* | *Treatment elsewhere?* | | |
| Yes | To be established under a 1963 statute (see Chapter 12) | See 6 | Before release on probation or parole | Committed to mental hospital |
| Yes | No | Unless psychotic, in prison while mingling | No | No statutory provision |
| No | No | In prison while mingling | (Unanswered) | Statutes provide for committal to mental hospital until sane |
| No | No | No special measures | No | Release forthwith |
| (Unanswered) | (Unanswered) | (Unanswered) | (Unanswered) | Committed to mental hospital |
| Yes | No | No special measures | Before release on parole | Committed to mental hospital |
| No | No | Psychiatric treatment in prison while mingling | No | Committed to mental hospital |
| Yes | No; if found insane, committed to mental hospital | No special measures | Before release on parole and after discharge from mental hospital or penitentiary | Committed to mental hospital |

gerous to other persons aged 12 or under because he may inflict injury or pain on the objects of his desire. The legal procedures afford full protection to the person accused, leaving disposition of the case to the court, with due regard to the examining psychiatrists' reports.

[18] The standard set forth by the statute is the finding or not finding of "abnormal mental illness which resulted in" the offense.

| | 1 | 2 | 3 | 4 |
|---|---|---|---|---|
| | *Psychiatric examination mandatory?* | *Place of examination?* | *Rule for determining sanity?* | *Permitted to plead guilty to lesser offense?* |
| VERMONT | Not mandatory, but before trial if insanity pleas anticipated | Vermont State Hospital | Rule derived from Model Penal Code[19] | If offense found to be less serious than originally charged |
| VIRGINIA | Not mandatory but may be requested by judge, prosecutor or defense and sentence deferred until report is made | Discretion of court or local authorities | M'Naghten Rule | Occasionally[20] |
| WASHINGTON | See page 349 for special procedures regarding sexual psychopaths | | | |
| WEST VIRGINIA | Mandatory before sentencing in serious sex crime | Discretion of court or local authorities | M'Naghten Rule | No data available |
| WISCONSIN (see Chapter 15) | Mandatory before sentencing | Usually at Wisconsin State Prison's special facility | No specific rule | No data available |
| WYOMING | Mandatory before sentencing | Discretion of court or local authorities; may be conducted in state hospital | No specific rule | Depends on individual case |

[19] Vermont rule:

A person is not responsible for criminal conduct if at the time of such conduct, as a result of mental disease or defect, he lacks adequate capacity either to appreciate the criminality of his conduct or to conform his conduct to the requirements of the law.

The terms "mental disease or defects" do not include an abnormality manifested only by repeated criminal or otherwise antisocial conduct. The terms "mental disease or defect" shall include congenital and traumatic mental conditions as well as disease.

| 5 Indeterminate sentence? | 6 Special institution? | 7 Treatment elsewhere? | 8 Psychiatric examination (*before or after release*)? | 9 Disposition of those found not guilty by reason of insanity? |
|---|---|---|---|---|
| Not as such but see below[19] | | See below[19] | Not mandatory at any stage but given before discharge when sanity is in question | At discretion of court may be confined in state prison or Vermont State Hospital at his own expense, if he has funds, otherwise at expense of state |
| (Not answered) | No | As much segregation as possible and treatment in prison | At court's discretion; by Department of Mental Hygiene and Hospitals; report available to prosecution and defense | Released forthwith |
| Yes | No, except state hospital for those found insane | No special measures | No | Action would be taken under another statute |
| Yes (a provision amounting to the same thing) | Special facility at Wisconsin State prison; special institution planned by 1965 or 1966 | Wisconsin State institution planned by 1965 or 1966 | See Chapter 15 for full description | Committed to mental hospital |
| Yes | No[21] | In prison while mingling or transferred to state mental hospital if sex problems serious | Mandatory before release on probation or parole | Committed to mental hospital |

Such persons must be institutionalized and treatment provided for them until such time as their mental condition no longer constitutes a threat to public welfare. They may be committed to mental or penal institutions within the state.

[20] With the consent of the attorney for the Commonwealth, the charge might be reduced to one such as contributing to the delinquency of a minor.

[21] State Board of Charities and Reform is empowered to enter into contracts with other states which maintain facilities. My informant unable to find that such a contract has ever been made and believes sex offenders of dangerous type are usually committed to the state mental hospital.

## Special procedures

Several states besides Wisconsin and California, whose systems have been described extensively in the text, have special procedures for dealing with sex offenders which cannot be fitted into tabular form.

### Iowa

The Iowa law permitting citizens to bring charges against persons they believe to be criminal sexual psychopaths calls for the following procedure:

"Any reputable person" may inform the county attorney of knowledge that an individual charged with a public offense is a criminal sexual psychopath, or that an individual has committed an act or acts which indicate he may be a criminal sexual psychopath. If the county attorney, after investigation, feels the charge has merit, he may file a petition to this effect. (The county attorney may also file such a petition of his own volition.)

Notice is given the individual charged, and a hearing is held at which the court shall determine whether the individual shall be medically examined, and, if so, by whom the examination shall be conducted and at what time and place.

In the event that a medical examination is ordered, the psychiatric report shall be filed as part of the court record but shall not be open for public inspection. A copy of the report shall be furnished without cost by the clerk of the court, upon request, to the person examined or his attorney.

If the medical examiners do not find proof of a propensity for sexual crime in the person examined, or the court is not satisfied with the proof, the petition shall be dismissed. If the court is satisfied with the proof submitted, the defendant is entitled to a jury trial. Or, if requested by the defendant, a hearing may be held before the court without a jury. The public may be excluded from the proceedings upon order of the court.

At this final hearing, the examining physicians may testify, but their reports, previously filed with the court, shall not be admissible in evidence. However, evidence of past acts of sexual deviation by the person charged shall be admissible.

It is mandatory that the person charged shall have counsel at every stage of the proceedings, shall have the right to present evidence in his behalf, and shall have full rights of appeal. If the defendant does not employ counsel, it is mandatory for the court to appoint a competent attorney to represent him, and a reasonable attorney's fee shall be included in the costs of the proceedings.

If the individual charged is found to be a criminal sexual psychopath in this final trial or hearing, the court is given two alternatives. The defendant may be committed to a state hospital for the mentally ill, under an indeterminate sentence, for treatment. Or the court may order the defendant to be tried on the criminal charges against him, "as the interests of substantial justice may require."

If the criminal sexual psychopath is committed to a state hospital, the hospital staff is required to make periodic examinations of the person committed under this statute, to determine the progress of treatment, and is required to report to the committing court not less than once a year.

At any time after commitment that the criminal psychopath has, in the opinion of three qualified psychiatrists, obtained maximum benefit from his hospitalization, and his release, in the opinion of the three psychiatrists, will not be incompatible with the welfare of society, an application for his release may be filed with the committing court.

Another hearing must be held similar in all respects to the original one that was held to determine the mental condition of the defendant. Following the hearing, the judge may either cause the defendant to be placed on probation for a minimum of three years or to be returned to the hospital, provided that, upon the expiration of the probationary period set by the court, the person may be discharged.

Special wards in the mental hospital are set aside for the men found to be criminal sexual psychopaths, and in 1958 a complete psychiatric unit was established at the maximum security hospital in the men's reformatory, for psychiatric diagnosis, care and treatment of men both in the security unit and in the rest of the prison population. It provides services to all the civil institutions through psychiatric teams stationed at the boys' training school at Eldora and the maximum security prison at Fort Madison. In 1960, a part-time out-patient parolee clinic was established in Des Moines to serve the parolees from the training school at Eldora.

## Missouri

Missouri has what is known as a Psychopathic Act, which provides that when a person is charged with a criminal offense and it appears to the prosecuting official that the defendant is a criminal sexual psychopath, the prosecuting official shall file a petition setting forth this fact to the court. In his petition he must show that the defendant is suffering from a mental disorder but is not insane or feeble-minded, and that the mental disorder has existed for a period of not less than one year immediately prior to the filing of his petition. If, after a hearing, the court finds the defendant is in fact a sexual psychopath, the court may direct that the individual be sent to the state mental hospital to remain there until cured.

In order for the individual to be released from the mental hospital, it is necessary for the committing court to hold a hearing and determine that the individual is in a condition to be released. A person thus released must be placed on probation for a minimum period of three years. However, it is expressly declared in the law that the operation of the criminal Sexual Psychopathic Act will not prevent the state from proceeding to try the defendant on the criminal charges, because it is expressly stated in the law that no one who is insane or feeble-minded can be handled as a sexual psychopath.

At time of writing, a bill was pending before the Missouri Legislature designed to overhaul the whole approach to the matter of legal insanity in Missouri, because at present Missouri is restricted to the M'Naghten Rule, except for the Sexual Psychopathic Act just noted. This is Senate Bill No. 143, 72nd General Assembly. In place of the ability to distinguish between right and wrong, which is the standard imposed by the M'Naghten Rule, the new bill would make the terms "mental disease or defect" include congenital and traumatic mental conditions as well as disease. It will hold that an individual is not responsible for criminal conduct if, at the time of such conduct, he, either as a result of mental disease or defect, did not know or appreciate the nature, quality or wrongfulness of his conduct (the gist of the M'Naghten Rule) or was incapable of conforming his conduct to the requirements of law, which is more in accordance with scientific thinking about the sex deviate.

## Michigan

Michigan is one of several states which conducted careful examinations into the problem before revising the statutes regarding the handling of sexual offenders. Since the present Michigan laws do not fit the questions I asked in my questionnaire to the Attorneys General but offer an interesting approach to the problem, I reprint the Michigan procedures as they were sent to me by Mr. Harold Kachelski, Research Analyst for the State of Michigan Department of Corrections.

We now have two distinctly different statutory provisions for treatment of the sex offender. We have a criminal sexual psychopath statute which provides for psychiatric examination of persons charged under the statute and commitment to the Ionia State Hospital for the Criminal Insane upon determination of meeting the description of a criminal sexual psychopath. Any person may be charged under the statutes who meets the following definition:

"Any person who is suffering from a mental disorder and is not insane or feeble-minded, which mental disorder has existed for a period of not less than one year and is coupled with criminal propensities to the commission of sex offenses is hereby declared to be a criminal psychopathic person."

The State Hospital Commission has the right to release such persons upon parole under such conditions as are deemed proper in the judgment of the State Hospital Commission. Persons found in an original hearing to be criminal sexual psychopaths may not thereafter be tried or sentenced for the offense originally charged.

Several sections of our Penal Code dealing with penalties for sex offenses, such as rape, gross indecency, incest, etc., have been amended to provide an optional sentence of from one day to life upon conviction, rather than the straight statutory penalty which, in most instances, carries a maximum penalty in terms of years less than life. These alternative sentencing provisions may be employed if the person is deemed a sexually delinquent person defined as:

". . . any person whose sexual behavior is characterized by repetitive or compulsive acts which indicate a disregard of consequences or the recognized rights of others, or by the use of force upon another person in attempting sex relations of either a heterosexual or homosexual nature, or by the commission of sexual aggressions against children under the age of 16."

The statutes provide that an indictment of a sexually delinquent person shall charge the offense and may also charge that the defendant was at the time of the offense a sexually delinquent person. Before sentence is imposed, the statute also provides that psychiatric examination may be made, but this is not mandatory. In practice, of course, it would be unusual to have sentence imposed without psychiatric examination. Persons sentenced as sexual delinquents are committed to the state prison system and must be re-examined psychiatrically at least every six months. Their release to the community is contingent upon the determination of the Parole Board which, of course, relies upon the findings of psychiatric examinations. While institutionalized, they may be confined in the Psychiatric Clinic of our largest institution or may be assigned to general functions along with the other inmates. Their program (work, education, etc.) and specific place of confinement within the institution is based upon individual requirements.

## Washington

Washington State also has a special body of laws regarding sexual psychopaths which differs from ordinary criminal procedures and also from those involving insanity. From the statutes that were furnished me, I deduced the following:

Psychiatric examination does not appear to be mandatory in all cases where defendants are charged with serious sex offenses. However, when an individual is charged with a sex offense and it appears that he is a sexual psychopath, the prosecuting attorney in a criminal proceeding may file a petition alleging that the defendant is a sexual psychopath and stating sufficient facts to support his allegation.

At a preliminary hearing, the court may require the testimony of two duly licensed physicians who have examined the defendant, and if the court finds there are reasonable grounds to believe the defendant is a sexual psychopath, the defendant is then confined at the nearest state hospital for observation.

After receiving the report from the institution, the court may then determine whether or not the defendant is a sexual psychopath. The law also states that a jury trial to determine the question may be demanded. If it is determined by the court proceedings that the defendant is a sexual psychopath, he is institutionalized in the Eastern Washington Hospital, which has maximum security facilities. There he receives treatment. Washington State has an indeterminate sentence, in the sense that a person found to be a sexual psychopath shall be retained by the superintendent of the institution involved until in his opinion it is safe for the man to be at large. The defendant may then be transferred to a penal institution to finish out his sentence for his crime or paroled, as the case may merit.

A similar body of laws applies to psychopathic delinquents. Any state institution may be designated for their care and treatment, provided they can receive treatment there. Treatment is mandatory.

If, after five years, the superintendent of the institution where the psychopathic delinquent is confined considers the offender safe to be at large, the superintendent shall discharge him. Temporary paroles may be granted by the superintendent for visits home, but the sheriff of the home county and the police chief of the home town or city must be notified that the delinquent may be visiting there.

# Bibliography

Out of the vast literature that has accumulated about the sexually sick man, I have selected here a number of titles which will give a broad view to persons new to the subject. A number of valuable books unfortunately are out of print but should be obtainable in professional or state libraries.

Banay, Ralph S., *We Call Them Criminals*. Appleton-Century-Crofts, Inc., New York, 1957.

Beck, Bertram M., *Five States*. American Law Institute, 133 South 36th Street, Philadelphia, Pa., 1951. A study of the Youth Authority program suggested by the American Law Institute in 1940 and now in operation, with some variations from the Model Law, in California, Wisconsin, Minnesota, Massachusetts and Texas.

Bromberg, Walter, *Crime and the Mind*. J. B. Lippincott Company, Philadelphia, 1948.

*California Sexual Deviation Research*. State of California Department of Mental Hygiene, Sacramento, Cal.

*California Sexual Deviation Research, Final Report on*. Langley Porter Clinic, San Francisco, Cal.

Clinard, Marshall B., *Sociology of Deviant Behavior*, 2nd. ed. Holt, Rinehart and Winston, Inc., New York, 1962.

*Crimes of Violence*. Report on a Conference on Crime, University of Colorado, Boulder, Colo.

*Current Projects in the Prevention, Control, and Treatment of Crime and Delinquency*. National Council on Crime and Delinquency, 14 East 23rd Street, New York, N. Y.

Ellis, Albert, and Brancale, Ralph, *The Psychology of Sex Offenders*. Charles C Thomas, Publisher, Springfield, Ill., 1956.

Guttmacher, Manfred S., *Sex Offenses: The Problem, Causes and Preven-*

*tion.* W. W. Norton & Company, Inc., New York, 1951. In addition to a discussion of sexual sickness from a psychiatric standpoint, this recognized authority also contributes a great deal of information about specific laws of the various states.

Karpman, Benjamin, *The Sexual Offender and His Offenses.* Julian Press, Inc., New York, 1954. Dr. Karpman illustrates his discussion of sexual sickness with many cases handled by himself and others and presents a review of the literature on the subject through 1951.

Lindman, Frank T., and McIntyre, Donald M., Jr., eds., *The Mentally Disabled and the Law.* University of Chicago Press.

Lindner, Robert, *The Fifty-Minute Hour.* Rinehart & Company, Inc., New York, 1955.

*Mental Illness and Due Process.* New York City Bar Association. Cornell University Press.

*Michigan: The Governor's Study Commission on the Deviated Criminal Sex Offender; A Citizen's Handbook of Sexual Abnormalities and the Mental Hygiene Approach to Their Prevention.* Michigan Department of Mental Health, Lansing, Mich.

Overholser, Winfred, *The Psychiatrist and the Law.* Harcourt, Brace and Company, New York, 1953.

Ploscowe, Morris, *Sex and the Law.* Prentice-Hall, Inc., New York, 1951. The subject reviewed by a legal expert and former magistrate.

*Psychiatric Characteristics of Sex Offenders.* A statistical analysis of 250 sex offenders examined at the New Jersey State Diagnostic Center at Menlo Park. Department of Institutions and Agencies, Trenton, N. J., mimeographed, 1950.

*Psychiatrically Deviated Sex Offenders.* Committee on Forensic Psychiatry, Group for the Advancement of Psychiatry, 3617 West Sixth Avenue, Topeka, Kansas, Report No. 9, May, 1949, rev. February, 1950.

Redl, Fritz, and Wineman, David, *Children Who Hate.* The Free Press of Glencoe, Illinois, 1951.

Roche, Philip Q., *The Criminal Mind.* Farrar, Straus and Cudahy, New York, 1958. An attempt by a psychiatrist to establish communication between criminal law and psychiatry.

Schneider, Kurt, *The Psychopathic Personality.* Charles C Thomas, Publisher, Springfield, Ill.

*Sing Sing Prison, Report on the Study of 102 Sex Offenders at, as Submitted to Governor Thomas E. Dewey.* Albany, N. Y., March, 1950. The first Sing Sing study, directed by David Abrahamsen.

*Study and Treatment of Persons Convicted of Crimes Involving Sexual Aberrations, Final Report on Research Project for the.* The second

Sing Sing study, directed by Bernard C. Glueck, Jr., under the jurisdiction of the New York State Department of Mental Hygiene, in co-
operation with the New York State Department of Correction, Albany, N. Y.

Tappan, Paul W., *The Habitual Sex Offender*. New Jersey State Department of Institutions and Agencies, Trenton, N. J.

Wertham, Frederic, *The Circle of Guilt*. Rinehart & Company, Inc., New
York, 1956. The eminent psychiatrist, through the case of a 17-year-
old Puerto Rican who shot and killed a younger boy with no apparent provocation, illustrates the way in which a psychiatric examination is conducted and the use of psychological tests. Dr. Wertham's
thesis is that understanding of a case cannot be gained merely from
interviews with a patient but that all possible sociological factors
should also be obtained.

————, *Seduction of the Innocent*, Rinehart & Company, Inc., New
York, 1954. A study of comic books prepared for children, and the
effect they have upon youngsters.

————, *The Show of Violence*. Doubleday & Company, Inc., New York,
1949. Descriptions of a number of the most sensational murder
cases of our era, in which Dr. Wertham acted as an expert witness.

White, Robert W., *The Abnormal Personality: A Textbook*, 2nd ed. Ron-
ald Press Company, New York, 1956.


In addition to those listed below, the magazines *Federal Probation* and
*Journal of Social Therapy* (now called *Corrective Psychiatry and Journal
of Social Therapy*) are a continuing source of articles, as are the professional magazines, too numerous to mention here, in the medical, legal
and sociological fields.


Banay, Ralph S., "Profile of a Sex Offender." *Journal of Social Therapy*,
Vol. 2, No. 2 (2nd quarter, 1956), pp. 85-92.

Brancale, Ralph, and Heyn, Louis L., "Detection, Classification, and
Treatment of the Youthful Offender." *Federal Probation*, Vol. 21,
No. 1 (March, 1957). A description of the work of the New Jersey
Diagnostic Center at Menlo Park.

Coogan, Matt J., "Wisconsin's Experience in Treating Psychiatrically-
Deviated Sexual Offenders." *Journal of Social Therapy*, Vol. 1, No.
2 (January, 1955), pp. 3-6.

Frisbie, Louise V., "The Treated Sex Offender." *Federal Probation*, Vol.
22 (1958).

Guttmacher, Manfred S., "Psychiatric Examination of Offenders." *Bulle-*

tin of the *World Health Organization,* Vol. 2 (1950), pp. 8743-749.

————, "What Can the Psychiatrist Contribute to the Issue of Criminal Responsibility?" *Journal of Nervous and Mental Disease,* Vol. 136, No. 2 (February, 1963), pp. 103-117.

Halleck, Seymour L., "The Physician's Role in Management of Victims of Sex Offenders." *Journal of the American Medical Association,* Vol. 180 (April 28, 1962), pp. 273-278.

Johnson, Adelaide M., and Robinson, David B., "The Sexual Deviant (Sexual Psychopath)—Causes, Treatment, and Prevention." *Journal of the American Medical Association,* Vol. 164 (August 3, 1957), pp. 1559-1565.

Karpman, Benjamin, "A Case of Paedophilia (Legally Rape) Cured by Psychoanalysis." *Psychoanalytic Review,* Vol. 37, No. 3 (July, 1950), pp. 235-276.

Kennedy, F., Hoffman, H. R., and Haines, W. H., "A Study of William Heirens." *The American Journal of Psychiatry,* Vol. 104, No. 2 (August, 1947), pp. 113-121.

Meyer, A. F., Apfelberg, B., and Sugar, C., "Men Who Kill Women." *Journal of Clinical Psychopathology,* Vol. 8 (January, 1947), pp. 481-517.

Reifen, David, "The Sexual Offender and His (Child) Victim." *International Child Welfare Review,* 1958.

"Sex Offenses." *Law and Contemporary Problems,* Vol. 25, No. 2 (Spring, 1960). Duke University School of Law, Durham, N. C.

Wertham, Frederic, "The Matricidal Impulse." *Journal of Criminal Psychopathology,* Vol. 2 (April, 1941), pp. 455-464.

————, "Psychiatry and the Prevention of Sex Crimes." *Journal of Criminal Law and Criminology,* Vol. 28, No. 6 (March-April, 1938).

Further publications with regard to Wisconsin's experience in treating sex offenders since 1951, on which the author drew in describing the Wisconsin system, are:

Glover, Benjamin, "Control of the Sex Deviate." *Federal Probation,* Vol. 24, No. 3 (September, 1960), pp. 38-45.

Halleck, Seymour L., "Juvenile Delinquents: 'Sick' or 'Bad'?" *Social Work,* Vol. 7, No. 2 (April, 1962).

———— and Pacht, Asher R., "The Current Status of the Wisconsin Sex Crimes Law." *The Wisconsin Bar Bulletin,* December, 1960.

Hersko, Marvin, Halleck, Seymour L., Mosenberg, Marshall, and Pacht, Asher R., "A Three-Way Process." *Journal of Social Therapy,* Vol.

7, No. 1 (1st Quarter, 1961). A study of three young incest victims, which included thorough study of the father and mother in each case.

Pacht, Asher R., Halleck, Seymour L., and Ehrmann, John C., "Diagnosis and Treatment of the Sexual Offender: A Nine-Year Study." *The American Journal of Psychiatry,* Vol. 118, No. 9 (March, 1962), pp. 802-808.

———, ———, and ———, "Psychiatric Treatment of the Sex Offender." *Current Psychiatric Therapies,* Grune and Stratton, Inc., Vol. 2 (1962), pp. 173-179.

Powers, Sanger B., "A Statement Prepared for the United States Subcommittee on Juvenile Delinquency with Respect to the Wisconsin Sex Deviate Law." Submitted upon request of the Committee by the Director, Division of Corrections, Wisconsin State Department of Public Welfare.

Uehling, Harold F., "Group Therapy Turns Repression into Expression for Prison Inmates." *Federal Probation,* Vol. 26, No. 1 (March, 1962), pp. 43-49.

*Wisconsin's Experience with Its Sex Crimes Law, 1951 to 1958, A Statistical Picture.* Statistical Bulletin C-26, State of Wisconsin Bureau of Research and Statistics.

Fuller descriptions of the California system, as exemplified by Atascadero State Hospital, and the way in which order was restored from the chaotic condition into which the new venture had fallen, can be found in the following, which may be obtained by writing to the Superintendent and Medical Director, Atascadero State Hospital, Atascadero, Cal. (requests will be referred to the proper office):

*An Introduction to Atascadero State Hospital.*

Blain, Daniel, *The Evaluation, Treatment, and Disposition of Mentally Abnormal Offenders* (by the California State Director of Mental Hygiene).

*ESP Newsletters* (Emotional Security Program patient publications).

*Introduction to the Operating Manual of Atascadero State Hospital* (setting forth the policy on the relative aspects of therapy and security).

*Legal Summary* (parts of the legal code governing the California program).

*The Mentally Ill Offender* (a publication briefly describing the aims of the hospital).

"Mentally Ill Offenders." *California Mental Health Progress,* published by the California State Department of Mental Hygiene (January, 1963).

*Progress Report, Atascadero State Hospital* (from March, 1961, to March, 1962).

*Questions and Answers about Atascadero State Hospital.* Prepared by a committee of patients in the hospital, this publication contains a full description of the hospital and also gives the patients' reaction to the system.

Sandritter, G. Lee, *Administration: Is It Treatment?* (by the hospital superintendent).

————, *Program Evaluation of Atascadero State Hospital* (November, 1962).

*Types of Admission to Atascadero State Hospital.*

Wolfe, Sheldon B., *The Emotional Security Program* (by the hospital public relations officer).

# Index